Emerging Themes in Cognitive Development

Volume II

Robert Pasnak Mark L. Howe
Editors

Emerging Themes in Cognitive Development

Volume II: Competencies

Springer-Verlag
New York Berlin Heidelberg London Paris
Tokyo Hong Kong Barcelona Budapest

Robert Pasnak, Ph.D.
Department of Psychology
George Mason University
Fairfax, VA 22030-4444
USA

Mark L. Howe, Ph.D.
Department of Psychology
Memorial University
St. John's, Newfoundland, A1B 3X9
Canada

With 8 illustrations.

Library of Congress Cataloging-in-Publication Data
Emerging themes in cognitive development/edited by Mark L. Howe and Robert Pasnak.
p. cm.
Includes bibliographical references and indexes.
Contents: v. 1. Foundations—v. 2. Competencies.
ISBN-13: 978-1-4613-9225-5 e-ISBN-13:978-1-4613-9223-1
DOI: 10.1007/978-1-4613-9223-1
1. Cognition in children. 2. Human information processing in children. I. Howe, Mark L. II. Pasnak, Robert.
BF723.C5E48 1992
155.4′13—dc20 92-297

Printed on acid-free paper.

Production managed by Natalie Johnson and James Harbison; manufacturing supervised by Vincent Scelta.
Typeset by Best-set Typesetter Ltd., Hong Kong.

9 8 7 6 5 4 3 2 1

Preface

Emerging Themes in Cognitive Development presents two volumes of the newest research and theory in cognitive development available at the outset of the 1990s. These ideas are firmly rooted in research from the 1980s and, in some sense, these volumes represent a culmination of that research and of even earlier work. Nevertheless, these volumes are offered as catalysts more than summaries, because each presents the freshest and most recently gathered data of many scientists whose insights have had an important impact on the field.

The latest ideas of these researchers will, in some cases, immediately prove to be dominant themes of research and theory. In other cases, of course, it will take longer for the concepts presented to capture the imagination of students and colleagues who are still invested in meritorious research on other themes. In either case, the syntheses and innovations proposed are not likely to escape the careful study of the serious scholar, and it is to such scholars that these volumes are dedicated.

The first volume provides a foundation by describing some fundamental aspects of cognitive development. In part, this proceeds through the development of theories and explanations that make sense out of extant and new data. Dempster describes how the common process of resistance to interference underlies many cognitive performances. This theoretical approach is advanced with sufficient precision and detail to reveal relations among phenomena previously thought unrelated, and thus it provides a welcome step toward a unitary theoretical explanation of diverse expressions of cognitive development. Harnishfeger and Bjorklund present an equally welcome analysis of the development of efficiency in inhibition, leading to a carefully constructed theory that inefficient inhibition is a major cause of poor cognitive performances by young children. Finally, fuzzy-trace theory, an outgrowth of recent trends in cognitive development, is presented in its most complete and up-to-date form. Brainerd and Reyna offer theoretical explanations of the development of a broad range of memory and reasoning phenomena. An excellent summary of this theory, exemplified by illustrations of age changes on a variety of reasoning tasks, is presented, and implications for developmental trends in memory are discussed.

This first volume also contains several demonstrations of formal modeling. The gains in prediction and precision that can be won by such mathematical analyses is the hallmark of cognitive developmental psychology as a maturing science. First, the reader is asked to consider the basic issue of speed of processing from a developmental perspective. Kail presents evidence that there is a common mechanism in cognitive processing that permits mathematical prediction of age differences. This model is designed to permit at least a first approximation to prediction of differences in processing rates at all ages from childhood to old age. It is followed by Thomas' analysis of individual differences on a variety of cognitive tasks. This advance in methodology is potentially quite important, particularly as it may lead to more accurate prediction of individual performance instead of merely accounting for group tendencies. This section ends with Cooney and Constas' superb analysis of the complex determinants of learning even simple cognitive skills. The nonlinear dynamic modeling approach they use is proving to be extremely productive and it is significant that at this time cognitive developmental psychology is joining other sciences in profiting from it.

This volume proceeds to the development of memory, a foundation for cognitive competence. Leichtman and Ceci describe the development of early memory capabilities and show how fuzzy-trace theory can be applied to the problem of infantile amnesia. Lehman and Bovasso explore another area of research that is just blossoming, namely, the intentional control of forgetting. They are able to show that improved methods uncover developmental trends that were previously hidden and identify the mechanisms by which children intentionally forget. Finally, Ausley and Guttentag present some of the first studies using indirect assessments of memory to identify developmental changes in associative learning. They are able to demonstrate indirect memory for associations during childhood and suggest that this paradigm may be an important tool for studying developmental changes in memory.

The first volume thus provides a foundation for understanding cognitive development. The most recent theories and models of cognitive development are described and key discoveries in new areas of research are presented. The second volume builds on this foundation by revealing new insights into the continued development of cognitive skills. We have labeled the improvements in cognitive performance that occur throughout the child's development cognitive "competence," a term that signifies simply a change or increment in cognitive proficiency, understanding, or mastery. The chapters in this volume provide descriptions of how cognitive abilities increase or may be increased on either narrow or broad fronts as children mature; these disparate gains in capacities and prowess may collectively be considered to represent competence.

The second volume begins with three chapters that present new analyses of children's cognitive competence and proceeds to five chapters that suggest how that competence may be changed. Gelman and Kalish's chapter introduces the volume by offering new insight into the ways in which children organize knowledge intelligently and efficiently. The chapter focuses on the link between children's understanding of causality and the categories by which they classify aspects of their environment. Their use of noncausal, statistical information to draw inferences based on categorizations is also described with a presentation of recent data.

The next chapter, by Siegel, deals with a significant cognitive deficit from which many children suffer. The cognitive basis of dyslexia is discussed, and evidence for and against alternative explanations is described. A model of this cognitive handicap as a modular processing deficit independent of general cognitive functioning is ultimately developed. This chapter leads into a consideration of differences in cognitive ability and how they should be assessed. A novel, modern theory of intelligence underlies Project Spectrum, which has developed new techniques for assessing a wide range of cognitive abilities. In their chapter, Adams and Feldman discuss the distinctive theoretical underpinnings and describe the assessment techniques of this innovative project. Implications for classroom observation and program planning are outlined, and the latest theoretical and research developments are described.

The next five chapters present new research and theory on children's increasing cognitive competence. These chapters offer cogent descriptions of the educational responsibilities and challenges now facing experts in cognitive development. Bjorklund, Gaultney, and Green lead off with a discussion of children's inferences about their own performances. Innovative and previously unpublished studies of children's predictions and interpretations of their own ability to duplicate another person's actions are analyzed in this research on meta-imitation. Surprising developmental trends are noted and interpreted in terms of the adaptive nature of cognitive immaturity.

A model of parental guidance of children's performance of cognitive tasks is presented by Rosengren, Behrend, and Perlmutter in the next chapter. Interactions of parental style, the cognitive ability and age of the child, and the cognitive performance desired are described, predicted, and tested empirically. This pioneering research is followed by Pressley and Van Meter's masterful description and analysis of the circumstances that favor discovery of cognitive strategies. This chapter describes the nature of this aspect of cognitive development and competence and explains the conditions that favor either unassisted acquisition of new strategies or that make explicit instruction necessary.

O'Sullivan's chapter develops the theme that principles of cognitive development can be used to enrich educational theory and practice. Examples of such applications in reading and memory are offered, and a recently developed program for young school children is used to emphasize this point. The view that developmental psychologists have the responsibility to ensure that the latest theory and research in cognitive development is incorporated into education, and the variety of challenges such efforts face, are elaborated.

Finally, Weikart and Hohmann describe two classic efforts to use principles of cognitive developmental psychology to assist disadvantaged children. The renowned Perry Preschool Project and Preschool Curriculum studies are described in depth, and follow-up data spanning nearly two decades are presented. This research, based on a Piagetian framework but fully anticipating Vygotskian perspectives, has valuable implications for efforts to apply cognitive developmental psychology to assist needy children today.

The second volume thus traces the development of cognitive competence and examines conditions that support or assist cognitive development. The primary challenge issued by many of these authors is to ensure the incorporation of our knowledge of cognitive development into educational practices.

Each volume also contains an afterword in which we, the editors, have done our best to draw together the major points contained in the different contributions to each volume. We have also tried to identify the emerging themes in cognitive development today, the final decade of the 20th century. How well we have succeeded only you can judge. Meanwhile, we thank the contributors for being responsive to both of us throughout the editorial process and for presenting their latest views and research in these volumes. It is our hope, as it must be theirs, that you the readers will reap the benefits.

Acknowledgment. Preparation of these volumes was facilitated by a research grant from the Natural Sciences and Engineering Research Council of Canada (OGP0003334) to Mark L. Howe.

Robert Pasnak and Mark L. Howe

Contents

Contents of Volume I

Contributors

MARGARET L. ADAMS Eliot-Pearson Department of Child Study, Tufts University, Medford, MA 02155, USA

DOUGLAS A. BEHREND Department of Psychology, University of Arkansas, Fayetteville, AK 72701, USA

DAVID F. BJORKLUND Department of Psychology, Florida Atlantic University, Boca Raton, FL 33431, USA

DAVID HENRY FELDMAN Eliot-Pearson Department of Child Study, Tufts University, Medford, MA 02155, USA

JANE F. GAULTNEY Department of Psychology, University of North Carolina at Charlotte, Charlotte, NC 28223, USA

SUSAN A. GELMAN Department of Psychology, University of Michigan, Ann Arbor, MI 48109, USA

BRANDI L. GREEN Department of Psychology, Florida Atlantic University, Boca Raton, FL 33431, USA

MARY N. HOHMANN High/Scope Educational Research Foundation, Ypsilanti, MI 48198, USA

MARK L. HOWE Department of Psychology, Memorial University of Newfoundland, St. John's, Newfoundland, A1B 3X9, Canada

CHARLES W. KALISH Department of Psychology, University of Michigan, Ann Arbor, MI 48109, USA

JULIA T. O'SULLIVAN Faculty of Education, Memorial University of Newfoundland, St. John's, Newfoundland, A1B 3X8, Canada

ROBERT PASNAK Department of Psychology, George Mason University, Fairfax, VA 22030, USA

MARION PERLMUTTER Institute of Gerontology, University of Michigan, Ann Arbor, MI 48109, USA

MICHAEL PRESSLEY Department of Human Development, University of Maryland, College Park, MD 20742, USA

KARL S. ROSENGREN Department of Psychology, University of Illinois, Champaign, IL 61820, USA

LINDA S. SIEGEL Ontario Institute for Studies in Education, Toronto, Ontario, M5S 1V6, Canada

PEGGY VAN METER Department of Human Development, University of Maryland, College Park, MD 20742, USA

DAVID P. WEIKART High/Scope Educational Research Foundation, Ypsilanti, MI 48198, USA

Contributors to Volume I

JAYNE ANN AUSLEY Department of Psychology, University of North Carolina at Greensboro, Greensboro, NC 27412, USA

DAVID F. BJORKLUND Department of Psychology, Florida Atlantic University, Boca Raton, FL 33431-0991, USA

MARGARET BOVASSO Department of Psychology, George Mason University, Fairfax, VA 22030, USA

C.J. BRAINERD Department of Educational Psychology, University of Arizona, Tucson, AZ 85721, USA

STEPHEN J. CECI Human Development and Family Studies, Cornell University, Ithaca, NY 14853, USA

MARK A. CONSTAS Department of Educational Psychology, University of Northern Colorado, Greeley, CO 80639, USA

JOHN B. COONEY Department of Educational Psychology, University of Northern Colorado, Greeley, CO 80639, USA

FRANK N. DEMPSTER Department of Educational Psychology, College of Education, University of Nevada, Las Vegas, NV 89154-3003, USA

ROBERT E. GUTTENTAG Department of Psychology, University of North Carolina at Greensboro, Greensboro, NC 27412, USA

KATHERINE KIPP HARNISHFEGER Department of Psychology, University of Georgia, Athens, GA 30602, USA

MARK L. HOWE Department of Psychology, Memorial University, St. John's, Newfoundland, A1B 3X9 Canada

ROBERT KAIL Department of Psychological Sciences, Purdue University, West Lafayette, IN 47907, USA

ELYSE BRAUCH LEHMAN Department of Psychology, George Mason University, Fairfax, VA 22030, USA

MICHELLE D. LEICHTMAN Human Development and Family Studies, Cornell University, Ithaca, NY 14853, USA

ROBERT PASNAK Department of Psychology, George Mason University, Fairfax, VA 22030, USA

V.F. REYNA Department of Educational Psychology, University of Arizona, Tucson, AZ 85721, USA

HOBEN THOMAS Department of Psychology, Pennsylvania State University, 513 Moore Building, University Park, PA 16802, USA

Part I
New Definitions of Competence

1
Categories and Causality

SUSAN A. GELMAN AND CHARLES W. KALISH

Sganarelle: We great doctors diagnose correctly at once. An ignoramus would have hemmed and hawed. He would have said: *It's this* or: *It's that.* But I put my finger on the trouble straight away, and tell you that your daughter is dumb.
Geronte: Yes, but I want you to tell me the cause.
Sganarelle: Nothing easier. The cause of her dumbness is the loss of her powers of speech.

—Molière, *The Reluctant Doctor*

[The doctors] know all about the Classics, and they speak fluent Latin, and they know the names of all the illnesses in Greek and they can define them and classify them. The one thing they can't do is cure them.

—Molière, *The Imaginary Invalid*

One does not have to share Molière's skepticism for doctors to appreciate his basic insight about illness categories. If a diagnosis is to be useful, it must do more than merely apply a label to a set of symptoms. Categorizing a disease in a way that fails to identify underlying causes is an empty gesture or "mere words."

The metaphor of symptom and disease illustrates the powerful link between categories and causality more generally. To put it simply, causal notions are central to how we organize experience into categories and how we use words that encode such groupings. Categories are not simply the products of feature lists and statistical correlations; rather, categorizers construct explanatory theories for how the world operates, and categories are embedded in these causal structures. The link between cause and category emerges in many domains, including those as diverse as medicine, biology, psychology, and law. In medicine, as we have seen above, the most useful and informative classification is one that provides information about the underlying cause of a disease, not merely its symptoms. In biology, species groupings reflect causal understandings; for example, red pandas are not classed with raccoons (which they resemble) but rather with giant pandas (with whom they share ancestry that causes their appearance). In psychology, the distinction between authoritative and authoritarian parenting styles is thought to reflect different etiologies and causal influences, not simply different patterns of behavior. And in law, whether or not people are "guilty" depends on their intentions (the underlying cause of their actions), and not simply their surface behaviors. The concept of "cause" is thus central to the way adults understand the world (Kant, 1958) and construct categories. We will argue that an understanding of causality also has important implications for the acquisition of categories by children.

Recently several investigators have proposed that categories are embedded in theories throughout development (see Carey, 1985; Gelman & Coley, 1991; Keil, 1989; Murphy & Medin, 1985; Quine, 1969; Wellman, 1990; Wellman & Gelman, 1992). Much thoughtful work focuses on characterizing children's theories, and causality is assumed to be an important element of such theories. Yet surprisingly little work on children's theories focuses on causality directly. Thus, questions such as the following remain unanswered: Precisely what role does causality play in the construction and evolution of categories? What would a category completely free of cause look like? Do developmental changes in children's understanding of causality have implications for how they classify?

In contrast, there is a rich literature focusing specifically on children's understanding of causality. In such work, causality is typically examined not as a component of particular theories (at least not explicitly), but rather as a disembedded, context-free notion. Moreover, unlike the work on children's theories, which implicitly assumes that causality is represented from an early age, the work on causal understandings often suggests that important changes take place with development.

The purpose of this chapter is to integrate these two seemingly disparate literatures—how causes inhere in theories, and the development of causality per se—to examine the role of causality in categories. We first review what is known about the developmental appreciation of causality as a critical cognitive construct in its own right. We then turn to an analysis of how causality is manifested in theories. In the third section, we describe recent evidence suggesting that causality plays a powerful and specific role in the structure and employment of children's categories. Finally, we briefly consider some implications of this framework for research on categorization.

Causality as a Developmental Primitive

Early Appreciation of Causality

How do children conceptualize causes? As a starting point, it is useful to consider the status of causality as a psychological construct. Causality can be directly perceived by adults (Michotte, 1963), as illustrated by certain illusions. For example, a pattern of lights moving in a particular manner evokes the inescapable sense that one light *causes* another to turn on—even when the observer is aware that such is not really the case. For adults, then, causality may be considered a primitive notion, one that is elicited automatically and below the threshold of awareness. Is it also a "developmental primitive" in Carey's (1982) sense? That is, do young children easily appreciate that events can be related as cause and effect? Or does this understanding emerge only with age and experience? To the extent that causality is a developmental primitive, we can be more confident that it plays a central notion in the structure and acquisition of children's categories.

Recent research with infants suggests that sensitivity to causality emerges early. Children are aware of the effects of their own behaviors, in that they prefer consequences that they control directly over those that are uncontrollable (see Parritz, Mangelsdorf, & Gunnar, 1992). For example, a child interacting with a noisy mechanical monkey perceives it as mildly threatening when it moves unpredictably, but enjoys it when its movements are controlled by the child (Gunnar-vonGnechten, 1978). A related phenomenon has also been demonstrated with social causes and effects (Mangelsdorf, in press). Infants 12 and 18 months old respond more positively to strangers who act in predictable ways that allow them more control than to strangers who are less predictable, although 6-month-olds were more sensitive to positive affect than controllability. Thus, by 1 year of age infants appear to appreciate causal relations that involve their own agency.

Studies that specifically isolate cause also find sensitivity to causal relations in infancy. For example, Leslie and Keeble (1987) showed 27-week-old infants events that were either causal (one object colliding into another, causing it to move; also known as *direct launching*) or noncausal (an object changing color). After infants habituated to the display, they were shown the same event run backward. Leslie and Keeble found more recovery of attention to the backward causal sequences than to the backward noncausal sequences. This indicates that cause and effect are viewed as nonequivalent. The authors argue that this perception cannot be reduced to spatiotemporal properties, but rather appears to be specifically causal. In contrast, Oakes and Cohen (1990) failed to find an appreciation of causality in 6-month-old infants. They did, however, find that 10-month-olds who habituated to a noncausal event (e.g., an event in which one object moved without being struck) showed more recovery of attention to a causal event (direct launching) than to another noncausal event (e.g., in which there was a time delay between when the object was struck and when it moved). These data clearly indicate that, within the first year of life, infants are sensitive to causal relations between objects.

Presumption of Cause

Although the developmental work provides evidence that infants are aware of causality, this does not necessarily imply that causality is a developmental primitive. For example, it could be a fragile understanding that emerges only under special conditions, and that is invoked less often in children than in adults. In other words, an early appreciation of causality does not preclude the existence of strong developmental changes in how often causal links are assumed.

The question of how often children invoke causal explanations has rarely been addressed directly. Interestingly, however, scattered pieces of evidence suggest that young children may invoke causal links at least as readily as older children and adults. Indeed, there is some evidence that children overattribute causality to events, so that occurrences with no apparent cause are presumed to be nonrandom. Brown (1990) states it this way: "Fundamental to learning is a search for cause, for determinism, and mechanism. Children assume (implicitly) that events are caused, and it is their job to uncover potential mechanisms" (p. 112). Evidence for this possibility is found in children's interpretation of random physical events, in their concepts of immanent justice and animism, and in studies of early story comprehension.

On Piaget's (1930) account, the mere co-occurrence of two events is enough for a young child to imagine a causal connection between them. Thus, children tend to assume there are causes underlying many phenomena that appear unpredictable to an adult (Piaget, 1952). Piaget and Inhelder (1951/1975) studied this issue by presenting children with random devices and asking them to predict and explain their outcomes. For example, one device was a spinning pointer that could stop on any one of eight colors; another device was a pivoting table containing marbles of two colors. What was striking about the predictions and explanations given by children up until age 7 years was their insistence that the machines had causally determined outcomes (see also Green, 1978). Children often reported that they could predict which color the pointer would stop on. They were insistent—even in the face of counter-evidence—that the devices were rule-bound and nonrandom. It appears that children readily assume that events are causally determined, and that this assumption could account for children's poor performance. However, it is not the case that randomness is beyond the capacity of young children. More recent work by Kuzmak and Gelman (1986) demonstrates that preschoolers do appreciate this concept when the experimental paradigm is simple and clear.

Piaget's (1951, 1952) concepts of finalism (that everything has a purpose) and artificialism (that everything has a maker) likewise imply that children assume that events are caused. Piaget noted that children relentlessly ask "why" questions ("Why do they [bodies] always fall?" "Daddy says it [lightning] makes itself all by itself in the sky. Why?"), further suggesting a presumption that such questions have answers. Of course, there may also be pragmatic rules that encourage children to pose "why" questions (as an acceptable means of initiating or continuing a conversation), so this phenomenon deserves closer inspection.

A similar framework exists for interpreting children's notions of immanent justice, again suggesting that preschoolers often find causal relations where none exist. Immanent justice is the principle that moral wrongdoings will cause negative outcomes to the wrongdoer. In these studies, children hear a story about a character who performs a morally negative deed (the "transgression," e.g., stealing cookies) and then experiences a misadventure (the "adversity," e.g., tripping over a rock). Children are asked why the adversity occurred and whether it would have occurred had the story character not transgressed. The usual finding is that children younger than 7 years tend to infer a causal relation between the transgression and the adversity (Karniol, 1980; Kister & Patterson, 1980; White, Elsom, & Prawat, 1978). Jose (1990) presents evidence suggesting that this response is also occasionally found in older children. Immanent justice explanations arise because children base their causal attributions on contiguity information: it is the close temporal connection between the transgression and the adversity that leads children to assume that the two are causally linked. Karniol (1980) suggests that younger children rely on immanent justice because they are trying to uncover a causal link, but fail to understand the possible mechanisms that could provide such a link. Older children also strive to establish a causal link, but in contrast to the younger subjects are able to construct plausible mechanisms. They either construct a "causal chain" (e.g., the boy felt guilty for stealing cookies, so he was careless and tripped) or, if that is not possible, they ascribe the co-occurrence to chance.

The findings from studies of immanent justice, although provocative, must be viewed with caution because the methodologies pose problems. Perhaps the most troubling aspect of these studies is that there may be powerful task demands suggesting to children that they should link transgressions to adversities. Consider that typically children hear only two pieces of information (transgression and adversity). By standard rules of conversational implicature (see Grice, 1975), the subject might reasonably assume that the experimenter intended a link between transgression and adversity to be inferred; otherwise, why would he or she describe the scenario in this way? To illustrate, consider the sentence, "The boy fell off his bicycle and skinned his knee." Normal language processing would license the bridging inference that the first event (falling off the bicycle) caused the second (skinning the knee; see Clark & Clark, 1977). Much the same reasoning process could be at work in the studies of immanent justice. It would be interesting to reexamine this phenomenon, but with a more neutral task in which a noncausal relation is also pragmatically feasible.

Miller and Aloise (1989) note that children overascribe intentionality to events (Berndt & Berndt, 1975; Smith, 1978); for example, reporting that sneezing is an intentional act. They suggest that this error is due to a heavy reliance on causal explanations. On their account, children may not understand the cause of a particular event (e.g., sneezing). Nonetheless, they firmly believe the event must have a cause, and so explain it by using their limited repertoire of causes, foremost among which is intentional causality. Far from not appreciating causality, this research suggests that children are misled by their tendency to reason causally.

Other support for children's overreliance on causality comes from studies of story comprehension. Fein (1973) showed children and adults series of pictures depicting either social or physical interactions. Some of these series related causal sequences; others related noncausal sequences. In this study, 4-year-olds tended to describe all sequences as causal. Seven-year-olds correctly distinguished between causal and noncausal social events but continued to ascribe causality to all physical sequences. By the age of 11 years, children were able to distinguish all causal and noncausal sequences. In a related study conducted by Poulsen and her colleagues (Poulsen, Kintsch, Kintsch, & Premack, 1979), 4- and 6-year-olds were shown series of pictures that included two or more causally and temporally related events. Children at both ages interpreted the series as stories. When the order of pictures was then scrambled, 6-year-olds continued to try to interpret the series as a story by providing causal links between pictures. Further, studies of children's memory for story events have shown that stories with more causal connections are remembered better and are judged as more important (Trabasso & Sperry, 1985; Trabasso & Van den Broek, 1985). Younger children may rely especially heavily on causal connections for recall of an event (Copple & Coon, 1977).

Summary

We have reviewed several lines of research suggesting that children are biased to view phenomena causally. We propose that young children often assume that even random events have causal underpinnings. Altogether, this hypothesis is consistent with the suggestion that causality is a developmental primitive. Carey's (1985) formulation states this concisely: "The evidence now available suggests that there is no developmental change in the foundational notions that underlie all theory building. Human beings are theory builders; from the beginning we construct explanatory structures that help us find the deeper reality underlying surface chaos" (p. 194).

Causality and Domain-Specific Mechanisms

Evidence that children assume causal links provides only half the picture, however. We still need to know how causal relations are understood. Do children and adults share the same notion of causality? Certainly children are not fully adult-like, as seen by the developmental changes that have been repeatedly documented in children's ability to reason about a variety of causal mechanisms (e.g., laws of physics, Kaiser, McCloskey, & Proffitt, 1986; McCloskey, 1983). How profound are these differences? Below we review several lines of evidence regarding children's conception of causality.

Bullock, Gelman, and Baillargeon (1982) propose three components of a mature understanding of causality. First, there are principles that define when two things are related causally (e.g., the principle that causes temporally precede their effects). Second, there is domain-specific knowledge that allows the identification of candidate causes for an effect (and vice versa). Third, there are rough-and-ready rules for deciding whether two events are causally connected. Regarding the third component, we have already reviewed evidence that children apply heuristics differently than adults; children tend to assume causal links between events more frequently than do adults. Regarding the second component, adults and children certainly differ in the specific knowledge they bring to bear on judgments of causality. The issue we are concerned with here is whether these are the only differences between causal concepts of children and those of adults (Carey, 1984), or whether there are additional differences as well. Thus, the most interesting component of Bullock et al.'s formulation is the first one: the principles used to define causality.

In particular, Bullock et al. (1982) describe three principles that undergird adults' definition of causality. Adults are said to believe in determinism, that all physical events are caused. A second principle, priority, states that causes must precede their effects in time. The third principle states that there must be some transfer of "causal impetus" between a cause and its effect. In other words, causes operate via discoverable, domain-specific *mechanisms*.

All three of these principles are important for adults. However, the third principle, that causes have mechanisms, is particularly at issue when considering children's cognition. Recall that Piaget had claimed that children reason about causation in a phenomenalistic way, by attending solely to outward links between events. If this analysis were correct, then children could not recognize the importance of mechanisms linking cause and effect. Instead, they would infer causality from factors that merely gave the appearance of causal connection. Features such as spatial or temporal contiguity or regularity of covariation between events would be sufficient to infer the presence of a causal link. On this view, children use general-purpose heuristics rather than attending to particular mechanisms. Because of the centrality of this principle in developmental theory, we will focus here on the question of whether children recognize the importance of causal mechanisms.

Bullock et al. (1982) report several studies investigating the role of mechanisms in children's causal reasoning. For example, Bullock (1979, reported in Bullock et al., 1982) conducted a study in which 3- and 5-year-old children were asked to decide what caused a jack-in-the-box to jump. Children saw a ball roll through a long box. At the same time, they saw a light moving through the box. Both the ball and the light disappeared, and a few seconds later the jack jumped. The ball and the light are both candidate causes on the basis of temporal and spatial information, yet subjects consistently chose the ball as the cause of the jumping. Children knew how a ball can cause another object to move (via physical collision), but did not know a mechanism whereby a light could cause movement. The presence of a means of transmission is thus an important part of children's attributions of causality.

Further evidence for the importance of mechanism in young children's reasoning about causality comes from the work of Shultz and his colleagues (e.g., Shultz, 1982; Shultz & Kestenbaum, 1985; Shultz, Pardo, & Altmann, 1982). Their concern has been to demonstrate that children recognize the need for a mechanism of transmission by which a cause produces its effect (what they term *generative transmission*). Their studies require children to choose which of two possible causes produced an effect. In a typical paradigm, one possibility lacked a mechanism to produce the effect but did have some other property that would make it a likely candidate, based on general-purpose heuristics (e.g., temporal or spatial contiguity). The second possible cause had the mechanism but lacked the other, domain-general attributes. For example, in one study children were asked which of two fans caused a candle to extinguish. A three-sided plexiglass screen surrounded the candle. One fan was turned on, but the screen prevented it from extinguishing the candle. Later, a second fan was turned on. At the same time, the screen was turned so that the opening faced the first fan. Thus, the turning on of the second fan came closer in time to the extinction of the candle, but only the first fan had the opportunity to transmit its effect. Children reliably chose the first fan as the cause of the candle going out. Children recognized that without a means of transmission, one event cannot cause another.

Summary of Causality Literature

In sum, children do seem to understand basic principles of causality in much the same way as do adults. One of the most important principles that children grasp is that a cause must have some means of producing its effect. Stated differently, children assume generative transmission rather than wholly abstract principles such as contiguity. There are also developmental differences in how children assign causality to events. Some of children's reasoning errors seem to stem from a relative difficulty in appreciating random phenomena, as well as a tendency to expect events to have causes (a tendency we term *presumption of cause*). One implication is that children may supply explanations (because they feel compelled to explain events) using inappropriate domains (when they do not know the correct mechanisms). In other cases, when children fail to grasp the appropriate mechanism, they may appear to be at an utter loss to explain the cause. However, many of these developmental differences can be attributed to differences in domain-specific knowledge (Carey, 1984) or in children's limited abilities to construct verbal explanations (Bullock et al., 1982), rather than to fundamental differences in how causes are understood. The most important point is that causal understandings are potent from early childhood. We turn now to how causality is manifested in categories.

Causality as a Central Component to Categories

Categories are central to the most complex, sophisticated forms of human reasoning as well as the most fundamental survival skills of all animals. We categorize when we recognize that a piece of food is edible, when we name things, or when we invent a new word to refer to a technical concept. Without the capacity to organize experience into categories, we would have extremely limited abilities to extend knowledge to new examples, and so to learn from experience.

Intuitively, it often seems that we classify instances together because they are "alike" in some obvious way such as appearance or function. Certainly this intuitive sense of similarity has powerful effects throughout the lifetime (Smith, 1989), and may be the most powerful way of organizing experience when processing demands are heavy or time constraints are severe (E.E. Smith, personal communication). Yet closer scrutiny reveals that similarity is not a sufficient basis to explain human categorization. Murphy and Medin (1985) argue that similarity fails for two reasons. First, there are epistemological problems in deciding what features to consider (see also Goodman, 1972). Any two objects are as similar as any other two objects, depending on what counts as a feature. For example, a mouse and a lawnmower have infinitely many features in common, in that both weigh less than 500 pounds, are found on earth, have a long appendage, spend time outdoors, are typically not purple, etc. The second difficulty with similarity is that, even were we to decide what counts as a feature, how we weight those features cannot be known in a theory-neutral way. Size, shape, and texture are all relevant features in a classification of common objects, yet depending on the particular content we may weight size more heavily (e.g., dime vs. nickel), shape more heavily (e.g., ball vs. block), or texture more heavily (e.g., cotton vs. silk) (see also Becker & Ward, 1991; Jones, Smith, & Landau, 1991; Soja, Carey, & Spelke, 1991; Ward, Becker, Hass, & Vela, 1991). What is needed instead is an analysis of how categories fit into larger theories.

Recent work in cognitive development has suggested that much of children's knowledge can be characterized in the form of naive theories (Carey, 1985; Keil, 1991; Wellman, 1990; Wellman & Gelman, 1992). By naive or commonsense theory, we mean a system of beliefs that specify causal relations among a set of entities. These beliefs are used both in explaining events and in defining component terms. While naive theories are not identified with the more formal and elaborated theories of scientific disciplines (see Atran, 1990b, for limitations of analogizing from scientific theories to everyday knowledge), there are important similarities between naive and formal theories. In the following section we briefly review some proposed accounts of commonsense theories and causality. After this review we propose two principles by which causality can influence categorization within a theory.

Commonsense Theories and Causality

An intuitive example may clarify the importance of theory in classification. Consider the organization of symptoms into diseases in our culture. On one level, it might seem that different sufferers of the flu are classed together because they have similar symptoms (e.g., grogginess, sore throat, fever). However, for most adults there are clear causal assumptions underlying the assignment of symptoms to disease. We group symptoms together as "the flu" because they have a common cause (a virus) and common effects. Furthermore, the symptoms respond in common ways to perturbations from the world (e.g., an aspirin reduces its symptoms; a vaccine can prevent it). If someone has "flu-like symptoms" (e.g., fever, sore throat) but not the underlying cause, then the person does not have the disease. Conversely, someone may not experience the symptoms but may still suffer the effects of the disease eventually (or be a carrier). The symptoms are mere reflections; the critical commonality is the underlying cause. Interestingly, this assumption—that a disease has an underlying common cause that leads to the symptoms—appears to be held even when the term *disease* is applied only loosely (e.g., computer viruses) or when the underlying theory and etiology of a disorder are less well understood (e.g., autism). Thus, a theory of human physiology underlies our classification of symptoms into diseases. Similarity alone is insufficient.

More generally, Markman (1990) suggests that "richly structured categories" (which are essentially what we mean by "theory-laden categories") differ from arbitrary categories in six ways. Specifically, they promote many more inductive inferences; they are believed to capture something fundamental about what is being classified; they specify the object's identity, rather than simply what it is like; they are relatively enduring and permanent; they are more likely to enter into hierarchically organized taxonomies; they may be viewed as mutually exclusive with one another. Similarly, Gelman and Coley (1991) propose that theory-laden categories have a cluster of properties that distinguish them from more similarity-based categories, including rich inductive potential, a non-obvious basis, an assumed essence, potential for anomalies, division of linguistic labor (see Putnam, 1973), and openness to revision. Rothbart and Taylor (in press) suggest that social categories also function like theory-laden natural kinds (naturally occurring species that "carve up nature at its joints"; see Schwartz, 1979), particularly in their inductive potential and what they call *unalterability*. Unalterability, which is reinforced by psychological essentialism, states that category status cannot be changed (e.g., a cat cannot become a dog; members of one caste cannot become members of another).

Although the notion of "theory" is rarely articulated in detail (but see Carey, 1985, and Wellman, 1990, for in-depth treatments of children's theories of biology and the mind, respectively), there is widespread agreement that theories include causality as a central component (Carey, 1985; Wellman, 1990). Causal mechanisms specify the ways the component elements of the theory may interact.

Researchers who study the role theories play in categorization have generally accepted causality as a primitive notion and have not analyzed how causality works within theories. Within this framework, one proposal has been that theories provide constraints for the kinds of features used in category construction (Kalish & Gelman, 1990; Keil, 1991; Murphy & Medin, 1985; but see Smith & Heise, in press, for a defense of perceptual similarity). For example, the judgment that curvedness is a more central property of boomerangs than of bananas results because it is difficult to see how curvedness could be a causally relevant feature within a theory of biology (which is responsible for the classification of bananas), whereas it is easy to see how curvedness might have important functional consequences within a theory of physics.

In support of the notion that some features are more important than others, Medin and Shoben (1988) gathered two kinds of ratings from adults: typicality (how typical is feature X of category Y?) and possibility (how likely is it for Y *not* to have X?). They found that judgments of *possibility* could not be reduced to judgments of *typicality*. As in the above example, a feature that was equally likely to occur in two categories (e.g., bananas and boomerangs are equally likely to be curved) was not equally alterable (e.g., a straight banana is deemed more possible than a straight boomerang). Because adults could not have appealed to empirical regularities when judging possibility (otherwise, the two tasks would have yielded converging results), one strong possibility is that adults appealed to their understanding of the causal consequences of property violations (e.g., the atypical shape).

Another important function of theories, according to Murphy and Medin (1985), is to provide explanations for correlated attributes (e.g., having a heart and having a liver). Keil (1991) makes a similar point when he suggests that categories with features connected through causal relations may be preferred to those with features connected merely through covariation. These ideas hold promise yet require further elaboration if they are to make specific predictions. Similarly, the distinction between causal and correlational features, although intriguing, will require closer examination in the future (e.g., can a feature be clearly designated as one or the other? if so, how can one tell the difference between the two?).

Causality and Categorization: Two Principles

Current accounts of causality, theories, and categorization in psychology offer valuable insights, but they do not offer a unified picture of the relations between causality and categorization. In this section we derive two implications for categorization that we believe are primary. We illustrate with the process of classifying illness, although the principles are intended to apply to theory-based categorization more generally.

Principle 1: Causal Links Determine Which Features are Primary When a Classification is Constructed and Extended

Imagine traveling to a distant land with the goal of developing a taxonomy of the diseases that affect that population. One issue is how to decide among various ways of partitioning the diseases, in all of their messy and intricate complexities. As philosophers have pointed out, there are indefinitely many ways of organizing elements into sets (Peirce, 1935; Goodman, 1972). It is logically possible, for example, to classify illnesses by the day of the week of their onset. Yet such a grouping seems absurd. Why do we ignore the weekday onset versus weekend onset distinction in favor of the division between chronic and acute? Our preference for the latter means of categorization is based on the belief (perhaps entirely implicit) that time course of an illness is a more theoretically important feature than onset time. By "theoretically important" we mean "likely to enter into the causal laws and relations formulated by the theory."[1] Time

[1] Depending on the theory of interest, some features that are irrelevant to one domain may become critical in another domain. For example, day of the week may be critical for classifying a social interaction as either business-related or personal.

course is more causally relevant (in being both a cause and an effect of other relevant features). This principle has several related implications:

(1a) Theories constrain which features are considered at all. For example, a viral theory of pneumonia will include microscopic organisms as central entities, and will be unconcerned with psychological factors. More generally, the theory dictates what kinds of entities are relevant. It may be for this reason that psychosomatic illnesses are so difficult for people to conceptualize accurately. That is, it is often assumed that illnesses are either wholly physical or wholly psychological. If the latter, they are sometimes erroneously thought not to be "real" in some sense—with no real pain and no true physical effects. It is difficult for people to consider categories that cut across theory boundaries. Furthermore, it is difficult to understand the causal mechanism linking mental states to physical states, thus exacerbating our difficulty with allowing psychological features in our medical categories.

(1b) Once a domain is identified, those features that cause other features are relatively more important. Features that are responsible for many other features are viewed as most central and defining. Thus, we categorize an illness by the particular virus (in the case of viral infection) that gave rise to the observed symptoms. DNA structure is considered the most important feature in classifying plants and animals because it is the cause of many other properties. The causal relation is inherently asymmetric (if A causes B, B does not cause A). The cause is more fundamental than the effect.[2]

(1c) Both implications discussed above concern how a category is set up in the first place. How does causality affect modifications to an already

---

[2]The importance attached to causally responsible features may be a recent historical phenomenon. Classification of diseases in the Renaissance relied on identifying signs of affinity (Foucault, 1973), also known as the doctrine of signatures. Signatures were indications provided by God of the relations among things. The signatures themselves were neither causes nor effects of the relations. For example, aconite was identified as a cure for eye diseases on the basis of the appearance of its seeds (Foucault, 1973, p. 27). The appearance of the seeds was thought to be neither a result nor a cause of curative properties, but rather a helpful sign provided by divine providence. Neither was there an attempt to discover what the actual properties of aconite responsible for the cure were; the concern was the proper identification and interpretations of signs indicating the value of aconite as a medicine. Properties and features were important only as signals of true relations, and interrelations among properties were ignored. Thus, a natural history by Aldrovandi from the early 1600s for each animal "offered the reader, and on the same level, a description of its anatomy and of the methods of capturing it; its allegorical uses and mode of generation; its habitat and legendary mansions; its food and the best ways of cooking its flesh" (Foucault, 1973, p. 129). All these features are equally important indications of the true nature of the animal.

existing category? We know that categories change—sometimes radically—as the theories they enter into change. What is the precise role of cause in these revisions? Here we can only speculate, but we do so on analogy with disease categories.

There are two views of disease: the Hippocratic and the Platonic (Engelhardt, 1975). This distinction corresponds roughly to a distinction between viewing disease categories as invented versus viewing them as discovered. A Hippocratic approach assumes that diseases are convenient fictions that serve to emphasize certain commonalities among patients. A system of categorization is valid insofar as it fits the needs of the doctor using it. New discoveries will modify conceptions of a disease only to the extent that the doctor finds them useful in his or her practice. So, a doctor treating patients with influenza might be unmoved by the discovery that there are many separate viruses that cause the illness, unless that information had direct implications for treatment or prognosis.

A Platonist doctor, on the other hand, would take such new data as providing crucial information about the true underlying nature of the disease. Whereas before, he or she had mistakenly viewed influenza as a single disease, the new information indicates that there are many different diseases that deserve to be considered distinct categories. These disease categories are understood to reflect the causal structure of the world; they are "indexed" (Kripke, 1972) to this structure. Therefore, new discoveries about the world can mandate a change in categories.

The Hippocratic/Platonist distinction, which outside of medicine is best characterized as a Nominalist/Realist distinction, has clear implications for determining when categories undergo revision. If categories are seen as arbitrary labels with no necessary basis in reality (a Hippocratic or Nominalist view), then discoveries about the world need not force changes in the way things are categorized. If, however, categories are seen as discoveries about the world (a Platonist or Realist view), new information will require a change in the way things are categorized.

In short, the categorizer has at least two options when confronted with new information about a category: either to alter the category (and incorporate anomalies), or to construct a new category. We hypothesize that, to the extent that causal links are assumed to be powerful, the categorizer incorporates the anomaly and revises the category. In contrast, to the extent that the classification is a mere convenience (not the discovery of natural law), the categorizer is likely to attempt revision. To illustrate, consider the case of black swans, which violate the empirical observation that swans are white birds. When presented with a black swan for the first time, we do not revise our category of "white birds" to include the anomaly, but we do revise our category of "swans." Paradoxically, the more we believe a category to reflect natural law, the less we may acknowledge an anomaly. A physicist who observes some particular aberrant behavior of an electron might doubt her equipment, her methodology, or even her sanity, before questioning her understanding of electrons (see Quine, 1960). The more an individual believes that his representation of a category reflects reality, the more definitional that representation becomes and the less likely the anomaly is to be noticed. Nonetheless, once the individual accepts the aberration as real, then that should force a revision of a natural kind.

(1d) Causal relations specify which feature violations are possible, and so which anomalies to accept. This principle explains why a five-legged chair is still a chair, but a mechanical bird is not really a bird. In the case of the chair, the object still has the same function in all of the causal relations that serve to define chairs. The mechanical bird, however, would not fulfill the same role in the relations and generalizations that determine what it is for something to be a bird.

(1e) Another corollary is that causality allows conceptual combination. In deciding which features of a concept are carried into combinations, it is important to know which are the causal features and which are merely typical associates of the category. In judging the intelligence of a member of the combined category "Harvard-educated carpenter" we assign the intelligence value associated with "Harvard-educated" rather than that associated with "carpenter" (Kunda, Miller, & Claire, 1990) because we know that intelligence is a causally relevant feature for the first category but not the second. (For this example to work, however, requires the questionable assumption that carpenters do not need to be intelligent.)

Principle 2: Categories Have Underlying Causes (Essences)

The assumption that categories are organized around features that generate, cause, or are responsible for other features has been described as psychological essentialism (Medin, 1989; Medin & Ortony, 1989). Given a belief that regularities in the environment require causes (referred to earlier as the principle of determinism), the particular cluster of features characteristic of a given category must have some causal basis. We can ask why it is that one gets a runny nose, body aches, and a fever when one has the flu. What is it that causes these symptoms to appear together? This question initiates the search for an essence of the flu that gives rise to these other features.

Medin refers to this as *psychological essentialism* to emphasize that it is a belief that people hold rather than a fact about the structure of the world. Atran (1990a, 1990b) further distinguishes between phenomenal and metaphysical essentialism. The first is the belief that the categories we have constructed have an underlying (perhaps undiscovered) essence; the second belief also entails corrigibility—the status of our categories is in doubt, open to revision, depending on the essence that has not yet been discovered. For our purposes, we focus on phenomenal essentialism.

A belief in essences has several implications for categories. First, there will be something that all members of a category necessarily have in common, however much they may vary from one another. Second, the nature of the essence should unambiguously determine category membership. Thus, although a patient's disease may be difficult to classify, an inspection of the disease's essential feature (or the essential feature of the class to which one wishes to assign it) will reveal its proper category membership. The most important implication of a belief in essences, however, is the structure this provides for categories. Categories are seen to consist of an underlying feature or set of features that cause sets of characteristic features. There are two parts to a category: an essence (which is the real basis of the category) and a set of features that are diagnostic of the essence (because they are its effects) but not central to the category.[3] This conception of categories is consistent with theories that distinguish between the core of a concept and its identification procedure (Armstrong, Gleitman, & Gleitman, 1983; Miller & Johnson-Laird, 1976).

Summary of Principles

In a nutshell, we propose that causality exerts its effects on categorization in two central ways: first, in determining which features are considered, which are deemed central, and which are open to revision, and second, in promoting the search for an essence. The principles outlined in this section were drawn from considering the philosophical and psychological underpinnings of adult categories.

We do not wish to claim that all categories entail causal links between features. We can categorize in even very subtle ways without a background theory (cf. Brooks, 1978; Biederman & Shiffrar, 1987). Learning based on similarity of features and analyses of covariation probably accounts, at least initially, for many concepts, and does not require causal understandings. Nonetheless, such categories are only a subset of those we construct.

In order to assess the value of these ideas, it helps to consider how the above hypotheses could be disconfirmed. In particular, we consider what evidence would argue against these principles. Any of four demonstrations would provide counterevidence against our framework.

If, in a given classification, no features have priority, or the features that do have priority are determined purely by an unbiased similarity metric, or the features that have priority are independent of the

[3] This does not mean a return to classical definitions of necessary and sufficient defining features (see Medin, 1989).

features that have causal powers, then the hypothesis would be disconfirmed.

If the categorizer cannot abstract to anomalies in a principled way, then the hypothesis would be disconfirmed. For example, all anomalies that have not been empirically observed would be rejected or accepted at equal rates.

If categories are not open to revision, then the hypothesis would be disconfirmed. For example, categories could be viewed as conventional and invented, as mere conveniences rather than natural kinds.

Finally, the hypothesis would be disconfirmed if there were no expectation of a category essence. This could take the form of drawing no distinction between surface and underlying characteristics, or it could take the form of expecting no commonalities underlying surface variations.

It is important that these tests do not rest on examining category content (e.g., whether a category concerns animals or artifacts). Although there may be important domain differences in the theoretical richness of a category (e.g., Gelman & Coley, 1991), this is due to how the domain is understood, rather than intrinsically determined by how it can possibly be organized. For example, a horse falls into the classes *horse*, *pet*, *odd-toed creature*, *Equus caballus*, each with a different category structure. Even if we limit our attention to basic-level categories such as *horse* (cf. Rosch, Mervis, Gray, Johnson, & Boyes-Braem, 1976) to determine whether a category has causal underpinnings, one needs to see how the category is being used. Simply listing the set of instances most commonly grouped together would not be informative. The word *horse* can be understood in terms of surface features alone or causal connections.

The Developmental Picture

We now turn to the developmental implications of this work. A major conclusion from the first part of the chapter is that children pay close attention to causal relations. A review of children's understanding of causality suggests that their conception is much like that of adults. If anything, children may overascribe causality to events. We therefore expect causality to influence children's categories in much the same way as it influences those of adults. This raises the implications that children will (a) view features that are more causal as more central, (b) demonstrate a grasp of possibility, enabling predictions about anomalies and conceptual combinations, (c) treat categories as open to revision, and (d) expect categories to embody essences. Recent research from our laboratory provides some evidence for three of these predictions, namely (a), (b), and (d). We describe such evidence below.

Identifying Central Features

Several studies demonstrate that similarity alone is insufficient to characterize how children classify, and suggest that causality determines which features are central. Keil (1989) found that, when given a conflict between the superficial features of one category and the origins or essence of another category (e.g., parentage and internal features), elementary school children formed categories based on the essence. Younger children were more likely to categorize based on superficial features, yet even preschoolers could overlook appearances in the clear cases. For example, they would deny that a cactus could be transformed into a porcupine, or that a horse wearing a close-fitting striped suit could then be a zebra.

Similarly, Gelman and Wellman (1991) provide a demonstration that even 4-year-old children consider insides more important than outsides, for selected clear cases (e.g., turtles, cars). Children learned about items that had either insides or outsides removed (e.g., for a turtle, either blood and bones, or the shell). When asked whether the objects would retain their identity (e.g., would it still be a turtle) and characteristic functioning (e.g., would it still be able to walk), children overwhelmingly reported that inside removal would alter both. In contrast, outside removal—even if it greatly altered an animal's appearance—would leave identity and functioning relatively unaffected. On balance, these studies suggest that similarity alone cannot account for children's categories.

We have recently found that children as young as 3 years of age selectively focus on theory-relevant properties when forming a classification (Kalish & Gelman, in press). For example, children predict how likely an object is to break based on its substance (e.g., glass) rather than its object identity (e.g., frying pan), even when object identity is highly correlated with fragility. For instance, when asked whether a glass frying pan would or would not break when dropped, children report that it would break. These same children consistently assert that a frying pan (with substance unspecified) will not break when dropped. Thus, when the theoretical domain of interest involves breaking (which presumably enters into naive theories of matter; see Smith, Carey, & Wiser, 1985), children know that material properties are more relevant than object type. To put it differently, children have learned the causal implications of material properties such as "made of glass" and use these implications as relevant. In an additional study (Kalish & Gelman, in press) we found, not surprisingly, that children can ignore material composition and make judgments based on object type when appropriate (e.g., deciding that a frying pan belongs in the kitchen because it is a frying pan). We have suggested that these data provide evidence that theory determines which features are particularly important to a classification.

If indeed children impute causes more readily than adults and correspondingly have difficulties understanding randomness, we would expect that children may pay little heed to statistical information about category structure, when the statistical information is divorced from specific causal connections. Gutheil and Gelman (1990) explored children's ability to make category-based inferences based on statistical information. Following Nisbett, Krantz, Jepson, and Kunda (1983) and Osherson, Smith, Wilkie, Lopez, and Shafir (1990), they examined two statistical heuristics that are salient for adults. To illustrate: one principle, category diversity, states that a property known to be true of a diverse sample (e.g., wolves and horses) generalizes more broadly and leads to more confident inductions than a property known to be true of a homogeneous sample (e.g., wolves and dogs). In this example, after learning that wolves and horses have calcium inside, you should be more confident that mice do, too, than after learning that wolves and dogs have calcium inside. Children (ages 5 and 7 years) and adults were given a series of inductive inference problems on which they were taught a new fact about a sample that varied in diversity (e.g., the sample was either a single sparrow, five highly similar sparrows, or five different kinds of birds). Subjects' task was to say whether the properties were also true of each of several test pictures (including a different sparrow, other birds, and nonbirds). Whereas adults generalized more broadly when given a diverse training sample than when given either a single instance or a homogeneous set of instances, children completely ignored the statistical information. They seemed oblivious to the striking variation in diversity. Instead, they made use of both category membership and perceptual similarity. In fact, children gave category membership special weight, and were even more willing than adults to draw inferences to dissimilar members of the category (e.g., they more often inferred that other birds had X when told that a single sparrow had X).

All of the work described above is limited in that it includes no independent confirmation of the causal structure of categories for children. Specifically, we do not know whether the features that children assume are most central are in fact ones they believe to be causally prior. For example, children rate internal features as more important than external ones—do they correspondingly believe that internal features cause external features? In future work, it will be important to gather independent confirmation of these causal links.

A Grasp of Possibility

Medin and Shoben (1988), in their recent "banana–boomerang" study, found that adults consider possibility as well as empirical regularities when constructing categories. Recall that in this task, adults judged curvedness to be more important for boomerangs than for bananas, even though past experience would tell us that both are always curved. Using a variant of this task, Biderman (1989) found that preschool children, too, can reason about category potential. The question was whether children determine category membership strictly on the basis of observed empirical correlations, or whether category judgments are instead based at least in part on causal understandings that place constraints on possible variation. Children were presented with 16 anomalies that they had never observed previously, and were asked whether each could exist. Examples included a blue bear that was born blue (which adults judged impossible) and a blue pretzel (which adults judged to be possible). All children correctly reported that these anomalies did not currently exist. Yet even the youngest subjects (4-year-olds) agreed that certain anomalies *could* exist, especially the same anomalies that adults judged as possible.

It is also relevant to consider children's ability to compute conceptual combinations, given that complex concepts may also require an ability to attend to theory-relevant properties. Although not explicitly framed in terms of conceptual combinations, numerous studies of children's ability to interpret and produce noun–noun compounds (e.g., *mouse-hat* to refer to a hat worn by a mouse) suggest that children construct these combinations with ease. Clark (1982) has diary data of 2- and 3-year-old children spontaneously coining combinations like "plate–egg" versus "cup–egg" to distinguish scrambled from soft-boiled eggs. In an experimental task, Clark, Gelman, and Lane (1985) found that children's interpretations of these compounds were also excellent by early preschool. Interestingly, use and understanding of these forms requires remarkable flexibility, as their interpretations are heavily context-driven. There are no simple rules of interpretation that can be stated in advance (Downing, 1977), so children's ready use of these expressions is all the more impressive.

We assume that children's knowledge of the causal implications of these properties guided their ability to reason about possibility on the tasks described above. As before, however, the data to this point are limited in that they do not include any independent confirmation of the causal structure children represent.

In addition to the question of whether children can reason about category possibility independently of empirical regularities, there is the additional issue of whether children overrely on causality, as we have proposed earlier. If so, then they might be conservative with regard to the possible changes a category member could undergo. Children may assume—as a default—that any feature reliably associated with a category has important causal links, and so they might be less willing than adults to allow that the feature could be altered. Such conservatism would be consistent with Keil's (1989) finding that changes in surface features lead children to report that category membership has changed.

In further support of this interpretation, in their spontaneous comments children in Keil's experiments often seemed to express that feature correlations could not be broken; for example, an animal that looked like a horse had to have horse parents. Most strikingly, this at times led children either to misremember the story premises or even to insist that the experimenter must be mistaken. Consider, for example, the following conversation between experimenter (E) and child (C) (Keil, 1989, pp. 166–167):

E: How can two cat parents have a dog baby?
C: They can't.
E: This animal's parents were cats.
C: They probably think that two dogs are cats.
E: No, their parents really are cats.
C: Oh, that's funny.

This child seems to view the relation between appearance (looking like a dog) and parentage (having dog parents) as more than a correlation; rather, it is treated as a necessary (perhaps causally determined) link. A similar belief appears to be expressed by another child, who insisted (p. 168)," . . . if it was a cow, if it had a baby, then it has to be a cow! If it was a horse, then it would have to be a baby horse."

Conversely, Rosengren, Gelman, Kalish, and McCormick (1991) found that preschoolers are conservative in their expectations of the kinds of transformations that can occur as animals age. In these studies, children (3-, 4-, and 5-year-olds) viewed triads of animal pictures. The experimenter identified one picture in each triad as the "baby"; children were then asked to decide which of the two remaining pictures in each set was the individual as an adult. The two choice pictures varied across sets so as to reveal which transformations children considered most likely. At all ages, children realized that animals get larger with age rather than getting smaller or staying the same size. However, what is interesting in this context is that the youngest children were especially unwilling to accept any other than size changes with age. Whereas older children and adults accepted color change or metamorphosis if the alternative was selecting an adult that was smaller than the baby, the 3-year-olds were loathe to accept such dramatic appearance changes.

Although the Rosengren et al. (1991) findings at first may seem inconsistent with Keil's (1989) findings (note that children are less conservative than adults in Keil's work—accepting changes in category membership that adults deem impossible—but more conservative than adults in Rosengren et al.), the two sets of findings can be viewed as opposite sides of the same coin. In both sets of experiments, children treat feature correlations as stable, perhaps necessary, and unlikely to be disrupted. The result is a reluctance to accept category anomalies.

Promote Search for Underlying Essence

Two sets of studies provide indirect evidence consistent with the notion of psychological essentialism: studies of innate potential and studies of natural cause. A concept of innate potential arises in attempting to explain the often striking metamorphoses that take place with developmental change. Consider the vast changes that occur in a human newborn to yield a human adult, or in a helpless, gentle tiger cub to result eventually in a fierce, full-grown tiger. One powerful account for the course of development is to posit that the immature creature is born with a certain potential to grow and develop in predestined ways. Although a 2-month-old kitten and a newborn tiger cub may look remarkably alike, their innate potentials differ and so result in differing end states.

For adults, the notion of innate potential can become highly intertwined with notions of environmental influences, and some have argued that developmental systems do not permit easy distinctions of innate from environmental forces (Sameroff, 1983). Nonetheless, as adults we retain the sense that innate forces help guide the development of living things from infancy to adulthood.

A belief in innate potential is consistent with a belief in an underlying essence. The innate potential is the essence. Accordingly, in a series of studies in our laboratory (Gelman & Wellman, 1991), we examined when a belief in innate potential arises. There were two groups of subjects: younger and older 4-year-olds. In the first study, the children were presented with a series of "nature–nurture" problems in which innate potential was pitted against environmental factors. For example, children learned of a newborn pig who was taken to a farm that had only cows, and who never saw another pig. Subjects then had to decide how the pig (in this example) would grow: would it have a straight or curly tail, and would it say "oink" or "moo"? In every problem, one question concerned a static physical property, the other concerned a behavioral property. The results showed that children at both ages answered as nativists (e.g., the pig would have a curly tail and would say oink), although this was particularly true for behavioral properties. In other words, children seemed to show belief in innate potential.

Two control studies were also conducted, to make sure that children were fully familiar with the properties being tested, and that differences between static and behavioral properties could not be due to different levels of familiarity with the two kinds of properties. We presented children the same problems but with no conflict (e.g., a pig brought up among pigs, or a cow brought up among cows). Here, children answered on the basis of the animal's identity (e.g., a pig raised among pigs will have a curly tail and will say "oink"; a cow raised among cows will have a straight tail and will say "moo"), with no reliable differences between behaviors and static attributes.

The last piece of evidence for essentialism focuses on children's explanations, from work reported in Gelman and Kremer (1991). To begin with, consider our hypothesis that children assume and search for causal explanations. In the case of artifacts, nearly all properties can be explained in terms of human action and intention. A chair is green and four-legged because a human built and painted it that way, with the intention of creating a green chair. In contrast, properties of natural kinds cannot be explained by appeal to external human forces (at least for adults). Rather, natural kind properties can be explained by essences; the essence is the underlying property that gives rise to surface features. Thus, when children are attempting to explain the feature clusters characteristic of natural kinds (e.g., the many features that goats have in common), they may assume that some internal, intrinsic, or inherent force is at work (in other words, an essence). This notion is reminiscent of Gelman's *innards principle* (1990), but applies more broadly than to innards alone. As Locke (1894/1959) stated: "the real internal, but generally . . . unknown constitution of things, whereon their discoverable qualities depend may be called their essence" (p. 26). To repeat the example provided above, the essence of a tiger causes it to have stripes, a large size, the capacity to roar, etc.

At first it may seem unlikely that children would appeal to essentialist explanations. According to Piaget, children are both animistic and artificialistic, and so should couch explanations in terms of human or human-like desires and behaviors. Thus, natural kinds could be treated as if they were artifacts (i.e., resulting from human causes), and children would have no need to consider essences. However, recent evidence suggests that children are not as strictly animistic as Piaget had proposed (Gelman, Spelke, & Meck, 1983; Richards & Siegler, 1984, 1986). It is possible, then, that children are not strictly artificialistic either, and that they may understand natural causes from an early age.

To examine this question, Gelman and Kremer (1991) asked preschool and 7-year-old children to explain the origins of things (e.g., where birds, TVs, or oceans come from). They also asked a second set of children to explain the source of behaviors (e.g., why birds fly) and properties (e.g., why birds have wings). Several findings emerged. First, children showed little evidence for animistic explanations; that is, they rarely reported that behaviors or properties of natural kinds resulted from the intentions of the items in question. They also showed no evidence for pervasive artificialism; that is, they appealed to human cause much more often for human artifacts (e.g., TVs) than for natural kinds (e.g., dogs), as appropriate. Third, children were willing to impute internal agency to both natural kinds and artifacts. For example, some children said that muscles helped make a bird fly, or that wires made a telephone ring. For natural kinds, the less human agency was involved, the more internal agency was implicated. Animals were said to have the fewest human origins, followed by plants, followed by natural substances. Correspondingly, causally relevant internal parts were viewed as most central to animals, followed by plants, followed by natural substances.

The other point from these data is that children often appealed to essence-like qualities, including innate cause ("The egg made the [rabbit's] ears so that it had them when it hatched"), intrinsic nature ("The leaf just makes itself change colors"), and growth ("It grew that way"). Seventy-two percent of preschoolers and 73% of 7-year-olds appealed to the state of the animal when it was born (or hatched), or to its intrinsic state, or to aspects of its growth. Moreover, they did so significantly more often for natural kinds than for artifacts. Even for 4-year-olds, members of a natural kind category are assumed to hold together because of an essential nature, but members of an artifact category are not.

Conclusions

In this last section, we speculate briefly as to the broader consequences of the views set forth. Roughly, these consequences can be divided into implications for categories based on what we know about causal understandings, and implications for causality based on what we know about children's categories.

One important implication concerns children's propensity to view events as caused. If this assumption is even stronger for children than for adults, then we might expect children in particular to treat categories as theory-laden. Children, more than adults, may view categories as discovered rather than invented, as attempts to capture something about the causal structure of the world rather than as useful fictions. They may be more likely to assume that there are essences to their categories. Even those categories that are clearly inventions (e.g., social categories such as occupational or social status) may nonetheless be considered empirical discoveries by the child. Moreover, if children do assume that events are caused (as opposed to being random), then they may have difficulty grasping the arbitrariness of certain categories (e.g., pet, worm).

In other words, we speculate that children might be "categorical realists"; that is, realists about the distinctions made by the categories they are acquiring. This notion suggests commonalities with other aspects of children's thinking. Turiel (1983) has argued that children are moral realists: moral precepts and rules are taken to be universal truths independent of human decisions. Piaget (1932/1965) believed that young children would treat social conventions (e.g., game rules) as similarly real and immutable. Research has failed to support Piaget's claims entirely, but has shown that young children seem to be realists about the status of a wider range of norms and customs (e.g., table manners, Miller & Bersoff, 1988) than adults (see Gabennesch, 1990, for review). Children have also been described as realists about the content of beliefs (Johnson, 1988). They appear not to understand the constructive nature of mental representations, but take beliefs to be accurate reflections of the true state of the world (Flavell, 1988; Wellman, 1990). (Note, however, that children are not unremitting realists when it comes to appearance-reality judgments; Flavell, Flavell, & Green, 1987.) Examining the relation between causality and categorization offers a promising way of pursuing inquiries into issues of childhood realism.

The second direction we wish to suggest is a way that studies of categorization can be helpful for research on causality. Although the two remain separate endeavors, we suggest that they are importantly linked in the mind of the child. An understanding of the causal rules and mechanisms appreciated by children will help to identify the categories that they can be expected to form. Learning a new kind of causal relation can provide the opportunity to form new categories. For example, once you grasp that not all human actions are intentionally caused (e.g., accidents, mistakes), you can refine your categories in the domain of morality. Similarly, a child who learns about magnetism can use this causal understanding to reformulate some existing categories (e.g., to motivate distinguishing iron from aluminum). More generally, as new kinds of causal understandings develop, children should be able to make category distinctions on that basis.

In sum, a consensus is now emerging that similarity is insufficient to characterize how adults or children classify. This has led many researchers to assert the importance of theories. In the present chapter we have attempted to go beyond this insight to develop some more precise consequences of viewing categories as embedded in theories. We have done so by attending to the role of causality in the construction of theory-laden categories. One point that repeatedly emerged in our review is that more work is needed to delineate children's causal understandings and to examine the precise links to category structure. It would also be useful to expand the range of domains that are studied. Until recently, much of the work has focused on physical causality and, more recently, intentional causality. It would also be extremely instructive to examine domains in which causal mechanisms play little if any role (e.g., theories of contagion). In future work, it will be intriguing to examine how causes fit into domain-specific theories.

Acknowledgments. We thank Bob Pasnak and Mark Howe for their helpful comments on an earlier draft. This work was supported in part by NICHD grant HD-23378 to the first author, an NSF predoctoral fellowship to the second author, and an award from the W.K. Kellogg Foundation through the Presidential Initiatives Fund of the University of Michigan.

References

Armstrong, S.L., Gleitman, L.R., & Gleitman, H. (1983). What some concepts might not be. *Cognition*, *13*, 263–308.

Atran, S. (1990a). *Cognitive foundations of natural history: Towards an anthropology of science*. New York: Cambridge University Press.

Atran, S. (1990b). *Speculations on the structure, development, and integration of basic conceptual domains*. Paper presented at the conference on "Cultural Knowledge and Domain Specificity," University of Michigan. Ann Arbor, MI.

Becker, A.H., & Ward, T.B. (1991). Children's use of shape in extending novel labels to animate objects: Identity versus postural change. *Cognitive Development*, *6*, 3–16.

Berndt, T.J., & Berndt, E.G. (1975). Children's use of motives and intentionality in person perception and moral judgment. *Child Development*, *46*, 904–912.

Biderman, C. (1989, April). *Flexibility of children's animal and artifact categories when judging anomalous objects' possible existence*. Paper presented at the biennial meeting of the Society for Research in Child Development, Kansas City, MO.

Biederman, I., & Shiffrar, M.M. (1987). Sexing day-old chicks: A case study and expert systems analysis of a difficult perceptual-learning task. *Journal of Experimental Psychology: Learning, Memory, and Cognition*, *13*, 640–645.

Brooks, L.R. (1978). Nonanalytic concept formation and memory for instances. In E. Rosch & B. Lloyd (Eds.), *Cognition and categorization* (pp. 169–211). Hillsdale, NJ: Erlbaum.

Brown, A.L. (1990). Domain-specific principles affect learning and transfer in children. *Cognitive Science*, *14*, 107–133.

Bullock, M. (1979). *Aspects of the young child's theory of causation*. Unpublished doctoral dissertation, University of Pennsylvania.

Bullock, M., Gelman, R., & Baillargeon, R. (1982). The development of causal reasoning. In W.J. Friedman (Ed.), *The developmental psychology of time* (pp. 209–254). New York: Academic Press.

Carey, S. (1982). Semantic development: the state of the art. In E. Wanner & L.R. Gleitman (Eds.), *Language acquisition: The state of the art* (pp. 347–389). Cambridge: Cambridge University Press.

Carey, S. (1984). Cognitive development: The descriptive problem. In M.S. Gazzaniga (Ed.), *Handbook of cognitive neuroscience* (pp. 37–66). New York: Plenum.

Carey, S. (1985). *Conceptual change in childhood*. Cambridge, MA: MIT Press.

Clark, E.V. (1982). The young word maker: A case study of innovation in the child's lexicon. In E. Wanner & L.R. Gleitman (Eds.), *Language acquisition: The state of the art* (pp. 390–425). Cambridge: Cambridge University Press.

Clark, E.V., Gelman, S.A., & Lane, N. (1985). Noun compounds and category structure in young children. *Child Development*, *56*, 84–94.

Clark, H., & Clark, E.V. (1977). *Psychology and language*. New York: Harcourt Brace Jovanovich.

Copple, C.E., & Coon, R.C. (1977). The role of causality in encoding and remembering as a function of age. *Journal of Genetic Psychology*, *130*, 129–136.

Downing, P. (1977). On creation and use of English compound nouns. *Language*, *53*, 810–842.

Engelhardt, H.T., Jr. (1975). The concepts of health and disease. In H.T. Engelhardt Jr. & S.F. Spicker (Eds.), *Evaluation and explanation in the biomedical sciences* (pp. 125–141). Dordrecht, Holland: Reidel.

Fein, D.A. (1973). Judgments of causality to physical and social picture sequences. *Developmental Psychology*, *8*, 147.

Flavell, J.H. (1988). The development of children's knowledge about the mind: From cognitive connections to mental representations. In J.W. Astington, P.L. Harris, & D.R. Olson (Eds.), *Developing theories of mind* (pp. 244–267). Cambridge: Cambridge University Press.

Flavell, J.H., Flavell, E.R., & Green, F.L. (1987). Young children's knowledge about the apparent-real and pretend-real distinctions. *Developmental Psychology*, *23*, 816–822.

Foucault, M. (1973). *The order of things; an archeology of the human sciences*. New York: Vintage Books.

Gabennesch, H. (1990). The perception of social conventionality by children and adults. *Child Development*, *61*, 2047–2059.

Gelman, R. (1990). First principles organize attention to and learning about relevant data: Number and the animate-inanimate distinction as examples. *Cognitive Science*, *14*, 79–106.

Gelman, R., Spelke, E.S., & Meck, E. (1983). What preschoolers know about animate and inanimate objects. In D. Rogers & J.A. Sloboda (Eds.), *The acquisition of symbolic skills* (pp. 297–324). London: Plenum.

Gelman, S.A., & Coley, J.C. (1991). Language and categorization: The acquisition of natural kind terms. In S.A. Gelman & J.P. Byrnes (Eds.), *Perspectives on language and thought: Interrelations in development* (pp. 146–196). Cambridge: Cambridge University Press.

Gelman, S.A., & Kremer, K.E. (1991). Understanding natural cause: Children's explanations of how objects and their properties originate. *Child Development*, *62*, 396–414.

Gelman, S.A., & Wellman, H.M. (1991). Insides and essences: Early understandings of the nonobvious. *Cognition*, *38*, 213–244.

Goodman, N. (1972). Seven strictures on similarity. In N. Goodman (Ed.), *Problems and projects* (pp. 437–447). Indianapolis: Bobbs-Merrill.

Green, M. (1978). Structure and sequence in children's concepts of chance and probability: A replication study of Piaget and Inhelder. *Child Development*, *49*, 1045–1053.

Grice, H.P. (1975). Logic and conversation. In P. Cole & J.L. Morgan (Eds.), *Syntax and semantics, Vol. 3; Speech acts* (pp. 41–58). New York: Academic Press.

Gunnar-vonGnechten, M.R. (1978). Changing a frightening toy into a pleasant toy by allowing the infant to control its actions. *Development Psychology*, *14*(2), 157–162.

Gutheil, G., & Gelman, S.A. (1990, March). *The development of inductive inference: The importance of the law of large numbers and degree of category heterogeneity*. Conference on Human Development, Richmond, VA.

Johnson, C.N. (1988). Theory of mind and the structure of conscious experience. In J.W. Astington, P.L. Harris, & D.R. Olson (Eds.), *Developing theories of mind* (pp. 47–63). Cambridge: Cambridge University Press.

Jones, S.S., Smith, L.B., & Landau, B. (1991). Object properties and knowledge in early lexical learning. *Child Development*, *62*, 499–516.

Jose, P.E. (1990). Just-world reasoning in children's immanent justice judgments. *Child Development*, *61*, 1024–1033.

Kaiser, M.K., McCloskey, M., & Proffitt, D.R. (1986). Development of intuitive theories of motion: Curvilinear motion in the absence of external forces. *Developmental Psychology*, *22*, 67–71.

Kalish, C.W., & Gelman, S.A. (in press). On wooden pillows: Multiple classification and children's category-based inductions. *Child Development*.

Kant, I. (1958). *A critique of pure reason* (N. Kemp, trans.). New York: Random House. (Originally published 1790.)

Karniol, R. (1980). A conceptual analysis of immanent justice responses in children. *Child Development*, *51*, 118–130.

Keil, F.C. (1989). *Concepts, kinds, and cognitive development*. Cambridge, MA: MIT Press.

Keil, F.C. (1991). Theories, concepts, and the acquisition of word meaning. In S.A. Gelman & J.P. Byrnes (Eds.), *Perspectives on language and thought: Interrelations in development* (pp. 197–221). Cambridge: Cambridge University Press.

Kister, M.C., & Patterson, C.J. (1980). Children's conceptions of the causes of illness: Understanding of contagion and use of immanent justice. *Child Development*, *51*, 839–846.

Kripke, S. (1972). *Naming and necessity*. Cambridge, MA: Harvard University Press.

Kunda, Z., Miller, D.T., & Claire, T. (1990). Combining social concepts: The role of causal reasoning. *Cognitive Science*, *14*, 551–577.

Kuzmak, S.D., & Gelman, R. (1986). Young children's understanding of random phenomena. *Child Development*, *57*, 559–566.

Leslie, A.M., & Keeble, S. (1987). Do six-month-old infants perceive causality? *Cognition*, *25*, 265–288.

Locke, J. (1894/1959). *An essay concerning human understanding* (Vol. 2). New York: Dover.

Mangelsdorf, S. (in press). Developmental changes in infant-stranger interaction. *Infant Behavior and Development*.

Markman, E.M. (1990). *Categorization and naming in children*. Cambridge, MA: MIT Press.

Mayr, E. (1988). *Toward a new philosophy of biology: Observations of an evolutionist*. Cambridge, MA: Harvard University Press.

McCloskey, M. (1983). Intuitive physics. *Scientific American*, *248*, 122–130.

Medin, D.L. (1989). Concepts and conceptual structure. *American Psychologist*, *44*, 1469–1481.

Medin, D.L., & Ortony, A. (1989). Comments on Part I: Psychological essentialism. In S. Vosniadou & A. Ortony (Eds.), *Similarity and analogical reasoning* (pp. 179–195). Cambridge, MA: Cambridge University Press.

Medin, D.L., & Shoben, E.J. (1988). Context and structure in conceptual combination. *Cognitive Psychology*, *20*, 158–190.

Michotte, A. (1963). *Perception of causality*. London: Methuen.

Miller, G.A., & Johnson-Laird, P.W. (1976). *Language and perception*. Cambridge, MA: Harvard University Press.

Miller, J.G., & Bersoff, D.M. (1988). When do American children and adults reason in social conventional terms? *Developmental Psychology*, *24*, 366–375.

Miller, P.H., & Aloise, P.A. (1989). Young children's understanding of the psychological causes of behavior: A review. *Child Development*, *60*, 257–285.

Murphy, G.L., & Medin, D.L. (1985). The role of theories in conceptual coherence. *Psychological Review*, *92*, 289–316.

Nisbett, R.E., Krantz, D.H., Jepson, C., & Kunda, Z. (1983). The use of statistical heuristics in everyday inductive reasoning. *Psychological Review*, *90*, 339–363.

Oakes, L.M., & Cohen, L.B. (1990). Infant perception of a causal event. *Cognitive Development*, *5*, 193–207.

Osherson, D.N., Smith, E.E., Wilkie, O., Lopez, A., & Shafir, E. (1990). Category-based induction. *Psychological Review*, *97*, 185–200.

Parritz, R.H., Mangelsdorf, S., & Gunnar, M.R. (1992). Control, social referencing, and the infants' appraisal of threat. In S. Feinman (Ed.), *Social referencing and the social construction of reality in infancy* (pp. 209–228). New York: Plenum.

Peirce, C. (1935). *Collected papers of Charles Sanders Peirce*, C. Hartshorne and P. Weiss (Eds.). Cambridge, MA: Harvard University Press.

Piaget, J. (1930). *The child's conception of physical causality*. London: Kegan Paul.

Piaget, J. (1951). *The child's conception of the world*. London: Routledge and Kegan Paul.

Piaget, J. (1952). *The language and thought of the child*. London: Routledge and Kegan Paul.

Piaget, J. (1965). *The moral judgment of the child*. New York: Free Press (originally published 1932).

Piaget, J., & Inhelder, B. (1975). *The origin of the idea of chance in children*. (L. Leake, Jr., P. Burrell, & H. Fischbein, Trans.). New York: Norton. (Original work published 1951.)

Poulsen, D., Kintsch, E., Kintsch, W., & Premack, D. (1979). Children's comprehension memory for stories. *Journal of Experimental Child Psychology*, *28*, 379–403.

Putnam, H. (1973). Meaning and reference. *Journal of Philosophy*, *LXX*, 699–711.

Quine, W.V.O. (1960). *Word and object*. Cambridge, MA: MIT Press.

Quine, W.V. (1969). Natural kinds. In W.V. Quine (Ed.), *Ontological relativity and other essays* (pp. 114–138).New York: Columbia University Press.

Richards, D.D., & Siegler, R.S. (1984). The effects of task requirements on children's life judgments. *Child Development*, *55*, 1687–1696.

Richards, D.D., & Siegler, R.S. (1986). Children's understandings of the attibutes of life. *Journal of Experimental Child Psychology*, *42*, 1–22.

Rosch, E.H., Mervis, C.B., Gray, W.D., Johnson, D.M., & Boyes-Braem, P. (1976). Basic objects in natural categories. *Cognitive Psychology*, *8*, 382–439.

Rosengren, K.S., Gelman, S.A., Kalish, C.W., & McCormick, M. (1991). As time goes by: Children's early understanding of growth. *Child Development*, *62*, 1302–1320.

Rothbart, M., & Taylor, M. (in press). Category labels and social reality: Do we view social categories as natural kinds? In G. Semin & K. Fiedler (Eds.), *Language, interaction, and social cognition*. London: Sage Publications.

Sameroff, A.J. (1983). Developmental systems: Contexts and evolution. In W. Kessen (Ed.), *Handbook of child psychology* (P.H. Mussen, Series Ed.). Vol.

1: *History, theory, and methods* (pp. 237–294). New York: Wiley.
Schwartz, S.P. (1979). Natural kind terms. *Cognition*, *7*, 301–315.
Shultz, T.R. (1982). Rules of causal attribution. *Monographs of the Society for Research in Child Development*, *47*, Serial No. 194.
Shultz, T.R., & Kestenbaum, N.R. (1985). Causal reasoning in children. *Annals of Child Development*, *2*, 195–249.
Shultz, T.R., Pardo, S., & Altmann, E. (1982). Young children's use of transitive inference in causal chains. *British Journal of Psychology*, *73*, 235–241.
Smith, C., Carey, S., & Wiser, M. (1985). On differentiation: A case study of the development of the concepts of size, weight, and density. *Cognition*, *21*, 177–237.
Smith, L.B. (1989). From global similarities to kinds of similarities: The constructions of dimensions in development. In S. Vosniadou & A. Ortony (Eds.), *Similarity and analogical reasoning* (pp. 146–178). New York: Cambridge University Press.
Smith, L.B., & Heise, D. (in press). Perceptual similarity and conceptual structure. In B. Burns (Ed.), *Percepts, concepts, and categories: The representation and processing of information*. Elsevier, Advances in Psychology.
Smith, M.C. (1978). Cognizing the behavior stream. *Child Development*, *49*, 736–743.
Soja, N.N., Carey, S., & Spelke, E.S. (1991). Ontological categories guide young children's inductions of word meaning: Object terms and substance terms. *Cognition*, *38*, 179–211.
Trabasso, T., & Sperry, L.L. (1985). Causal relatedness and importance of story events. *Journal of Memory and Language*, *24*, 595–611.
Trabasso, T., & Van den Broek, P. (1985). Causal thinking and the representation of narrative events. *Journal of Memory and Language*, *24*, 612–630.
Turiel, E. (1983). *The development of social knowledge: Morality and convention*. Cambridge, MA: Cambridge University Press.
Ward, T.B., Becker, A.H., Hass, S.D., & Vela, E. (1991). Attribute availability and the shape bias in children's category generalization. *Cognitive Development*, *6*, 143–167.
Wellman, H.M. (1990). *The child's theory of mind.* Cambridge, MA: MIT Press.
Wellman, H.M., & Gelman, S.A. (1992). Cognitive development: Foundational theories of core domains. *Annual Review of Psychology*, *43*, 337–375.
White, E., Elsom, B., & Prawat, R. (1978). Children's conceptions of death. *Child Development*, *49*, 307–310.

2
The Cognitive Basis of Dyslexia

LINDA S. SIEGEL

Dyslexia is a condition in which individuals, despite average or above average intelligence, have great difficulty in learning to read. Dyslexia is a diagnosis by exclusion; dyslexics have average or above average IQ test scores, have had adequate instruction in reading, and do not have neurological problems such as seizure disorders or significant emotional disturbances that might be considered to be responsible for their difficulty in acquiring reading skills. There has been much discussion of, and controversy about, this disorder. In this chapter, I will review some of these controversial and definitional issues, and present a model of the underlying nature of the cognitive deficits involved in dyslexia. I will examine the empirical evidence for this model by reviewing a number of studies of dyslexic and normal readers.

Definitional Issues

There are three major issues in the definition of dyslexia that are critical to the understanding of this disorder. The first issue involves the nature of the reading process and the appropriate way to measure reading. The second is the role of intelligence, operationally defined by IQ test scores, in the definition of dyslexia, and the third issue involves the nature of the dyslexic population, specifically the degree of homogeneity and whether there are distinctive subtypes within this population.

The Measurement of Reading

Reading has been measured in a variety of ways (for an extended discussion see Siegel & Heaven, 1986). There are four types of material that are typically found in reading tests: nonwords (also called pseudowords), single words, sentences, and paragraphs. Pseudowords are pronounceable combinations of letters that are not real English words, and the reading of these pseudowords is a test of the acquisition of grapheme–phoneme conversion (GPC) rules. It is important to note that these pseudowords can be read only by the application of these GPC rules and not from visual memory, because, by definition, these pseudowords have never been seen before because they do not exist as words in the English language. Tests with single words involve the reading of isolated words and are called tests of word recognition. The words may be decoded; that is, read with the application of GPC rules, or they may be recognized through direct visual access with no intermediate phonological coding. The reading of sentences and paragraphs may involve the use of cues from the surrounding context and does not allow the determination of whether or not the correct reading involves a good guess because individual words are often predictable from the context. The issue of generalization from context is not relevant with words or pseudowords because there is no context. On these grounds, single-word or pseudoword reading represents purer tests of reading skill uncontaminated by guessing from surrounding context.

Paragraph and sentence reading tests are usually reading comprehension tests. Reading "comprehension" tests, as they are currently constructed, have a number of serious conceptual and methodological problems. First of all, most of the questions involve merely searching the text for the correct verbatim phrase rather than making an inference (Tal & Siegel, 1990). A number of the questions can be answered without reading the passage (Tal & Siegel, 1990). As these tests are timed, speed rather than quality of reading is probably being measured. For example, Biemiller and Siegel (1991) found that by giving children a little extra time their reading scores increased dramatically. However, the most serious problem with the use of low scores on reading comprehension tests as an operational definition of dyslexia is that it does not yield a clear and consistent picture of dyslexia. Specifically, children with a low score on a reading comprehension test and good word recognition skills are not different from normal readers on syntax and phonological processing tasks (Siegel & Ryan, 1989a). On the other hand, if dyslexia is defined on the basis of poor word recognition skills, children with dyslexia have significantly poorer phonological processing, syntactic awareness, and short-term and working memory skills than normal readers. For these reasons, it is important to use poor word recognition skills, and not poor "comprehension" skills, as the operational definition of dyslexia.

The Role of Intelligence

Although intelligence, or more properly IQ, has been conceptualized as an important part of the definition of dyslexia in that individuals must have average or above average IQ scores to be considered dyslexic and, even further, in some definitions have significantly lower reading scores than would be predicted by their IQ, recent accounts of dyslexia suggest that intelligence may not be a central construct. These issues are summarized in Siegel (1988b, 1989a, 1989b, 1990a, 1990b). For example, instead of emphasizing intelligence, Stanovich (1988a, 1988b) has proposed that a deficit in phonological processing is the core deficit of a reading disability. Stanovich characterized phonological processing as a modular function that "is not under the direction of higher level cognitive structures and is not supplemented by real world knowledge." Furthermore, according to Stanovich's model, phonological processing "may fail without disrupting the operations of central processes that do not depend on its output, and also that efficiently functioning central processes cannot remedy a module that is functioning inefficiently" (Stanovich, 1988b, p. 158). This theory would predict that a phonological processing deficit should be characteristic of all disabled readers, and that phonological processing deficits should be independent of general cognitive ability (operationally defined as IQ test scores). Regarding the first prediction, there is ample evidence, described later in this chapter, that difficulty with phonological processing is a pervasive characteristic of dyslexics. Regarding the second prediction, phonological processing should show a much stronger correlation with reading skills than general cognitive ability. Further, IQ scores should not contribute a significant amount of independent variance to the prediction of reading skills.

There is evidence from a number of sources that phonological processing skills are independent of general cognitive abilities. Reading disabled children at all IQ levels show equal difficulty with phonological processing tasks such as pseudoword reading, recognizing the visual form of a pseudoword, pseudoword spelling, and a phonological lexical task that involves distinguishing which of two pseudowords sounds like a real word (e.g., *kake-dake*, *joak-joap*) (Siegel, 1988a). That is, when reading disabled children at four IQ levels, <80, 80–90, 91–109, >109, were compared, there were no significant differences among these groups on tasks that involved phonological processing skills. All the reading disabled children performed at a level significantly below that of normally achieving children but there were no significant differences among the reading disabled groups, despite significant differences in IQ. The significance of this finding is that if phonological processing ability is impaired, as it was in these reading disabled children, even high levels of cognitive functioning cannot compensate for the deficit.

The traditional definition of an individual with dyslexia is one where there must be a discrepancy between the IQ and the reading score, such that the reading score is significantly lower than would be predicted by the IQ. That is, the reading score must be, in some way, "unexpected." For children who have low IQ scores and are poor readers, the expectation is that their poor reading skills are in some way related to their low IQ scores so their reading failure is not unexpected. A consequence of these assumptions is that children who are poor readers and who have high IQ scores are different from those who are poor readers and who have lower IQ scores. In order to examine these assumptions, I studied the differences between dyslexic children, children whose reading scores were significantly below their IQ, and poor readers, whose reading scores were not below the level that would be predicted from their IQ, on any of a variety of phonological processing, language, and memory tasks (Siegel, 1991). I found no differences between these two groups on tasks that were related to reading, syntactic awareness, and verbal short-term and working memory. However, both groups demonstrated significantly poorer performance than normal readers. These results suggest that high IQ scores do not protect an individual from reading problems or influence the nature of the reading problems when they occur.

Another approach to examining these issues involves comparing the relative contributions of IQ and pseudoword reading, one of the best measures of phonological processing skills, to word recognition and reading comprehension. If phonological skills contribute most of the variance and IQ scores contribute little independent variance, then this finding would suggest that phonological processing is the key component of reading and that general cognitive ability is not a significant factor. If, on the other hand, IQ is a significant correlate independent of phonological processing, this finding would suggest that IQ is important. When

TABLE 2.1 Results of the multiple regression analyses.

WRAT Reading n = 1106		
Order of entry	Multiple R	R^2
1. Pseudoword reading	0.81	0.65
2. IQ	0.82	0.67
1. IQ	0.43	0.19
2. Pseudoword reading	0.82	0.67
Gilmore Comprehension n = 412		
Order of entry	Multiple R	R^2
1. Pseudoword reading	0.51	0.26
2. IQ	0.54	0.30
1. IQ	0.40	0.16
2. Pseudoword reading	0.54	0.30
Stanford Comprehension n = 170		
Order of entry	Multiple R	R^2
1. Pseudoword reading	0.59	0.35
2. IQ	0.64	0.41
1. IQ	0.42	0.18
2. Pseudoword reading	0.64	0.41

the relative contributions of IQ scores and phonological processing were examined, IQ did contribute little independent variance to the prediction of word reading and reading comprehension scores (Siegel, in press). These results are shown in Table 2.1. As can be seen from the data presented in Table 2.1, when pseudoword reading is forced into the multiple regression first, IQ contributed relatively little independent variance but when IQ was forced in first, pseudoword reading contributed a great deal of independent variance. These studies have led to the conclusion that phonological processing deficits can exist at all levels of IQ scores and that the problems of the individual with dyslexia are similar whatever the IQ level.

Subtypes of Dyslexia?

Although it is often claimed that there are subtypes within the population of dyslexic individuals, there is no definitive evidence for the existence of subtypes within the population of dyslexic individuals. My colleagues and I have examined the evidence for the existence of these subtypes and have found significant definitional, methodological, and statistical problems with the existing studies of subtypes of reading disabled individuals. These issues are reviewed in Morrison and Siegel (1991b), Siegel and Heaven (1986), Siegel, Levey, and Ferris (1985), and Siegel and Metsala (1991). There are, however, subtypes within the learning disabled population and this heterogeneity within the learning disabled population is mistakenly interpreted as heterogeneity within the reading disabled population. There is a group of children who have difficulties with arithmetic and written work, and often spelling, but not with word recognition or pseudoword reading; these individuals are often labeled as dyslexic when, in fact, they are not (Morrison & Siegel, 1991a; Siegel & Feldman, 1983). In addition, as noted earlier in this chapter, we have found that children with reading comprehension problems are a heterogeneous group and if a deficit in reading comprehension is used to define a reading disability, subtypes will emerge (Siegel & Ryan, 1989a). However, we argue that the finding of subtypes is an artifact of the definition and that if a definition of reading disability is based on poor word recognition or pseudoword reading skills, then the group labeled dyslexic is quite homogeneous in regard to their performance on tasks that tap the basic cognitive processes related to reading.

Basic Cognitive Processes in Reading

The development of a clear and precise definition of dyslexia has resulted in a formulation of the cognitive aspects of this disability. Specifically, there are three processes that are significant in the development of reading skills in English. These processes are phonological processing, syntactic awareness, and working memory. *Phonological processing* involves a variety of skills but in the context of the development of reading skills, the most significant is the association of sounds with letters; that is, the understanding of grapheme–phoneme conversion rules and the exceptions to these rules. This ability is the basis of decoding print, and although there are other routes to obtain meaning from print, the phonological route is clearly an important one and critical in the early development of reading skills (e.g., Stanovich, 1988a, 1988b). *Syntactic awareness*, also called grammatical sensitivity, refers to the ability to understand the syntax of the language. This ability appears to be critical for fluent and efficient reading of text that requires making predictions about the words that come next in the sequence. *Working memory* refers to the retention of information in short-term storage while processing incoming information and retrieving information from long-term storage. In the context of reading, working memory is relevant because the reader must decode and/or recognize words while remembering what has been read and retrieving information such as grapheme–phoneme conversion rules. During the years in which reading skills are acquired, there is a significant growth in all these skills.

In the following sections, I will provide details of the growth of these skills in children who are normal readers and also in children with dyslexia. I will also examine the similarities and differences in the reading skills of dyslexic and normal readers. It has been a common belief that individuals with dyslexia have perceptual problems but, as outlined by Vellutino (1979), this assumption is an incorrect one. In fact, the difficulties experienced by dyslexics involve a variety of language skills, as Vellutino has argued and as I will illustrate in this chapter.

Phonological Processing

Current theories of the development of reading skills in English stress that phonological processing is the most significant underlying cognitive process. Arguments for this position are outlined in Stanovich (1988a, 1988b). Phonological processing is conceptualized as a modular process that is not under the control of higher level structures. Therefore, a deficit in phonological processing cannot be compensated for by high levels of cognitive functioning (e.g., as indicated by measured intelligence). Other skills cannot be mobilized to accomplish what the phonological processing module does. Phonological processing involves a variety of functions but, in the context of the development of reading skills, the most significant is the association of sounds with letters or combinations of letters, referred to as the understanding of grapheme–phoneme conversion (GPC) rules; because of the irregular nature of these correspondences in English, the learning of the GPC rules is a very complex process.

For children learning to read English, the learning of these correspondences is a result of systematic instruction and the extraction of the rules is a result of repeated encounters with print. There are no data available to provide evidence as to how much of the development of these skills is a result of specific instruction in the GPC rules and how much is a result of experience with print. In any case, the understanding of the GPC rules develops rapidly in the first years of experience with print under normal conditions, as will be illustrated in this chapter.

Measurement of Phonological Processing Skills

In an alphabetic language such as English, the best measure of phonological processing skills is the reading of pseudowords; that is, pronounceable combinations of letters that can be read by the application of GPC rules, but, of course, are not real words in English. Examples include pseudowords, such as *shum*, *laip*, and *cigbet*. All of these pseudowords can be read by anyone who is familiar with the GPC rules of English even though these are not real words and have not been encountered in print or in spoken language before.

There have been a number of studies of the development of the ability to read pseudowords (e.g., Calfee, Lindamood, & Lindamood, 1973; Hogaboam & Perfetti, 1978; Venezky & Johnson, 1973). There is ample evidence that children with dyslexia have a great deal of difficulty reading pseudowords. Studies such as those of Snowling (1980), Siegel and Ryan (1988), and Waters, Bruck, and Seidenberg (1985) have shown that dyslexics have more difficulty reading pseudowords than normal readers matched in either chronological age or reading level. For example, we have studied the development of the ability to read pseudowords in normal and dyslexic readers, aged 7 to 14 years (Siegel, 1986; Siegel & Ryan, 1988). By the age of 9 years, the normal readers are quite proficient and performing at almost a perfect level for even the most difficult pseudowords, with, in some cases, as many as four syllables. However, the performance of the dyslexic children was quite different. The children with dyslexia acquired these reading skills very slowly, and even at the age of 14 years were performing no better than normal readers at the age of 7 years. These data are shown in Figure 2.1.

The above comparisons are based on chronological age. An alternative way of studying both the development of reading skills and the differences and similarities between normal and dyslexic readers is the use of a match based on reading age, also called reading level. This type of design is used to attempt to equate experience with reading print. The theory of this type of comparison is that children who are poor readers probably read less and, therefore, do not have the same exposure to print so it would be

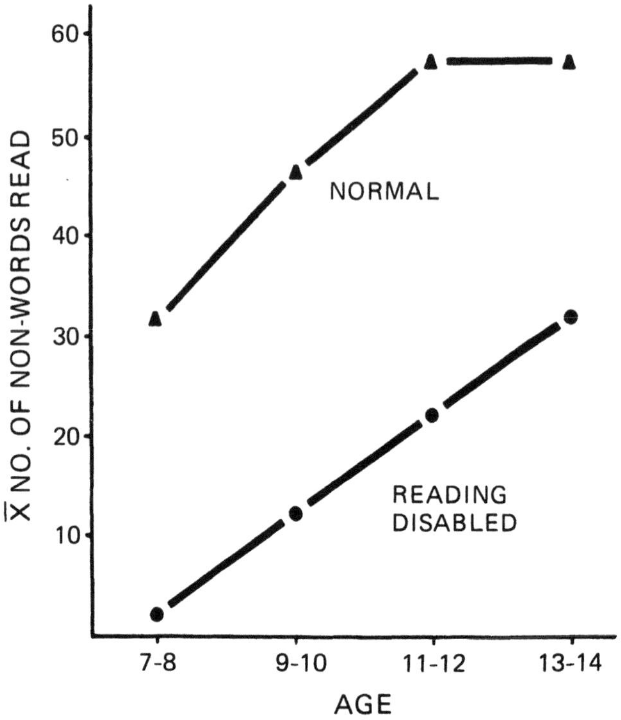

FIGURE 2.1. Accuracy of pseudoword reading as a function of chronological age and group.

expected that a chronological age match would put the disabled readers at a disadvantage. In order to control for experience with print, a comparison of dyslexic and normal readers matched on reading grade level was used. Even when the normal readers and the dyslexics were matched on reading level (hence the dyslexics were considerably older than the normal readers), the performance of the dyslexics on the reading of pseudowords was significantly poorer than the normal readers. That is, even at the same level of proficiency in reading words as normal readers, dyslexics experienced considerable difficulty reading pseudowords. These data are shown in Figure 2.2.

Thus, the acquisition of these phonological processing skills occurs very slowly in children with serious reading problems. This difficulty seems to be the fundamental problem of children with dyslexia and often continues even to adulthood. Many adults with dyslexia become reasonably fluent readers but still have difficulty reading pseudowords or read them very slowly (e.g., Barwick & Siegel, 1990; Bruck, 1990; Shafrir & Siegel, 1991).

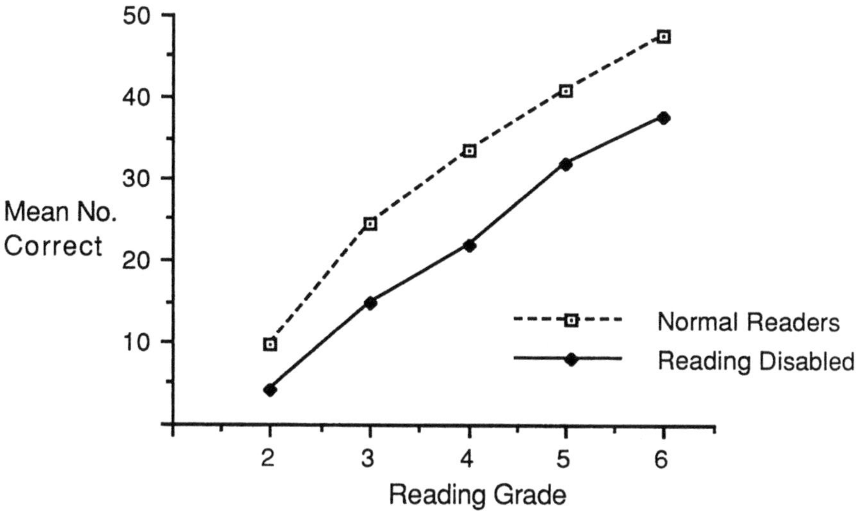

FIGURE 2.2. Accuracy of pseudoword reading as a function of reading grade level and group.

There are other kinds of tasks that have been used to measure the development of the understanding of grapheme–phoneme conversion rules. They provide additional evidence that dyslexics have difficulty with the phonological route and use other processes to read words. In one study, we contrasted the reading of pseudowords that could be read by analogy or by phonics, for example, *puscle*, *fody*, *risten* (Siegel & Geva, 1990). Dyslexics had a great deal of difficulty with these pseudowords. The dyslexics were significantly less likely than normal readers of the same chronological age to read these words correctly. Even when matched with normal readers of the same reading grade level, they had significantly lower scores. Compared to the normal readers of the same chronological or reading ages, dyslexics were significantly less likely to use a rule-based strategy and more likely to use an analogy strategy. This pattern suggests a greater reliance on the visual route.

Although we have evidence about the inadequate phonological skills of dyslexics, little is known about the manner in which the complex set of grapheme–phoneme conversion rules of the English language is acquired. The ascertainment of the order and nature of the acquisition of these rules is an important first step in the understanding and treatment of dyslexia. A number of investigators have begun to work on these issues (e.g., Guthrie & Seifert, 1979; Siegel & Faux, 1989; Snowling, 1980). To study this acquisition process, we presented dyslexics and normal readers with words and pseudowords that involved a variety of grapheme–phoneme conversion rules, such as consonant blends, r-influenced vowels, inconsistent vowels, etc. (Siegel & Faux, 1989). We found that complexity, as measured by the number of syllables in a pseudoword, was a significant determinant of the difficulty or reading the pseudoword. Pseudowords with two or more syllables were quite difficult for older dyslexics (11–13 years) even though normal readers had become quite proficient by the age of 9 to 10 years. Even simple vowels and consonant blends were not mastered by the oldest dyslexics in the study (ages 11–14 years) when they were required to read pseudowords such as *mog*, *lun*, and *spad*, although most of the 7- and 8-year-old normal readers had no difficulty with these features in words or pseudowords.

In most cases, even when the dyslexic readers appeared to demonstrate mastery of grapheme–phoneme conversion rules when they read a word, they were unable to read a pseudoword with the same rule. Dyslexics experienced unusual difficulty when reading pseudowords. Even when they could read words with particular letter sound correspondences in CVC words, such as *ran*, *wet*, and *sit*, they could not read pseudowords such as *han*, *fet*, and *rit*, and although they could read words involving consonant blends, such as *hunt*, *spot*, and *help*, they could not read pseudowords of a similar structure, such as *lunt*, *grot*, and *melp*.

This superiority of words over pseudowords suggests that the dyslexic children were using some sort of direct lexical access that, of course, they could use when they read words but that was not possible in the reading of pseudowords. It is probable that this direct lexical access involves processing each word as a picture (visual representation) rather than as a series of letters with sounds. This visual representation, rather than GPC rules, is retrieved from long-term memory.

One relatively simple "rule" of English, with few exceptions, is that a final "e" in a one-syllable word makes the vowel long. This rule was not mastered by the oldest dyslexics in this study. That is, the older dyslexics could correctly read the words that contained these rules (e.g., *like*, *cute*, *nose*) but could not read the comparable pseudoword (e.g., *rike*, *fute*, *mose*). This difficulty is quite surprising since this rule is repeatedly stressed in reading instruction and is normally mastered very early in the development of reading skills. When the reading disabled and normal readers were matched on reading grade level, there were many instances in which the scores of the reading disabled were significantly lower than those of normal readers who were the reading grade level controls. For example, the normal readers had significantly higher scores than the disabled readers of the same reading age on the following tasks: reading one syllable pseudowords at grade level 3, two-syllable pseudowords at grades 4 to 5, multisyllable pseudowords at grade 6, and pseudowords with consonant blends at grade levels 2, 3, and 6. There were some cases in which there were no diffierences between dyslexics and reading level matched normal readers; however, these instances were often ones in which there were floor or ceiling effects.

Words can obviously be read by some sort of direct visual access but pseudowords cannot be read without intermediate phonological processing, because, by definition, there is no word in the internal lexicon that matches a pseudoword. Hence, these data indicate that dyslexics have a severe deficit in phonological processing.

Pseudoword reading is not the only task that distinguishes dyslexics from normal readers. Another task is the spelling of pseudowords. Dyslexics make significantly lower scores on a task that involves the spelling of pseudowords, even when the dyslexics are at the same reading grade level as younger normal readers (Siegel & Ryan, 1988).

One type of evidence of phonological processing skills is the use of phonological recoding in short-term memory such that rhyming (confusable) stimuli are more difficult to remember than nonrhyming stimuli. A number of studies have found that younger poor readers are less disrupted by rhyming stimuli (e.g., Bryne & Shea, 1979; Mann, Liberman, & Shankweiler, 1980; Shankweiler, Liberman, Mark, Fowler, & Fischer, 1979; Siegel & Linder, 1984). However, Johnston (1982) and Siegel and Linder (1984) have found that older dyslexic children do show phonetic confusability although their short-term memory for letters was significantly poorer than age-matched controls. This latter finding is not surprising as phonological recoding skills are likely to be involved in any verbal memory task and the poor verbal memory of the dyslexics may be a function of inadequate phonological abilities.

Phonemic awareness, the ability to recognize the basic phonemic segments of the language, is obviously an important component of phonological processing. There is evidence that difficulties with phonemic awareness predict subsequent reading problems (e.g., Bradley & Bryant, 1983; Wallach & Wallach, 1976). Poor readers also have deficits in phonological production tasks; for example, naming of objects represented by multisyllable words, and with repetition of multisyllabic words and difficult phrases with alliteration. Pratt and Brady (1988) found differences between good and poor readers on the ability to segment words into phonemes and delete sounds from words. Good readers were more accurate in judging the length of a word or pseudoword.

Dyslexics also have difficulty recognizing the visual form of sounds (Siegel & Ryan, 1988). In the Gates McKillop test the children hear pseudowords such as *whiskate* and are asked to select the correct version of the word from among four printed choices: *iskate*, *wiskay*, *wiskate*, and *whestit*. Dyslexics had significantly lower scores than normal readers on this task.

Syntactic Awareness

Syntactic awareness is the ability to understand the basic grammatical structure of the language in question. Siegel and Ryan (1988) have investigated the development of these skills in normal and disabled readers using an Oral Cloze task, a Sentence Correction task, and the Grammatical Closure test of the Illinois Test of Psycholinguistic Abilities. In the Oral Cloze task, a sentence is read aloud to the child and the child is required to fill in the missing word in¨ sentence. Examples of sentences that we used are: "Jane __ her sister ran up the hill;" "Betty __ dug a hole with her shovel;" "The girl __ is tall plays basketball." In the Sentence Correction task, a sentence that is syntactically incorrect is read aloud to the child and the child is required to correct the sentence. Examples include: "Animal are kept in zoos," "Can you read them book?," and "It was very cold outside tomorrow." In the ITPA Grammatic Closure subtest, the child is required to supply the missing word in a sentence that is read aloud while the examiner points to pictures illustrating the sentence, for example, "Here the thief is stealing the jewels. Here the jewels have been __." In this example, the child must understand the irregular past tense of the verb *to steal* in order to supply the correct word.

When the dyslexics and the normal readers were compared on these three tasks, the dyslexics performed at a level that was significantly lower than the normal readers up to the age of 12 years, as shown in Figure 2.3

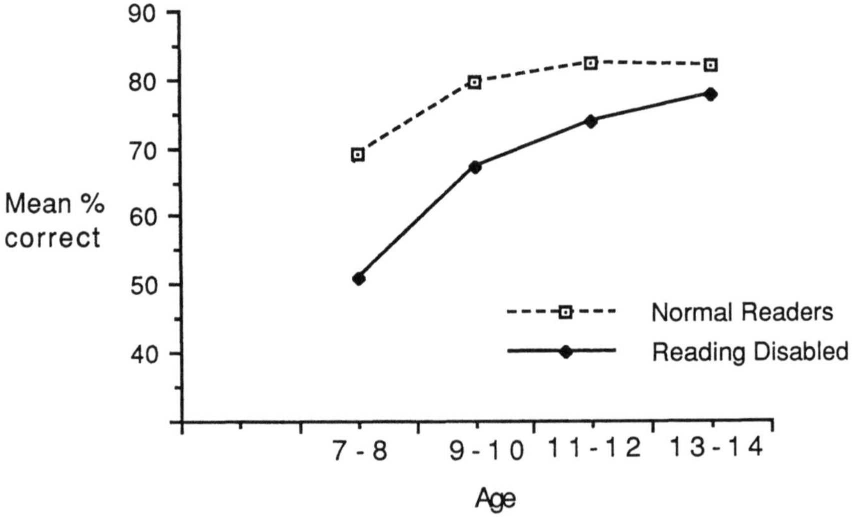

FIGURE 2.3. Mean percentage of correct responses on the Oral Cloze Task as a function of chronological age and group.

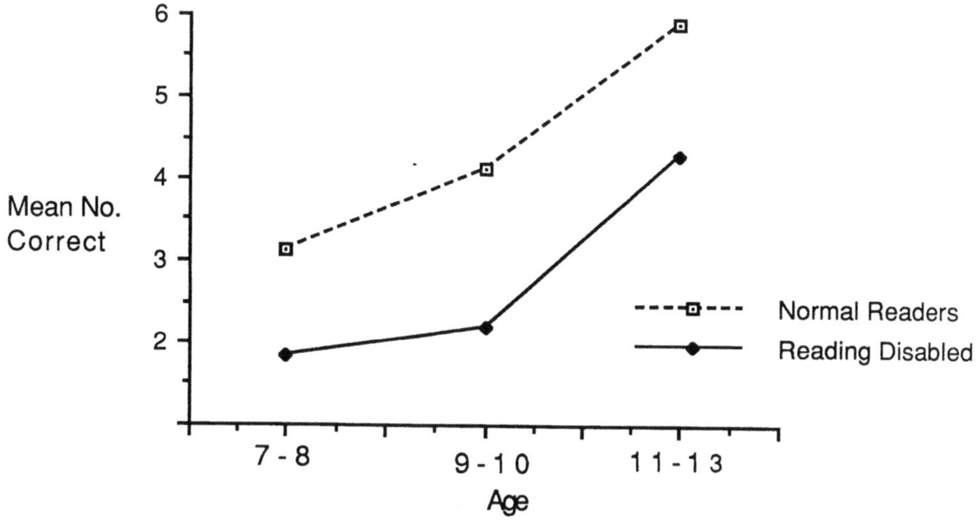

FIGURE 2.4. Performance on the working memory task as a function of chronological age and group.

for the Oral Cloze Task. These results show that after the age of 12 years, the performance of both groups was close to 100, so that this ceiling effect precluded the appearance of group differences. Therefore, it is not possible to determine if the differences between dyslexics and normal readers persists into adulthood. It is possible that with more difficult tasks differences might have appeared between the older normal readers and the dyslexics, but the differences were significant in the elementary school years.

Working Memory

Working memory is the ability to retain information in a short-term store while processing incoming information. In reading, this would mean the decoding or recognizing of words or phrases while remembering what has been read. We have studied working memory in normal readers and dyslexics by developing a task that we feel taps the type of memory processes that occur in reading (Siegel & Ryan, 1989b). In this task, the child is read aloud two, three, four, or five sentences and asked to fill in the missing word at the end of a sentence. The child is then required to remember the missing words. Examples of sentences were: "In the summer it is very ___. People go to see monkeys in a ___. With dinner we sometimes eat bread and ___." In this case, the child was then required to repeat the three words that he or she selected in the same order that the sentences had been presented. The dyslexics performed significantly more poorly than the normal readers on this task, indicating difficulties with working memory. The data for this task are shown in Figure 2.4. As can be seen in Figure 2.4, the dyslexics had significantly lower scores than the normal readers at each age level.

Other Processes

The three basic cognitive processes just described are important for the development of reading skills and are significantly disrupted in dyslexic readers. There are two other processes that are also relevant to the development of reading: semantics and orthographic processing. *Semantics* refers to the understanding of meaning; *orthographic processing* refers to the understanding of the writing conventions of the language and the correct and incorrect spellings of words. These processes are interesting for a variety of reasons but one of these is dyslexics do not seem to experience the same degree of difficulties in these areas that they do in other areas.

Semantics

There are two types of tasks that indicate that the semantic processing of poor readers is relatively intact. One of these involves is the analysis of errors made in reading single words; the other involves the understanding of the meaning of complex sentences I have shown that there is a small group of dyslexics who make semantic substitutions while reading single isolated words (Siegel, 1985). It is important to note that I am not discussing errors made in reading text but, instead, reading single words. There is no context for the child to use to make guesses in these situations. For example, they make errors such as reading *look* as *see*, *chicken* as *duck*, or *me* as *you* when reading single words that are not in any context. These dyslexics all had very poor, or nonexistent, phonological processing skills and were unable to read a single pseudoword. These types of semantic errors indicate that phonological processing is not used at all because none of the sounds present in the stimulus word are produced in the response. In addition, the response is not visually similar to the target word. However, these types of errors indicate that some semantic processing is occurring and that although the word is not being read correctly, some semantic information is being processed. These kinds of errors are made only in the early stages of reading acquisition and only by poor readers. Some examples of these types of errors are shown in Table 2.2. Normal readers do not appear to make these types of errors. The types of errors that normal readers make typically involve the substitution of a visually and/or phonologically similar word. Examples of

TABLE 2.2 Examples of semantic and normal reader errors.

Target word	Dyslexic semantic error	Normal reader error
Chicken	Duck	Children
Me	You	My
Away	Go	Way
Him	You	How
Around	Because	Round
She	Girl	See
Look	See	Book
Open	Up	Pine

the types of errors that normal readers make when reading these words are also shown in Table 2.2.

Only dyslexic readers make these kind of errors and only a small proportion of dyslexics do so. Normal readers, even at the earliest stages of reading, do not appear to make these semantic errors. These types of errors indicate that grapheme–phoneme conversion rules are not being used at all and that phonological processing is virtually nonexistent.

There is other evidence that the semantic processing skills in dyslexic children are adequate. In the sentence correction task described earlier some of the sentences were syntactically correct but meaningless; that is, they did not make sense. Examples are: "There are flowers flying in the garden"; "In the summer, it snows"; and "The moon is very big and bright in the morning". The dyslexics did not have any trouble correcting these sentences and performed at a level similar to the normal readers (Siegel & Ryan, 1984). This contrasts with their performance on the sentences where the correction of syntax was required. Therefore, the dyslexics have a deficit in the processing of syntactic information but this does not extend to processing of semantic information.

Orthographic Processing

Another aspect of reading is orthographic processing, which will be discussed in the context of dual route theories of reading. One of the popular theories of reading is the dual route theory, which proposes that there are two possible routes involved in gaining access to the meaning of print (e.g., Coltheart, 1978; Forster & Chambers, 1973; Meyer, Schvanevelt, & Ruddy, 1974). One of these routes involves direct lexical access; that is, visually reading a word without any intermediate phonological processing. The orthographic configuration of a word is directly mapped onto an internal visual store in lexical memory. This process is often referred to as *whole word recognition*. The other route involves the use of grapheme–phoneme conversion rules to gain lexical access to a print stimulus. Spelling-sound conversion rules are used to translate a graphemic code into a phonemic one. In this route, the application of the rules does not rely on word-specific spelling to sound pronunciations. Instead, grapheme-to-phoneme conversion rules are presumed to be stored explicitly and used to determine a word's pronunciation.

Olson, Kliegl, Davidson, and Foltz (1985) have developed two tasks that provide a direct contrast of the visual (orthographic) and phonological processing routes. In the phonological task, the child has to specify which of two pseudowords presented visually, sounds like a real word (e.g., *kake-dake*, *joap-joak*). In the visual task, the child is presented visually with a real word and a pseudoword (e.g., rain-rane, boal-bowl) and has to select the correct spelling. These tasks are designed so that only one process can operate in each task. That is, in the visual task both choices sound exactly the same, so that visual memory for the orthography of a word must by used; phonological processes are not helpful in this case because sounding out the words would produce the identical response to each word. For the phonological task, recall of the visual pattern would not be useful because neither alternative is a correct orthographic pattern in the English language. However, one of the alternatives, when sounded out, does produce an English word, although it is obviously not the correct orthographic form. These tasks were administered to dyslexic and normal readers, aged 7 to 16 years (Siegel, 1986). Not surprisingly, the dyslexics performed more poorly on the phonological task than the normal readers and did not catch up to the normal readers until the age of 13 years.

The dyslexics also had difficulty with the visual task and performed more poorly than the normal readers at ages 7 to 12 years, but the picture is different when a reading grade match was used. When the dyslexic readers are compared to normal readers of the same reading age, resulting in the dyslexics being much older than the normal readers, the dyslexics actually performed at a significantly higher level on the visual task than did the normal readers at reading grade level 2. This finding indicates good visual memory skills in the dyslexics in comparison to their level of word reading. It indicates that the dyslexics were paying attention to the visual aspects of a word rather than the phonological aspects.

To study another aspect of the awareness of orthographic structures, a task was developed (Siegel, Geva, & Share, 1990) in which the ability to recognize legal and illegal orthographic combinations of English letters was assessed. The task was a two-choice one in which the children were presented with 18 pairs of pronounceable pseudowords, one of which contained a bigram that never occurs in an English word in a particular position and the other one of which contained an orthographic string that occurs in English. Examples are *filv-filk*, *moke-moje*, *vism-visn*, and *powl-lowp*. This task was administered to normal and dyslexic readers aged 7 to 16 years.

The performance of the normal readers and dyslexics did not differ except at the youngest ages. At ages 7 to 8 years, the dyslexic children

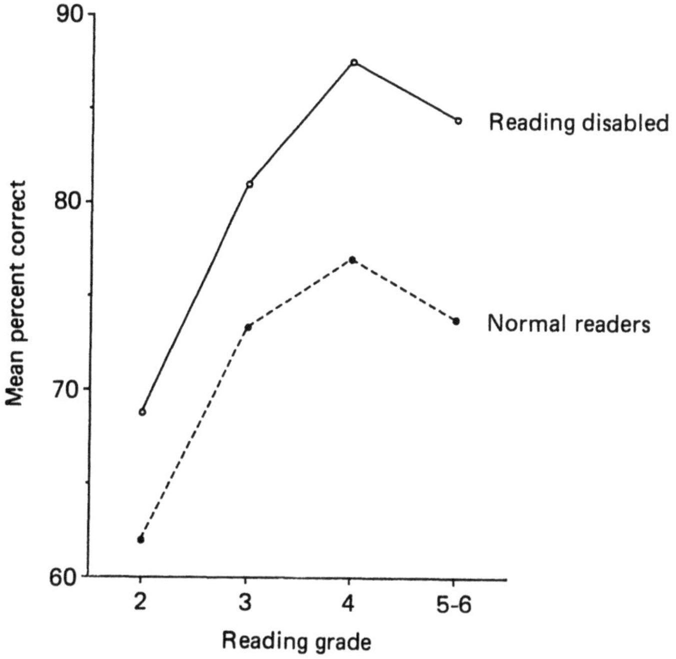

FIGURE 2.5. Performance on the orthographic task as a function of reading grade level and group.

made significantly more errors than did normal readers of the same chronological age. The dyslexic children did not perform more poorly than the normal readers ages 9 to 16 years. However, when the normal and dyslexic readers were matched on reading level, the dyslexics performed at a significantly higher level than the normal readers. These data are shown in Figure 2.5. Therefore, in comparison to the data on phonological processing, the orthographic processing of the dyslexics is quite good. These data indicate that orthographic processing is not as impaired in dyslexics as is phonological processing. Instead, the data show that semantic and orthographic processing occurs in reading but that the use of these processes can disrupt normal reading and cause errors to be made.

Summary

Three processes, syntactic awareness, phonological processing, and working memory are significantly disrupted in children who are dyslexic in English. Semantic and orthographic processes are not disrupted to the same extent. However, the underutilization of phonological processing and the consequent reliance on semantics and orthographic or visual processing disrupts reading. The deficitsin the three fundamental cognitive processes of phonological processing, syntactic awareness, and working memory constitute the basis of dyslexia.

Acknowledgments. The preparation of this chapter and the research reported in it was supported by a grant from the Natural Sciences and Engineering Research Council of Canada. The author wishes to thank Letty Guirnela for secretarial assistance.

References

Barwick, M., & Siegel, L.S. (1990). *The incidence and nature of learning disabilities in runaway, homeless youth*. Unpublished manuscript.

Biemiller, A., & Siegel, L.S. (1991). Developmental changes in relationships between reading comprehension, reading speed, reading accuracy, and working memory. Unpublished manuscript.

Bradley, L., & Bryant, P.E. (1983). Categorizing sounds and learning to read: A causal connection. *Nature*, *301*, 419–421.

Bruck, M. (1990). Word-recognition skills of adults with childhood diagnosis of dyslexia. *Developmental Psychology*, *26*, 439–454.

Byrne, B., & Shea, P. (1979). Semantic and phonemic memory in beginning readers. *Memory and Cognition*, *7*, 333–341.

Calfee, R.C., Lindamood, P., & Lindamood, C. (1973). Acoustic-phonetic skills and reading: Kindergarten through twelfth grade. *Journal of Educational Psychology*, *64*, 293–298.

Coltheart, M. (1978). Lexical access in simple reading tasks. In G. Underwood (Ed.), *Strategies of information processing* (pp. 151–216). London: Academic Press.

Forster, K.I., & Chambers, S. (1973). Lexical access and naming time. *Journal of Verbal Learning and Verbal Behavior*, *12*, 627–635.

Guthrie, J.T., & Seifert, M. (1979). Letter-sound complexity in learning to identify words. *Journal of Educational Psychology*, *69*, 686–696.

Hogaboam, T.W., & Perfetti, C.A. (1978). Reading skill and the role of verbal experience in decoding. *Journal of Educational Psychology*, *70*, 717–729.

Johnston, R. (1982). Phonological coding in dyslexic readers. *British Journal of Psychology*, *73*, 455–460.

Mann, V.A., Liberman, I.Y., & Shankweiler, D. (1980). Children's memory for sentences and word strings in relation to reading ability. *Memory and Cognition*, *8*, 329–335.

Metsala, J., & Siegel, L.S. (in press). Developmental dyslexia and hyperlexia: Attributes and underlying reading processes. In S. Segalowitz & I. Rapin (Eds.), *Developmental neuropsychology*. Amsterdam: Elsevier.

Meyer, D.E., Schvanevelt, R.W., & Ruddy, M.G. (1975). Loci of contextual effects on word recognition. In P.M.A. Rabbitt & S. Dornic (Eds.), *Attention and performance* (Vol. 5, pp. 98–118). New York: Academic Press.

Morrison, S.R., & Siegel, L.S. (1991a). Arithmetic disability: Theoretical considerations and empirical evidence for this subtype. In L.V. Feagans, E.J. Short, & L. Meltzer (Eds.), *Subtypes of learning disabilities: Theoretical perspectives and research*. Hillsdale, NJ: Erlbaum.

Morrison, S.R., & Siegel, L.S. (1991b). Learning disabilities: A critical review of definitional and assessment issues. In J.E. Orzbut & G.W. Hynd. (Eds.), *Advances in the neuropsychology of learning disabilities: A handbook of issues, methods, and practice*. New York: Academic Press.

Olson, R., Kliegl, R., Davidson, B.J., & Foltz, G. (1985). Individual and developmental differences in reading disability. In T.G. Waller (Ed.), *Reading research: Advances in theory and practice* (Vol. 4, pp. 1–64). New York: Academic Press.

Pratt, A.C., & Brady, S. (1988). Relations of phonological awareness to reading disability in children and adults. *Journal of Educational Psychology*, *80*, 319–323.

Shafrir, U., & Siegel, L.S. (1991). Short-term memory and phonological skills in reading and arithmetic disabled adults. Unpublished manuscript.

Shankweiler, D., Liberman, I.Y., Mark, L.S., Fowler, C.A., & Fischer, F.W. (1979). The speech code and learning to read. *Journal of Experimental Psychology: Human Learning and Memory*, *5*, 531–545.

Siegel, L.S. (1985). Psycholinguistic aspects of reading disabilities. In L.S. Siegel & F.J. Morrison (Eds.), *Cognitive development in atypical children*. New York: Springer–Verlag.

Siegel, L.S. (1986). Phonological deficits in children with a reading disability. *Canadian Journal of Special Education*, *2*, 45–54.

Siegel, L.S. (1988a). Evidence that IQ scores are irrelevant to the definition and analysis of reading disability. *Canadian Journal of Psychology*, *42*, 201–215.

Siegel, L.S. (1988b). Definitional and theoretical issues and research on learning disabilities. *Journal of Learning Disabilities*, *21*, 264–266.

Siegel, L.S. (1989a). IQ is irrelevant to the definition of learning disabilities. *Journal of Learning Disabilities*, *22*, 469–478, 486.

Siegel, L.S. (1989b). Why we do not need IQ test scores in the definition and analyses of learning disability. *Journal of Learning Disabilities*, *22*, 514–518.

Siegel, L.S. (1990a). IQ and learning disabilities: R.I.P. In H.L. Swanson & B. Keogh (Eds.), *Learning disabilities: Theoretical and research issues*. Hillsdale, NJ: Erlbaum.

Siegel, L.S. (1990b). Siegel's reply. *Journal of Learning Disabilities*, *23*, 268–269, 319.

Siegel, L.S. (1991). Dyslexics vs. poor readers: Is there a difference? In preparation.

Siegel, L.S. (in press). Phonological processing deficits as the basis of a reading disability. *Developmental Review*.

Siegel, L.S., & Faux, D. (1989). Acquisition of certain grapheme-phoneme correspondences in normally achieving and disabled readers. *Reading and Writing: An Interdisciplinary Journal*, *1*, 37–52.

Siegel, L.S., & Feldman, W. (1983). Non-dyslexic children with combined writing and arithmetic difficulties. *Clinical Pediatrics*, *22*, 241–244.

Siegel, L.S., & Geva, E. (1990). *Reading by analogy or rules: A comparison of poor and normal readers*. Unpublished manuscript.

Siegel, L.S., Geva, E., & Share, D. (1990). *The development of orthographic skills in normal and disabled readers*. Unpublished manuscript.

Siegel, L.S., & Heaven, R.K. (1986). Categorization of learning disabilities. In S.J. Ceci (Ed.), *Handbook of cognitive, social and neuropsychological aspects of learning disabilities* (Vol. 1). Hillsdale, NJ: Erlbaum.

Siegel, L.S., Levey, P., & Ferris, H. (1985). Subtypes of developmental dyslexia: Do they exist? In F.J. Morrison, C. Lord, & D.P. Keating (Eds.), *Applied developmental psychology* (Vol. 2). New York: Academic Press.

Siegel, L.S., & Linder, B.A. (1984). Short-term memory processes in children with reading and arithmetic learning disabilities. *Developmental Psychology*, *20*, 200–207.

Siegel, L.S., & Metsala, J. (1991). An alternative to the food processor approach to subtypes of learning disabilities. In N.N. Singh & I. Beale (Eds.). *Current perspectives in learning disabilities: Nature, theory, and treatment*. New York: Springer–Verlag.

Siegel, L.S., & Ryan. E.B. (1984). Reading disability as a language disorder. *Remedial and Special Education*, *5*, 28–33.

Siegel, L.S., & Ryan, E.B. (1988). Development of grammatical sensitivity, phonological, and short-term memory skills in normally achieving and learning disabled children. *Developmental Psychology*, *24*, 28–37.

Siegel, L.S., & Ryan, E.B. (1989a). Subtypes of developmental dyslexia: The influence of definitional variables. *Reading and Writing: An Interdisciplinary Journal*, *1*, 257–287(b).

Siegel, L.S., & Ryan, E.B. (1989b). The development of working memory in normally achieving and subtypes of learning disabled children. *Child Development*, *60*, 973–980.

Snowling, M.J. (1980). The development of grapheme-phoneme correspondence in normal and dyslexic readers. *Journal of Experimental Child Psychology*, *29*, 294–305.

Stanovich, K.E. (1988a). Explaining the differences between the dyslexic and garden variety poor reader: The phonological-core variance-difference model. *Journal of Learning Disabilities*, *21*, 590–604, 612.

Stanovich, K.E. (1988b). The right and wrong places to look for the cognitive locus of reading disability. *Annals of Dyslexia*, *38*, 154–177.

Tal, N., & Siegel, L.S. (1990). *The relationship between question-answer type and reading comprehension among good and poor readers*. Unpublished manuscript.

Vellutino, F.R. (1979). *Dyslexia: Theory and research*. Cambridge, MA: MIT Press.

Venezky, R.L., & Johnson, D. (1973). Development of two letter-sound patterns in grades one through three. *Journal of Educational Psychology*, *64*, 109–115.

Wallach, M.A., & Wallach, L. (1976). *Teaching all children to read*. Chicago: University of Chicago Press.

Waters, G.S., Bruck, M., & Seidenberg, M. (1985). Do children use similar processes to read and spell words? *Journal of Experimental Child Psychology*, *39*, 511–530.

3
Project Spectrum: A Theory-Based Approach to Early Education

MARGARET L. ADAMS AND DAVID HENRY FELDMAN

Project Spectrum is a collaborative research and development project codirected by David Henry Feldman of Tufts University and Howard Gardner of Harvard University. Research under the aegis of Project Spectrum is currently in its eighth year. In its first 4 years of work, Spectrum's goal was to develop new means of assessing the cognitive abilities of preschool children. This goal grew out of the cognitive-developmental theories of Feldman and Gardner.

Because Spectrum's work is theory-based, this chapter begins with a brief review of Feldman's and Gardner's theories. It proceeds with a description of Spectrum's approach to assessment. Some implications of this approach for classroom observations and curriculum development are also discussed. Possible future directions in research and application are presented in the final section.

Theoretical Foundations

Both researchers and practitioners in the field of child development have traditionally organized their understanding of development in terms of global areas. The areas typically identified include cognitive, social-emotional, and physical development (Berk, 1991; Bredekamp, 1987; Hendrick, 1980b; Sroufe, Cooper, & Marshall, 1988). Research in this field has included efforts to identify and describe universal sequences in the development of intellect (Piaget, 1967, 1970), moral reasoning (Kohlberg, 1987), artistic reasoning (Parsons, 1987), and social cognition (Damon, 1977; Selman, 1980). Increasingly, theorists and researchers, particularly those working in the area of cognitive development, have begun to argue that development is not only universal but also domain-specific (Case, 1985; Feldman, 1980; Fischer, 1980; Horowitz, 1987; Keil, 1986).

Simultaneous with this shift in the field, a growing number of researchers and practitioners have expressed dissatisfaction with the view

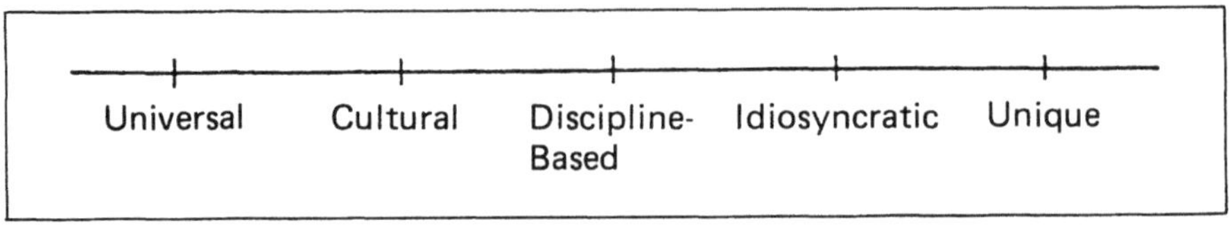

FIGURE 3.1. Developmental regions from universal to unique.

of intelligence as IQ (Baron, 1985; Feldman & Adams, 1989; Gardner, 1983; Sternberg, 1985). Maintaining that intelligence entails more than linguistic and logical-mathematical abilities, this group holds that IQ provides an incomplete description of cognitive ability.

Feldman's Theory of Nonuniversal Development

With his theory of nonuniversal development, Feldman (1980, 1981, in press) attempts to move the field of developmental psychology beyond an exclusive consideration of universals in development. By *nonuniversal development*, Feldman means development that is neither spontaneous nor fully achieved by all individuals. In fact, a distinguishing feature of nonuniversal development is that its achievement requires specific types of input and support from the environment. In large measure, cultural values shape the extent to which such support is available from the environment. Also important in shaping the course of nonuniversal developments is the element of individual choice (Feldman with Goldsmith, 1986).

Feldman's universal-to-unique continuum maps the territory encompassed by his theory of development (see Fig. 3.1). This continuum identifies four regions of nonuniversal development. Cultural domains are bodies of knowledge that all individuals within a given culture are expected to acquire. Examples of cultural domains in the United States include reading and writing. Discipline-based domains involve the development of expertise in a particular discipline, such as medicine or psychology. Idiosyncratic domains include subareas of a discipline, craft, or profession. These domains represent one's specialty. Patent law and ice sculpting are examples of idiosyncratic domains. Unique developmental achievements are creative advances that result in substantial new contributions to bodies of knowledge. Einstein's theory of relativity is a case of unique developmental achievement.

Feldman's theory of nonuniversal development both broadens and integrates the subject matter of the field of cognitive development. It broadens our understanding by asserting that many disciplines, professions, and hobbies, although not universal, are nevertheless developmental. The theory differentiates our understanding of cognitive development by incorporating into an overall framework those areas of development through which we distinguish ourselves as individuals as well as those that are common to all humanity. The perspective afforded by recognition of nonuniversal development thus complements our understanding of universal development.

According to Feldman, achievement in nonuniversal domains is not, as Piaget maintained, "mere learning" (Ginsburg & Opper, 1979). Rather, achievement in these domains is also developmental in the sense that progress in these domains is sequential and can be characterized in terms of qualitatively distinct levels of mastery. An individual's movement through this sequence of hierarchical levels is achieved, as in universal development, through a process of constructive transformation. However, in nonuniversal development, the organization that the individual constructs reflects the structure of the particular domain in which development occurs. Accordingly, Feldman maintains that there can be diversity among an individual's levels of development across domains.

Arguing that development can be domain-specific entails the premise that domains themselves have coherent, distinctive structures that evolve over time; these structures are referred to as *stages* or *levels*. Feldman characterizes the structure of a nonuniversal domain by analyzing it in terms of its constituent *elements* at each developmental *level*. To identify elements and levels, it is typically necessary to consult experts in the particular domain under study (Benjamin, 1989/1990; Mockros, 1989; Walton, Adams, Goldsmith, & Feldman, 1988).

Snyder and Feldman's (1980, 1984) description of a sequence of transition phases between levels, based on the movement of elements, provides a model for tracking development in a nonuniversal domain. An individual's status in the domain is described by evaluating ability in relation to each element. The same individual typically demonstrates differing degrees of ability in relation to different elements. An individual's developmental advance in the domain is assessed by comparing successive evaluations of ability in relation to each element.

Snyder and Feldman (1980, 1984) model a dynamic system and propose that shifts in its configuration over time follow certain patterns. The sequence of transition phases in their model suggests how developmental states are transformed as an individual moves toward mastery of a domain. This sequence is illustrated in Figure 3.2.

Based on Snyder and Feldman's (1980, 1984) study of children's development in the nonuniversal domain of map drawing, Figure 3.2 shows a hypothetical distribution of abilities in a child's map drawing system at six succeeding points in time. In phase 1, the majority of the child's skills are operating on developmental level III. In phases 2 and 3, incremental forward movement of elements occurs; Snyder and Feldman refer to this process as *elaboration*. In phase 4 of the transition cycle, the majority of the child's skills now operate on level IV. In phase 5, additional elements

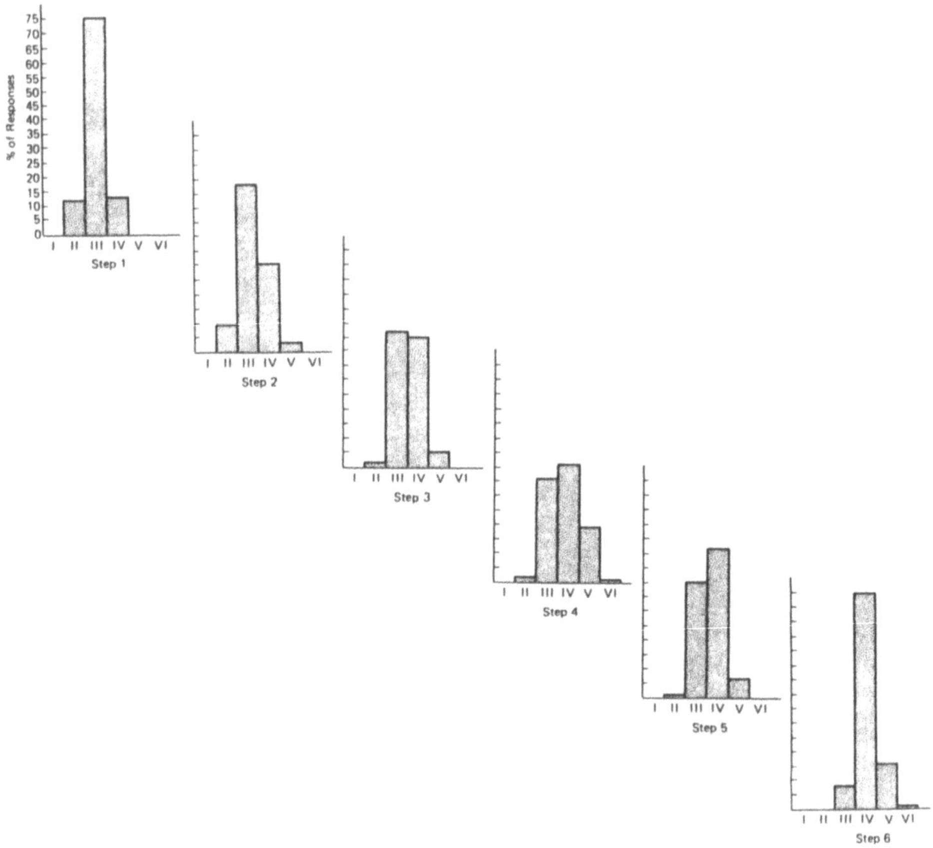

FIGURE 3.2. An illustration of the six steps in the transition process based on group data. (Note that steps 1 and 6 are essentially the same shape, indicating a complete transition cycle.)

move to level IV; Snyder and Feldman describe this as *consolidation*. In phase 6, all elements in the system have moved to the succeeding developmental level.

According to Snyder and Feldman's model, the individual is always in transition; development in the domain is an ongoing, dynamic process. Thus, although it is possible to describe an individual's developmental state at a particular moment in time, it is also necessary to recognize that this state is transient.

As previously stated, achievement in nonuniversal domains is largely a function of exposure to particular environmental conditions. Among the relevant environmental variables are the availability of systematic instruction, supporting technologies, mentors, and institutional subcultures

(Feldman with Goldsmith, 1986). In order to advance in nonuniversal domains, an individual must master a set of distinctive concepts as well as particular methods and media. Such advance cannot, of course, be attempted unless the domain's structure is communicable and the culture at least tolerates the pursuit of its mastery.

Feldman's theoretical work is based, in part, on his study of child prodigies (Feldman with Goldsmith, 1986). In this research, Feldman found that a child's ability in his area of prodigious achievement typically far outdistanced his general academic ability (e.g., IQ) and his universal developmental level as measured by Piagetian tasks (Feldman, 1979). Thus, it is not possible to account for prodigies' achievements by reference only to high IQ or accelerated universal development.

Exhibiting extreme variations in ability, prodigies violate traditional expectations about intellect and its development. Rather than viewing prodigies as anomalies, Feldman questioned traditional expectations. Feldman's study of prodigies provided the impetus for his proposal of a broader developmental framework and the more differentiated view of cognitive ability represented in the universal-to-unique continuum.

Gardner's Theory of Multiple Intelligences

A strong critic of psychometrics, Gardner is particularly skeptical of the idea that there is a central mental organization that controls the functioning of the mind. He argues that the mind is organized in terms of relatively independent realms of functioning. Gardner calls these realms of functioning *intelligences*. He purposefully uses the term *intelligence* to describe each of these realms in order to underscore his assertion that all of the realms are of potentially equal import.

In *Frames of Mind* (1983), Gardner defines intelligence as "the ability to solve problems, or to create products, that are valued within one or more cultural settings" (p. X). He identifies a number of criteria for judging whether or not a competence is to be considered an intelligence. These criteria include the isolated loss of function as a result of brain damage, the existence of *idiots savants* and prodigies, an identifiable set of core operations that deal with specific kinds of input, and a distinctive developmental history. Meeting these criteria strengthens Gardner's contention that each intelligence is relatively autonomous.

Based on such criteria, Gardner proposes that there are at least seven distinct intelligences. These are linguistic, logical-mathematical, musical, spatial, bodily-kinesthetic, interpersonal, and intrapersonal. The first two intelligences capture much that is represented in traditional IQ tests. The core components of musical intelligence are pitch, rhythm, and timbre. Spatial intelligence is the set of capacities that makes it possible to form and manipulate representations of the world. Bodily-kinesthetic intelligence is displayed by dancers, mimes, and athletes. Interpersonal intelligence refers to the ability to understand others; intrapersonal intelligence centers around the understanding of self.

Gardner does not claim that this roster of intelligences is exhaustive; rather, his aim is to establish support for a pluralistic view of intelligence. Gardner suggests that the failure to award certain of these abilities the status of an intelligence reflects a constraining cultural emphasis on logical, rational thought rather than a scientific conclusion based on evidence. (For a more extensive discussion of Gardner's theory as foundation for the work of Project Spectrum, see Krechevsky & Gardner, 1990, and Ramos-Ford & Gardner, 1991.)

Summary

Both Feldman and Gardner argue that cognition entails a broader range of abilities than psychometric IQ measurements identify. It is in recognition of such a diversity of intellectual strengths that their joint Project selected the name *Spectrum*. Both theorists also maintain that cognitive abilities are better thought of as specific rather than as one general capacity. This assertion entails the prediction that individuals often exhibit uneven profiles of ability when a wide range of domains is assessed. Finally, both theorists view cognitive ability as developing, not remaining static. Rather than identifying a fixed amount of something that is stable over time, Feldman and Gardner locate cognitive abilities in particular contexts and examine how these abilities change over time.

Spectrum's Assessment System

A more differentiated view of cognition, articulated in both Feldman's and Gardner's theories, requires appropriate means of assessing a wider range of abilities. Although many traditional forms of assessment are designed to identify deficits (Sattler, 1988), Spectrum aims to identify strengths and interests as well as relative weaknesses. Spectrum's view is that every individual has strengths; the challenge is to sample from a wide enough range of possibilities that the expression of strength can be detected. Implicit in this view is the notion that individuals need to be supported in the development of existing capabilities as well as provided with remediation in areas of difficulty (Malkus, Feldman, & Gardner, 1988; Ramos-Ford, Feldman, & Gardner, 1988).

Spectrum began the development of its assessment techniques at the preschool level. One reason for the choice of this age group was theoretical; namely, to determine whether individual differences in a wide range of abilities can be reliably discerned and assessed early in life. A second reason was more practical: preschool environments tend to be more open to innovations than more formal school settings. Although

TABLE 3.1 Project Spectrum assessment system: domains and activities.

Language	**Numbers**
Narrative measure: Storytelling board	Counting measure: Dinosaur game
Descriptive measure: Reporter task	Calculating measure: Bus game
Movement	**Social**
Creative movement measure: Biweekly movement curriculum	Social analysis measure: Classroom model activity
Athletic measure: Obstacle course	Social roles measure: Peer interaction checklist
Music	**Science**
Production measure: Singing activity	Hypothesis testing measure: Water activity
Perception measure: Pitch discrimination	Logical inference measure: Treasure hunt game
Visual Arts	Mechanical measure: Assembly activity
Art portfolios	Naturalist measure: Discovery area

its work began with preschoolers, in principle Spectrum's approach to assessment could be adapted for use with students of all ages.

Feldman and Gardner's theories provided a framework for thinking about the range and content of areas that Spectrum could assess. Observations of classrooms informed identification and definition of the specific ways in which preschool children demonstrate competence in a variety of domains. During the initial 4 years of research, children, teachers, and parents at the Eliot-Pearson Children's School at Tufts University were important sources of feedback about the validity and utility of the assessments being developed.

Spectrum's assessment system includes 15 measures that yield information about a child's bodily-kinesthetic skills, musical talents, natural science abilities, and social analytic capabilities as well as linguistic and logical-mathematical abilities (see Table 3.1). The areas chosen for assessment were based on both Gardner's theory of multiple intelligences and Feldman's theory of nonuniversal development, although not a direct application of either. For example, Spectrum assesses scientific reasoning skills such as hypothesis testing, not specifically found in either theory. Therefore, it is appropriate to say that the two founders' theories guided Spectrum's choices of areas to assess but did not dictate them.

Spectrum's measures range from relatively structured activities to more informal observations (see Table 3.2). The structure of the tasks varies with the structure of the domains they tap. What constitutes an appropriate means of assessing a child's ability in visual arts, for example, is different from what is required for assessing a child's creative movement ability.

TABLE 3.2 Descriptions of Spectrum activities.

Storyboard activity: This activity provides a concrete but open-ended framework in which a child creates stories. The activity measures a range of language skills including complexity of vocabulary and sentence structure, use of connectors, use of descriptive language and expressive dialogue, and ability to pursue a storyline. The materials for the storyboard include a landscape with foliage, dwellings, and assorted figures, creatures, and props (e.g., king, dragon, and jewel box).

Reporting activities: This activity assesses a child's ability to describe experiences. In the activity, the child is asked to report on a movie shown to the class. The child is asked a series of questions about the movie; answers are scored in terms of coherence, ability to report literal content accurately, level of detail, sentence structure, and vocabulary. "Weekend News" is a supplemental reporting activity, carried out as a part of the year-long curriculum. At the beginning of each week, children are asked to tell what they did over the weekend. The accounts are recorded by an adult and collected in a notebook. The recording of Weekend News insures the availability of multiple samples of a child's reporting skills. These samples are informally reviewed throughout the year.

Creative movement: Children participate in biweekly creative movement sessions throughout the school year. This curriculum focuses on children's abilities in five areas of dance and creative movement: sensitivity to rhythm, expressiveness, body control, generation of movement ideas, and responsiveness to music. Each session lasts approximately 20 min. Teachers use a balance of semistructured and more open-ended activities, as well as a mix of their own and the children's ideas.

Athletic movement: An outdoor obstacle course provides children with the opportunity to participate in sequences involving complex and combined movements. The obstacle course involves the types of skills found in many different sports such as coordination, timing, balance, and power. The course includes a balance beam, a ramp, a climbing structure, and a bean-bag toss.

Singing activity: This activity is designed to assess the child's ability to maintain accurate pitch and rhythm while singing, and the ability to recall a song's musical properties. During the activity, the child is asked to sing a favorite song and the "Happy Birthday" song. The child is also asked to recall a song taught to the class before the activity.

Music perception activity: This activity assesses a child's ability to discriminate pitch. The activity consists of three main parts: song recognition, error recognition, and pitch discrimination. In Part I, phrases of familiar tunes are played on a tape recorder and the child is asked to identify the tune as soon as it is recognized. During the error recognition component of the task (Part II), the child listens to different versions of a familiar tune and is asked to identify which are correct and which are incorrect. In Part III, Montessori Bells are used to measure a child's ability to discriminate pitch. The child is asked to find the bells that match the sounds of the teacher's bells.

Art portfolios: Throughout the school year, each child's art work is collected in a portfolio. These portfolios include drawings, paintings, collages, and three-dimensional pieces. Twice a year the contents are reviewed and assessed in terms of level of representation, degree of exploration, and level of artistry (e.g., expressivity). The child's preferred medium is also noted.

Dinosaur game: This game is designed as a measure of the child's understanding of number concepts, counting skills, and use of strategy. The game consists of a board with a picture of a large dinosaur on it, wooden dice, and small plastic dinosaurs for game pieces. The object of the game is for the small dinosaurs to escape from the mouth of the large dinosaur. Two players take turns rolling dice, which determine the direction and the number of spaces to be moved. The child is given the opportunity to manipulate the dice in order to optimize moves and to articulate understanding of the rules of the game.

TABLE 3.2 *Continued*

Bus game: This game assesses the child's ability to create a useful notation system, perform mental calculations, and organize number information for one or more variables. The game consists of a cardboard bus, a board with four bus stops, human figures, and two sets of colored chips. In the game, the child is asked to keep track of how many people ride a bus, which makes a number of stops. Each trip becomes increasingly challenging. For example, people can only get on the bus during the first trip but they can get on and off during the second trip.

Classroom model: The purpose of this activity is to assess the child's ability to observe and analyze social events and experiences in the classroom. In the activity, the child is presented with a small replica of her classroom, complete with furnishings and wooden figures with photographs of classmates and teachers on them. The child is asked questions about personal preferences for activities and relationships with peers as well as the preferences and relationships of classmates. Awareness of social roles is also probed.

Peer interaction checklist: Teachers use a checklist to assess the behaviors in which children engage when interacting with peers. After completing the checklist, the teacher reviews it in order to determine whether or not the child consistently assumes a distinctive social role. Each role is described by means of a general definition and a list of characteristic behaviors. For example, a child who is identified as a facilitator is able to share information and skills effectively with other children.

Water activity: This activity is used to assess a child's ability to generate hypotheses based on observations and to conduct simple experiments. Presented with a tub of water and an assortment of floating and sinking materials, the child is asked to predict what each object will do when placed in the water. After seeing each object in the water, the child is challenged to think of ways to make a floating object sink and a sinking object float. The child is also asked which object is hidden inside an opaque container placed in the water.

Treasure hunt game: This game assesses the child's ability to make logical inferences. In the game, each of several different kinds of objects is hidden on a board under a flag of a particular color. The child begins the game by looking under one flag of each color. The child is provided with a color-coded box, which may be used to keep track of the "treasures" uncovered. The child is then asked to predict what will be found under other flags and to specify where particular treasures can be found. Use of the color-coded box reflects how each child organizes the information gathered and whether the child is able to use this information to discover the rule governing the placement of objects.

Assembly activity: This activity is designed to measure the child's mechanical ability. The child is presented with two food grinders to take apart and put back together. Successful completion of the activity requires fine motor skills as well as visual-spatial, observational, and problem-solving abilities. More specifically, one can look at whether the child notices causal connections, uses a systematic approach, infers relationships based on observations, and demonstrates an understanding of the overall structure of simple mechanical objects.

Discovery area: This is a year-round area of the classroom devoted to natural science activities. Activities include caring for small animals, growing plants, and observing natural materials such as rocks and shells. An informal checklist posted in the area provides the teacher with a means of recording information about each child's observations, appreciation, and understanding of natural phenomena. For example, some children notice similarities and dissimilarities between materials and exhibit sensitivity to change over time; others ask questions based on their observations in order to find out more about something in the area.

Characteristics of Spectrum Assessment Tasks

Although the structure of the tasks varies, all of the tasks share several critical characteristics. The materials used are attractive to children and actively involve them in the assessment process. For example, in a task designed to assess children's understanding of number concepts, Spectrum responds to preschoolers' fascination with dinosaurs. The materials for this task include a game board picturing a large dinosaur and game pieces in the form of small plastic dinosaurs. The object of the game is to escape the mouth of the large dinosaur pictured on the board. Dice are rolled to determine the direction and number of spaces moved; the child's consequent manipulation of the game piece reveals the child's understanding of the concepts being assessed.

The contexts, designed to enable adults to gather information systematically about children's abilities and interests, are meaningful to children. That is, Spectrum's approach to assessment does not involve asking children to exhibit isolated behaviors (e.g., to hop on one foot). To learn about the child's athletic ability, an obstacle course is used. To gather information about a child's ability to generate hypotheses and conduct simple experiments, Spectrum engages the child in water play.

All of the tasks are designed to accommodate a range of ability. Recall that, in Feldman's terms, Spectrum assesses nonuniversal development. Accordingly, although children are of similar chronological age and typically in the same universal stage of cognitive development, their levels of ability in the domains that Spectrum assesses are expected to differ. When children tell stories, an activity designed to sample narrative language skills, their productions range from an entry level of simply labeling actions as they manipulate figures to a more advanced level of creating an elaborated story structure that entails the development of characters and plot.

What is Measured

To be specific about what the tasks measure, experts in the particular domains assessed were consulted to assist in the identification of elements or key abilities. In the domain of music, for example, the elements are pitch and rhythm. In the area of visual arts, the elements assessed include level of representation and degree of exploration.

In addition, as a child participates in a specific activity, strengths in other areas may be revealed. For example, some children sing during parts of the story they tell. Although this is not captured by formal scoring procedures, taking note of such an occurrence is important for a more complete understanding of a child's abilities. Similarly, the keen adult observer will gather rich incidental information about the child's interaction with the assessment materials. The nature of this information will be particular to the individual child involved. It might include the child's ideas about other materials that could be used in the activity, the child's observations about other activities that are similar to the one in which the child is currently engaged, or the child's spontaneous reflections about the frustrations caused by the activity.

Although for convenience we refer to Spectrum's assessment of a child's ability, Spectrum explicitly acknowledges that a child's participation in the assessment tasks reflects not only ability but also experience and interest (Krechevsky & Gardner, 1990; Malkus et al., 1988). When possible, Spectrum recommends that children be given an opportunity to explore and experiment with materials before the materials are used for assessment purposes. When children are not familiar with the materials, the results of the assessment may reflect children's difficulty with the task structure rather than their capability in the domain. Attending to the child's interest in the task is also necessary for rendering an accurate interpretation of the child's performance. A child who does not complete a task will likely get a lower score than one who does, but may or may not be as capable in the domain. Through explicit recognition of the important role that a child's interest plays in shaping performance, Spectrum's approach yields information that may be vital to capturing individual nuances and subtle variations in children's abilities.

Working Styles

Upon completion of each assessment task, the child's "working style" during the task is described. The construct of working style encompasses the process dimension of the child's involvement in each of the assessment tasks. It refers to the way in which a child interacts with the materials of a content area. After the child completes the task, working style is described in such terms as levels of engagement, confidence, and persistence (Wexler-Sherman, Gardner, & Feldman, 1988).

The assessment of working style enables the observer to compare a child's approach across a variety of tasks. Rather than assuming that the child's approach persists across all domains, Spectrum recognizes that style can be influenced by the demands and opportunities of particular domains. By comparing the child's working style across domains, it is possible to gather information systematically about style without the risk of inaccurately describing a child's behavior in terms of general traits.

The identification of a child's working styles also makes it possible to determine better to what extent a child's difficulty with a particular task is rooted in style rather than content. That is, styles themselves may facilitate or hinder performance. As an example, children who primarily focus on interacting with the adult during the activity may not be demonstrating their highest level of competence in relation to the demands of the activity itself.

The Role of Ongoing Observations

Because its assessment tasks are seen as only one source of information about a child, Spectrum recommends that its activities be supplemented by additional activities in each area and also by informal observations (Hatch & Gardner, 1986). Furthermore, because the information gained from the tasks describes the child's place in a developmental process at a particular point in time, it is necessary to reassess the child's progress regularly.

Consistent with its theoretical bases, Spectrum maintains that informal observations are most useful when they are domain-specific. Thus, rather than making observations of a child's "problem-solving ability," Spectrum suggests that teachers observe a child's problem-solving behavior when playing with construction materials or resolving a conflict with a peer. Similarly, a teacher making observations based on a Spectrum approach describes a child's attention span when engaged with particular materials rather than drawing conclusions about a child's attention span in general (Gardner, 1987).

When adopting this approach, teachers can use the elements that Spectrum identifies in each domain as focal points for observation. Many teachers gather information through informal observation, but they may not always be clear about what they are looking for and so may be limited in what they see. As a result, the information gathered may be of limited use for both guiding further assessment and developing curriculum. By focusing observations in terms of domains, elements, and working styles, Spectrum's approach insures that observation will be specific, content-relevant, and in-depth.

Documentation

Spectrum's documentation of the child's performance on the assessment activities takes a variety of forms. These forms include score sheets, observation checklists, and portfolios. The method used for recording and scoring a child's performance on individual tasks is determined by the nature of the task and the characteristics of the domain from which it samples.

For some activities, Spectrum has devised techniques for converting the child's performance into a quantitative score. This conversion is most often based on determining at what level the child is operating in relation to each of the elements assessed by the activity. Because the child's status in nonuniversal domains is typically characterized by a mixture of levels, rather than one uniform level (Feldman, 1986; Snyder & Feldman, 1980, 1984), it is necessary to recognize this differentiation in performance in order to be accurate in assessing the child's status.

One important consequence of this technique is that two children who have the same quantitative scores often have distinctive capabilities. Interpretation of the scores, in substantive terms, then requires a closer examination of how they are earned. As an example, two children score 16 points when their art portfolios are evaluated. One child earns nine points for level of representation, three points for degree of exploration, and four points for level of artistry (e.g., expressivity). The second child earns three points for level of representation, six points for degree of

TABLE 3.3 Excerpt of a sample Spectrum Profile.[a]

Meg

Meg was an active and enthusiastic participant in all Spectrum activities presented this year. The areas in which Meg showed the most interest and ability were creative movement, visual arts, and logical inference.

Meg participates enthusiastically in creative movement sessions. She has shown an unusual responsiveness to different kinds of music and is able to move in subtle and intriguing ways. She is able to move her whole body, as well as isolated body parts, with feeling and precision. While listening to folk music, Meg did an expressive dance by moving only her shoulders and hips. She moves freely and feels comfortable and confident dancing alone when other children in the group have chosen not to. Throughout the year, Meg also offered many inventive suggestions for movement experiences and games.

In addition to her interest and ability in creative movement, Meg has shown an equal ability in more athletic forms of movement. She frequently offered to show her classmates new things she had mastered at gymnastics class and encouraged others to try a variety of movement challenges such as cartwheels and somersaults. She exhibited skill in maneuvering her way through an outdoor obstacle course, walking swiftly across a balance beam, and running around obstacles.

Meg also shows a strong interest in the visual arts, particularly in painting and drawing with markers. Her art work is, for the most part, characteristic for a child her age. She has explored design and simple representations throughout the year. What makes Meg's work distinctive is her use of the color spectrum in almost every drawing and painting. Each time it is used in a slightly different way: as a rainbow, for outlining figures with color after color, and in a variety of different patterns and designs. The color spectrum has become, in a sense, Meg's trademark.

Meg exhibited unusual ability for a child her age in a Spectrum activity focused on logical inference. While playing the Treasure Hunt Game, she was one of the few children able to gather and organize information systematically, and use the information to draw conclusions and make predictions. She was able to "break the code" and articulate the underlying rule for the game, including the abstract association that particular treasure boxes were always empty.

exploration, and seven points for level of artistry. By examining how each child earns the score of 16 points, it is possible to describe more precisely what capabilities each child demonstrates.

In order to appreciate children's abilities in a range of activities, Spectrum recommends writing a report (Ramos-Ford & Gardner, 1991). This report, called a *Spectrum Profile*, describes each child's relative strengths and weaknesses in terms of that child's own range of capabilities, and occasionally in relation to peers (see Table 3.3). The child's profile is described not only in terms of capacities, but also preferences and inclinations. Included in the profile are descriptions of the child's working styles across the tasks. When writing the profile, suggestions are offered about ways in which parents can follow through in the home with readily available materials and in the community with public resources (e.g., museums, libraries, parks). When Profiles are shared with parents, it is stressed that the Profile describes a child at a particular point in time and, especially at young ages, profiles can shift dramatically in relatively short periods of time (Gardner, 1990).

In Spectrum's view, its quantitative and qualitative methods of documentation complement and support each other. Each method has both strengths and limitations. Deriving quantitative scores necessitates the reduction of information; much of what is uniquely expressed is lost as a consequence. Narrative description provides richness of detail, but this strength makes summary comparisons cumbersome. In the field, the purpose for which Spectrum assessments will be used determines the most appropriate form of documentation.

When Spectrum's approach to ongoing observations is adopted, teachers continue to collect information about children and how they spend their time. In order to document children's progress, teachers may choose to construct portfolios of work samples (e.g., collections of dated drawings or paintings, a book of stories, tape recordings of singing). Classroom photograph albums and videotapes are other means of recording what children do. In each instance, children can be involved in selecting what to keep a record of and reflecting on the progress their recordings document. All of these forms of documentation also provide a basis for staff discussions and communicating with parents. The developmental emphasis in portfolio assessment is particularly important to Spectrum, as befits a project created by two developmentalists.

The Spectrum Field Inventory

Currently under development, the Spectrum Field Inventory is a condensed version of Spectrum's assessment effort. Designed to be easily transportable, the Inventory includes six tasks that can be administered in two 1-hour sessions. The Inventory, like its parent technique, samples from a wide range of distinct domains, thus providing a richer understanding of a child's cognitive abilities than is afforded by many standardized measures of children's intelligence. Because it is transportable and relatively time efficient, the Inventory can be used in a variety of contexts, including school, home, and laboratory.

Despite a superficial resemblance to traditional psychometrics, the Inventory is not a test in the traditional sense. There is no assumption that what it measures is definitive or exhaustive. Although it yields some quantitative information, the child's scores reflect development at a particular point in time, not fixed abilities. The Inventory is not designed for the purposes of ranking, tracking, or labeling children. Its primary purpose is to provide access to the diversity that characterizes the extended range of young children's cognitive abilities and interests. Through such access it is possible to initiate the effort to perceive what distinguishes children as individuals and to begin to provide more sensitively for the full range of their developmental potentials.

We describe Spectrum's approach to assessment as a system because it is more than a set of assessment tasks. It is also a system of principles based on theory and educational philosophy. The administration of the tasks and interpretation of the information gathered is, under optimal conditions, guided by these principles. The principles that guide Spectrum are as follows: every child has strengths, assessment measures experience and interest as well as ability, assessment is most accurate when children are experienced with the materials used for assessment purposes, assessment occurs in contexts that are meaningful to children, assessment is an ongoing process, and assessment and curriculum should both be seen in developmental context, both universal and nonuniversal.

Implications for Curriculum Development

Although Spectrum concentrated on the development of assessment techniques in its first 5 years of research, implications for curriculum development have always been part of Spectrum's agenda. Spectrum's approach to assessment intentionally blurs the traditional line between assessment and curriculum. From Spectrum's perspective, in order for assessment to be accurate children must have opportunities to explore materials and become familiar with the possibilities and challenges they present. Assessment information is most useful for teachers when it can help in the planning of learning experiences. The recognition that developing an appropriate curriculum requires ongoing assessment is gaining acceptability in the field of early education (Bredekamp, 1987).

Spectrum's approach to assessment potentially influences curriculum development in several areas: selection of materials, organization of subject matter into domains and elements, and individualization of instruction.

Materials

At the most concrete level, some of the same materials that are used for assessment can also be used as regular classroom activities. Spectrum uses both familiar and novel materials for assessment purposes. The storytelling board and the classroom model afford novelty that both teachers and children can explore. Materials for the storytelling board include landscape features, dwellings, human figures, animals, and simple props. The classroom model, suggested and developed by former Spectrum staff member Janet Stork, is designed to tap children's understanding of social dynamics in the classroom. The materials include a replica of the child's classroom and small wooden blocks with attached photographs of the children and teachers. In addition to its more formal assessment function, the classroom model offers many opportunities for children to process their interactions with their peers as well as their teachers.

For all Spectrum activities, the materials can be used in simpler or more challenging versions. For instance, to simplify the dinosaur game, children can play using only the die that indicates the number of spaces to move (rather than also using the die that indicates the forward or backward direction of the movement). To make the game more difficult, the teacher might provide a board with more spaces and two number dice as well as the directional die.

The same materials may also be used in different ways. As children become familiar with the story board, they may have ideas about other materials that could be used for storytelling. In one classroom, an entire curricular unit was built around constructing, outfitting, and using story-boards for creating stories.

Domains and Elements

At a more conceptual level, Spectrum's areas of assessment offer teachers potentially different ways of looking at and planning for children's school experiences. An illustration of this is the observational checklist that Spectrum designed for teachers to use when assessing the nature of children's interactions with their peers. The checklist suggests thinking of children's interactions with each other in terms of social roles. A child who is having difficulty relating to peers may have the requisite skills but be frustrated by not being able to play a certain role. A child may want to be a leader in the class, but may be unsuccessful because, although able to initiate activities, the child may not be flexible in responding to other children's ideas as play continues. Seeing this, the teacher may be able to provide specific support and guidance in particular situations rather than remaining informed only at a more general level such as whether or not the child is engaging in cooperative play.

Spectrum's descriptions of domains in terms of elements or core capacities provides a framework for curriculum development. Its conceptual analysis makes it possible for teachers to move beyond the structured tasks that Spectrum provides and generate further experiences that involve the same elements and processes. This framework is particularly helpful for areas in which teachers themselves feel less comfortable. We have found that bodily movement activities are particularly useful to teachers.

According to a position statement issued by the National Association for the Education of Young Children (1988), the selection of an assessment instrument must be based, in part, on its utility for ensuring that children benefit from their educational experiences. Spectrum assessments are more easily translated into specific curriculum plans than are many traditional forms of assessment because the areas assessed are organized in terms of the same sorts of areas that many teachers use to organize their curriculum.

Individualizing School Experience

Early childhood educators generally recognize individual differences and are committed to be responsive to these differences (Bredekamp, 1987; Hendrick, 1980a; Pitcher, Feinburg, & Alexander, 1984; Robison, 1983). The ways in which individuals are generally known to differ include stage and rate of development, style of learning, specific areas of talent, personality, and family background. But it has proven difficult to articulate how to be responsive to these differences (Hendrick, 1980a).

One way to individualize school experience is to let children choose what to do (Hendrick, 1980b). Thus, many teachers build into the daily schedule indoor and outdoor choice times. Another way to individualize is to let children determine the pace or rate of learning. In traditional Montessori programs, for example, the use of materials is prescribed but the rate at which the child moves through the sequence defining their use is individually determined (Montessori, 1962). A third way is to provide for a range of developmental ability (Bredekamp, 1987). As an example of this strategy, a teacher might put puzzles with differing numbers and sizes of pieces in the manipulative area.

Using the findings of the Spectrum assessment process, it is possible to design more specifically and more practically a match between a program of instruction and a particular child. The child may still choose from available materials but now the child's performance in Spectrum activities also influences and helps direct what materials are made available. Rate of development is still assumed to vary and therefore children will not necessarily be engaged with the same sorts of materials, nor will the same materials always be used in the same ways by different children. The range of ability for which provision is made will vary in terms of specific children and across specific domains. Information about a child's working styles guides selection of the most effective contexts for learning (e.g., size of group, degree of structure) and the most appropriate means of instruction (e.g., encouraging engagement, directing focus, providing models). That Spectrum's approach yields such information distinguishes it from many traditional forms of psychometric assessment that, according to Sattler (1988), usually do not provide information about the conditions that facilitate children's learning.

It is important to note again that from Spectrum's perspective individualization is accomplished through responsiveness to strengths as well as provision for relative weaknesses. If a child is able to do something and it is acknowledged by her teacher, the child feels valued and experiences a sense of success. This sense of success contributes to continuing participation, which then affords opportunities for further achievements (Briggs, 1970). In some instances, the sense of success in one area of the curriculum may make the child more likely to take the risk of engaging in areas where she feels less confident. Similarly, a child who is more generally having difficulty in the classroom may have a different experience once the teacher discovers and then helps the child to recognize her strengths.

Sustaining the Effort

Although making a match between an individual child and an educational experience is a challenging and critical first step, it is only one phase of the educational process. The realization of children's full potentials requires thoughtful, sustained efforts to design experiences that engage and support the expression of their capabilities (Feldman with Goldsmith, 1986). To capture the dynamics of what is involved, Feldman (1976) has suggested that the metaphor of the "child as craftsman" be adopted to guide the educational process. Another metaphor recently proposed (Rogoff, 1990) is the child as "apprentice"; both metaphors express the idea of relationship between teacher or mentor and student, a more experienced and expert person guiding the experience of the neophyte.

In adopting these metaphors, a main purpose of education is to provide conditions under which each child can pursue more advanced levels of mastery within chosen fields of work. According to Feldman, the matter of how much the child can learn must be considered in relation to a particular field of endeavor at a particular point in time. For children to experience the sense of satisfaction from earned mastery that the metaphor implies, it is necessary for teachers to be prepared to help children move beyond surface encounters with subject matter. Exploration must be followed by sustained, supervised experience in a specific domain in order for true engagement to occur.

Developmental Education

To design an educational program that is developmentally sound, it is necessary to have a clear picture of a child's developmental status. When assessing this status, it is critical to be aware of the concept of development that underlies the structure and content of the assessment instrument used. Every assessment instrument is based on either explicit or implicit assumptions; none provides a simple reflection of a child's abilities.

Many developmental assessment techniques assess a child's development only in terms of universal stages (Feldman with Goldsmith, 1986). Yet, the design of an educational program includes decisions about materials, activities, and modes of instruction that impact both universal and nonuniversal development. Making these decisions for a particular group of children necessitates going beyond an understanding of universals in child development (Feldman, 1976; Fowler, 1980). Spectrum's approach aims to equip teachers with knowledge that will guide them beyond thinking in terms of what is appropriate for typical 4-year-olds and 5-year-olds, and enable them to consider what is appropriate for each 4- and 5-year-old.

When attention is given only to universal dimensions of development, there is the risk that children will not be challenged enough, and that an artificial ceiling will constrain their growth. The rich information gathered through Spectrum's assessment activities will enable teachers to design curricula that are developmental, in both universal and nonuniversal domains.

Spectrum proposes that there are multiple ways to respond to the implications of its approach when developing curricula. Just as Spectrum recognizes the distinctiveness of individual children, it also recognizes that teachers have different interests, styles, strengths, and weaknesses. Furthermore, the needs of differentially structured programs (e.g., public and private, full-day and half-day) vary. The wide range of Spectrum's potential implications for curriculum development are intended to reflect this positive diversity in the field.

Future Directions

Research

To understand and enhance young children's universal and nonuniversal development, studies of the content and sequence of their advances in all regions of the universal to unique continuum of developmental domains must be carried out. Although much has been learned about universals in young children's development, we have only begun to appreciate the more specific expressions of ability that even young children display (Feldman with Goldsmith, 1986; Krechevsky & Gardner, 1990; Ramos-Ford & Gardner, 1991). Thus, for example, there is a substantial database documenting the milestones of young children's gross motor development (Cohen & Gross, 1979); however, much less is known about how young children develop in the domain of creative movement, or even more specifically, in a particular dance form such as ballet.

To study children's development in nonuniversal domains such as those that Spectrum assesses, it will be necessary to conduct longitudinal research. Feldman's (in press) technique of domain analysis offers a promising methodology for beginning such work. As domains are "mapped" (i.e., as their elements, levels, sequences, and skills are explored), it will be necessary to study more specifically how transitions in these domains are accomplished. Although it is a reasonable working assumption that the same basic mechanisms operate in both universal and nonuniversal development, empirical work may reveal that more subtle processes are also involved (Vygotsky, 1978). When development in nonuniversal domains is better understood, we will also be better equipped to address the questions of how universal and nonuniversal development are related, and how change in one kind of domain facilitates or impedes progress in others (Vygotsky, 1978; Wertsch, 1985). Spectrum offers the possibility of exploring nonuniversal domains that are key to the school curriculum.

Practice

Spectrum currently is pursuing a number of objectives. Description of its assessment techniques in forms that will be useful to educators, as well as further development work, are among the project's current goals. The project is investigating the effectiveness of a Spectrum-based intervention program for children at risk for school failure. Plans for refinement of the Spectrum Field Inventory include further work on the measure of children's social understanding and the development of more efficient scoring systems. To extend the utility of Spectrum's 15 tasks, plans for translating their structures into guides for ongoing classroom observations are being formulated. Designing and field testing techniques for teacher education is also an important priority for the project.

Conclusions

A risk to any innovation is the danger that it will be assimilated to traditional forms and distorted in the process. Project Spectrum's approach to early education is based on Feldman's transformative view of the nature of development and Gardner's distinctive model of multiple intelligences. Were its approach to assessment to be assimilated in terms of the view of intelligence as IQ or another psychometrically inspired approach, children would actually be at increased risk for early tracking and could be subjected to inappropriate performance pressures.

Many children already experience difficulty meeting the demands of school environments (Bredekamp & Shepard, 1989; Cardenas & First, 1985). As concerned developmental psychologists and educators, we have an opportunity to try to increase the likelihood that children will succeed by designing environments that broaden the range of cognitive ability recognized and supported in school and in doing so, recognize and validate the rich diversity that exists in our multicultural society.

If Spectrum's approach to assessment and its implications for curriculum development can be understood and implemented with consistent reference to its theoretical bases, we will move one step closer to development of the full range and variety of forms of valuable human potential. At the least, we will reduce the likelihood that children will fall by the wayside in dangerously large numbers, neither understood nor nurtured in the schools they are required to attend.

Acknowledgments. The support of the William T. Grant Foundation and the Rockefeller Brothers Fund is gratefully acknowledged. The members of our research team, the Developmental Science Group, made important contributions; thanks to Ann Benjamin and Jie-Qi Chen. We appreciate the help and cooperation of the Spectrum staff. For their comments, we also thank Robert Pasnak and Mark Howe.

References

Baron, J. (1985). *Rationality and intelligence.* New York: Cambridge University Press.

Benjamin, A.C. (1990). Levels of expertise in early childhood teaching: An initial field test of a diagnostic instrument (Doctoral dissertation, Tufts University, 1989). *Dissertation Abstracts International, 50*, 3843A.

Berk, L.E. (1991). *Child development* (2nd ed.). Boston: Allyn/Bacon.

Bredekamp, S. (Ed.). (1987). *Developmentally appropriate practice in early childhood programs serving children from birth through age 8* (expanded ed.). Washington, DC: National Association for the Education of Young Children.

Bredekamp, S., & Shepard, L. (1989). How best to protect children from inappropriate school expectations, practices, and policies. *Young Children, 44*(3), 14–24.

Briggs, D.C. (1970). *Your child's self-esteem.* Garden City, NY: Doubleday.

Cardenas, J., & First, J.M. (1985). Children at risk. *Educational Leadership, 43*(1), 4–8.

Case, R. (1985). *Intellectual development: Birth to adulthood.* New York: Academic Press.

Cohen, M.A., & Gross, P.J. (1979). *The developmental resource: Behavioral sequences for assessment and program planning* (Vol. 1). New York: Grune/Stratton.

Damon, W. (1977). *The social world of the child.* San Francisco: Jossey-Bass.

Feldman, D.H. (1976). The child as craftsman. *Phi Delta Kappan, 58*, 143–149.

Feldman, D.H. (1979). The mysterious case of extreme giftedness. In H. Passow (Ed.), *The gifted and the talented: Yearbook of the National Society for the Study of Education* (pp. 335–351). Chicago: University of Chicago Press.

Feldman, D.H. (1980). *Beyond universals in cognitive development.* Norwood, NJ: Ablex.

Feldman, D.H. (1981). Beyond universals: Toward a developmental psychology of education. *Educational Researcher, 11*, 21–31.

Feldman, D.H. (1986). How development works. In I. Levin (Ed.), *Stage and structure: Reopening the debate* (pp. 284–306). Norwood, NJ: Ablex.

Feldman, D.H. (in press). *Beyond universals in cognitive development* (2nd ed.). Norwood, NJ: Ablex.

Feldman, D.H., & Adams, M.L. (1989). Intelligence, stability, and continuity: Changing conceptions. In M.H. Bornstein & N.A. Krasnegor (Eds.), *Stability and continuity in mental development* (pp. 293–309). Hillsdale, NJ: Erlbaum.

Feldman, D.H., with Goldsmith, L.T. (1986). *Nature's gambit.* New York: Basic Books.

Fischer, K.W. (1980). A theory of cognitive development: The control and construction of hierarchies of skills. *Psychological Review, 87*, 477–531.

Fowler, W. (1980). *Infant and child care: A guide to education in group settings.* Boston: Allyn/Bacon.

Gardner, H. (1983). *Frames of mind: The theory of multiple intelligences.* New York: Basic Books.

Gardner, H. (1987). The theory of multiple intelligences. *Annals of Dyslexia, 37*, 19–35.

Gardner, H. (1990). Assessment in context: The alternative to standardized testing. In B.R. Gifford & M.C. O'Connor (Eds.), *Future assessments: Changing views of aptitude, achievement, and instruction* (pp. 2–44). Boston: Kluwer.

Ginsburg, H., & Opper, S. (1979). *Piaget's theory of intellectual development* (2nd ed.). Englewood Cliffs, NJ: Prentice-Hall.

Hatch, T.C., & Gardner, H. (1986). From testing intelligence to assessing competences: A pluralistic view of intelligence. *Roeper Review, 8*, 147–150.

Hendrick, J. (1980a). *Total learning for the whole child.* St. Louis: C.V. Mosby.

Hendrick, J. (1980b). *The whole child: New trends in early education* (2nd ed.). St. Louis: C.V. Mosby.

Horowitz, F.D. (1987). *Exploring developmental theories: Toward a structural/behavioral model of development.* Hillsdale, NJ: Erlbaum.

Keil, F.C. (1986). On the structure-dependent nature of stages in cognitive development. In I. Levin (Ed.), *Stage and structure: Reopening the debate* (pp. 144–163). Norwood, NJ: Ablex.

Kohlberg, L. (1987). *Child psychology and childhood education: A cognitive-developmental view.* New York: Longman.

Krechevsky, M., & Gardner, H. (1990). The emergence and nurturance of multiple intelligences: The Project Spectrum approach. In M.J. Howe (Ed.), *Encouraging the development of exceptional skills and talents* (pp. 222–245). Leicester, England: British Psychological Society.

Malkus, U., Feldman, D.H., & Gardner, H. (1988). Dimensions of mind in early childhood. In A.D. Pellegrini (Ed.), *The psychological bases for early education* (pp. 25–38). Chichester, England: Wiley.

Mockros, C.A. (1989). *Aesthetic judgment: An empirical comparison of two stage developmental theories*. Unpublished master's thesis, Tufts University, Medford, MA.

Montessori, M. (1962). *The discovery of the child* (M. Johnstone, Trans.). Adyar, India: Vasanta Press.

National Association for the Education of Young Children. (1988). Position statement on standardized testing of young children 3 through 8 years of age. *Young Children*, *43*(3), 42–47.

Parsons, M.J. (1987). *How we understand art: A cognitive developmental account of aesthetic experience*. Cambridge: Cambridge University Press.

Piaget, J. (1967). *Six psychological studies*. New York: Random House.

Piaget, J. (1970). Piaget's theory. In P. Mussen (Ed.), *Carmichael's manual of child psychology* (Vol. 1, pp. 703–732). New York: Wiley.

Pitcher, E.G., Feinburg, S.G., & Alexander, D. (1984). *Helping young children learn* (4th ed.). Columbus, OH: Charles Merrill.

Ramos-Ford, V., Feldman, D.H., & Gardner, H. (1988). A new look at intelligence through Project Spectrum. *New Horizons for Learning*, *8*(3), 6–7, 15.

Ramos-Ford, V., & Gardner, H. (1991). Giftedness from a multiple intelligences perspective. In N. Colangelo & G.A. Davis (Eds.), *Handbook of gifted education* (pp. 55–64). Boston: Allyn/Bacon.

Robison, H. (1983). *Exploring teaching in early childhood education* (2nd ed.). Boston: Allyn/Bacon.

Rogoff, B. (1990). *Apprenticeship in thinking: Cognitive development in social context*. New York: Oxford University Press.

Sattler, J.M. (1988). *Assessment of children* (3rd ed.). San Diego: Sattler.

Selman, R.L. (1980). *The growth of interpersonal understanding*. New York: Academic Press.

Snyder, S.S., & Feldman, D.H. (1980). Individual developmental transitions: A film metaphor. In D.H. Feldman, *Beyond universals in cognitive development* (pp. 41–85). Norwood, NJ: Ablex.

Snyder, S.S., & Feldman, D.H. (1984). Phases of transition in cognitive development: Evidence from the domain of spatial representation. *Child Development*, *55*, 981–989.

Sroufe, L.A., Cooper, R.G., & Marshall, M.E. (1988). *Child development: Its nature and course*. New York: Alfred Knopf.

Sternberg, R.J. (1985). *Beyond IQ*. New York: Cambridge University Press.

Vygotsky, L.S. (1978). *Mind in society: The development of higher psychological processes*. Cambridge, MA: Harvard University Press.

Walton, R.E., Adams, M.L., Goldsmith, L.T., & Feldman, D.H. (1988, June). *Affect and development in a nonuniversal domain*. Paper presented at the meeting of The Jean Piaget Society Philadelphia, PA.

Wertsch, J.V. (Ed.). (1985). *Culture, communication, and cognition: Vygotskian perspectives*. Cambridge: Cambridge University Press.
Wexler-Sherman, C., Gardner, H., & Feldman, D.H. (1988). A pluralistic view of early assessment: The Project Spectrum approach. *Theory into Practice*, *27*, 77–83.

Part II
Advances in Competence

4 "I Watch, Therefore I Can Do": The Development of Meta-Imitation During the Preschool Years and the Advantage of Optimism About One's Imitative Skills

DAVID F. BJORKLUND, JANE F. GAULTNEY, AND
BRANDI L. GREEN

Although language may be the quintessential human skill, our ability to learn through observation serves to distinguish us from other species and likely played an important role in our cognitive evolution. We are not the only species to learn through watching, of course, but the extent to which we have perfected observational learning is unmatched in the animal kingdom. It is primarily through observational learning over an extended childhood that we acquire the skills and knowledge needed to survive in human culture.

Although we learn many things through watching that we never try to reproduce (opposite-sex stereotypic behavior, for example, see Money, 1988), observational learning is most readily noted when children imitate a model's behavior. Many theorists from a variety of perspectives have acknowledged the role that imitation plays in the acquisition of novel behavior (e.g., Bandura, 1989a; Bandura & Walters, 1963; Piaget, 1962), with the cognitive function of imitation being "to help children understand the challenge presented by the model's behavior that lies just beyond their level of competence" (Kuczynski, Zahn-Waxler, & Radke-Yarrow, 1987, p. 276). Imitation obviously plays an importance social role as well, serving in early life as a form of parent–child communication (Pawlby, 1977) and in later childhood to initiate, sustain, and strengthen social bonds (e.g., Grusec & Abramovitch, 1982; Thelen, Dolinger, & Roberts, 1975). Although imitative abilities certainly improve with age, the frequency of imitation in young children's lives is impressive, with mothers easily noting examples of imitation even among toddlers (Kuczynski et al., 1987). Naturalistic studies of preschoolers in the classroom have also reported a high incidence of imitation. For example, Abramovitch and Grusec (1978) found an average of 14.82 imitative acts per hour by 4- to 5-year-old children during periods of free play (see also Miller & Thelen, 1986).

Observational learning is not a single ability. Bandura's (1989a) social cognitive model proposed that imitation is composed of several subprocesses, all of which develop over childhood. These components include attentional processes, retention processes, production processes, and motivational processes. In this chapter we introduce a cognitive process that influences children's observational learning, that of *meta-imitation*—children's knowledge of their own imitative abilities. Meta-imitation would be included among the production processes in Bandura's model, affecting how the imitative acts are represented, how feedback about one's performance is processed, and how children perceive the match between the model's behavior and their enactment. In this chapter we present data from two naturalistic studies and an experiment indicating that preschool children generally overestimate how well they will be able to imitate a modeled behavior (i.e., their predictions of their imitative skills). Further, after attempting to reproduce the observed behavior, they overestimate how well they imitated the behavior in question (i.e., their postdictions). We argue that such overestimation is in all likelihood adaptive, and should be viewed not so much as ineffective thinking skills that must eventually be overcome, but rather as a reflection of an immature cognitive system that plays a beneficial role in development. This overestimation of imitative ability leads, as parents know to their distress, to children attempting activities that are clearly (to the adult) inappropriate (e.g., the child who is certain he can back the car out of the garage just like Daddy). As Bandura (1989a) has noted, it is this inflated self-efficacy that requires parents to be ever watchful of their young children.

Before discussing our data, we will review research examining children's evaluation of their motor and cognitive abilities, demonstrating a general tendency of young children to overestimate their actual competencies. We will also present some arguments concerning why being out of touch with one's physical or cognitive abilities may be advantageous for young children.

Young Children's Estimation of Their Cognitive Abilities

How well we think we can perform a task, and how good a job we think we did after performing a task, would seem to be important factors in both cognitive and social development. The confidence a person has in his or her competence in a particular domain will influence what tasks that person chooses to perform and how long one persists at those tasks (Bandura, 1989b). Thus, the degree of confidence a child has will determine not only the type of tasks attempted and the duration of the attempt, but also what is learned as a result.

Children's ability to predict (and postdict) their cognitive performance has been studied under the rubric of *metacognition*, which refers to a person's knowledge of his or her own cognition and the factors that influence thinking. For every form of cognition, it is possible to think of a corresponding metacognition, and metacognition has been studied with respect to memory, communication, reading, and attention, among others (e.g., Flavell & Wellman, 1977; Garner, 1990; Miller, 1985; Whitehurst & Sonnenschein, 1986). A general finding of developmental metacognitive research is that there is a concomitant age-related improvement in cognitive and metacognitive abilities (see Flavell, 1978; Schneider, 1985). It has also been generally assumed that being "in touch" with one's mental abilities affords greater cognitive benefits than being "out of touch."

In studies asking children to predict their level of performance on cognitive tasks, a general finding is that the frequency and degree of overestimation declines with age. This has been most consistently noted in studies of metamemory (for reviews, see Cavanaugh & Perlmutter, 1982; Flavell & Wellman, 1977; Schneider, 1985; Schneider & Pressley, 1989). In experiments where children are shown sets of items and asked to predict how many they will be able to recall, preschoolers are highly prone to overestimate their actual recall abilities, with many professing that they will remember 100% of the items correctly (Flavell, Freidrichs, & Hoyt, 1970; Levin, Yussen, De Rose, & Pressley, 1977; Yussen & Levy, 1975). With age, children's estimations of their memory abilities come closer to reality, with their predictions being more influenced by their previous performance than that of younger children. Although children are typically more accurate when it comes to evaluating their memory performance than predicting it, several researchers have found that this postdiction ability also increases with age (Moynahan, 1976; Pressley, Levin, Ghatala, & Ahmad, 1987; Schneider, 1988). The higher degree of overestimation for prediction as opposed to postdiction tasks is probably because it is more difficult to imagine cognitive acts that have not yet taken place than it is to evaluate an event that has already occurred (see Moynahan, 1976).

Researchers of metacognition have not been the only ones examining children's estimations of their cognitive ability. Prediction-performance contrasts of abilities have also been a staple of the achievement motivation literature (see, e.g., Stipek, 1984; Stipek & Mac Iver, 1989). Schneider (1988) and Weinert (1986) have each noted the similarity in the metacognition and achievement motivation paradigms and findings, with studies from both traditions reporting overestimation of performance by young children, with accuracies of their abilities gradually improving with age.

Research dating back at least to the 1960s (Phillips, 1963) has found that young children overestimate how well they will do on psychomotor tasks, such as putting Xs into squares, completing puzzles, or balancing balls on a moving platform (Clifford, 1978; Parsons & Ruble, 1977; Stipek & Hoffman, 1980). This research has shown that young children do not use feedback about their past performance to guide their subsequent predictions as well as older children do, although when the feedback is made particularly salient, young children can make more accurate assessments of their own ability (Clifford, 1978; Levin et al., 1977; Stipek & Daniels, 1988). Similar patterns of results have been found when children are asked to judge their own "smartness" or ability on some academic task. In research by Stipek and her colleagues (Stipek, 1981, 1984; Stipek & Hoffman, 1980; Stipek, Roberts, & Sanborn, 1984), children in first grade and younger generally rated themselves as being "one of the smartest kids in their class." It was not until second or third grade that children's estimations of their own abilities became more realistic, correlating significantly with those of their teachers and classmates. Furthermore, young children seem to wear rose-colored glasses only when assessing their own performance. Their assessments of other children's intellectual abilities are more realistic, indicating that they are capable of making reasonably accurate judgments of children's abilities; they just reserve their overly optimistic appraisals for themselves.

Why are Young Children So Optimistic?

Perhaps the most straightforward explanation for children's overly optimistic opinions of their competencies is that such overestimation reflects cognitive limitations. This explanation would hold that children are unable to use feedback from their past performance in their expectancy judgments, and thus their initial opinions are only slightly modified by experience. This explanation does not seem to be accurate, however. As we mentioned above, young children will attend to feedback when their performance is made particularly salient (Clifford, 1978; Levin et al., 1977), and they are able to make relatively accurate ability judgments of other children (Stipek, 1981; Stipek & Hoffman, 1980). As with so many other aspects of cognition, young children seem to have the ability to perform well, but do so only under certain conditions (see Bjorklund, 1989). Thus, although young children's limited cognitive abilities must certainly contribute to their pattern of performance, such limitations alone cannot adequately explain the research findings.

One reason for young children's poor estimation of their own behavior has to do with how they define success and failure. Stipek (1984) has suggested that young children enjoy performing a task for its own sake and are less concerned about achieving a specific goal. Simply performing a task, therefore, may constitute a success in the child's eyes, whereas the adult would rate the act a success or failure on the basis of the outcome.

Related to this is how children view ability and effort in evaluating success. Evidence from a variety of sources indicates that young children do not differentiate effort from ability (e.g., Harter & Pike, 1984; Heckhausen, 1984; Nicholls, 1978; Stipek & Mac Iver, 1989; Wellman, 1985). Trying hard is as important to perceived success as doing well, a message that most preschool children are likely to get from their teachers and parents (Stipek & Mac Iver, 1989). A parallel finding is that young children generally hold an incremental theory of their own intelligence, believing that they can become smarter with effort (Dweck & Elliott, 1983). Also, many tasks young children attempt are done poorly initially, but their performance improves with practice. Thus, despite previous failures, children may believe, based on past performance and comments from adults, that they will do better "next time," a way of thinking that accounts for their failure to adjust their estimations of past or future performance as a result of feedback. This can account for their more accurate assessment of other children's ability. They are unable to know how hard the other children are trying, and therefore consider only the observable performance. Thus, they make more accurate judgments of the performance per se.

Stipek (1984) has proposed an explanation of young children's overestimations based on Piaget's (1930) idea of "wishful thinking." According to this concept, preschool children often do not differentiate between their wishes and their expectations. They believe that their desires are efficacious in and of themselves, and therefore judge future performances by how well they would like them to be. Although wishful thinking can explain why children are more accurate judging other children's abilities than their own, it runs into some of the same problems that the *cognitive limitations* explanation does. With salient feedback, children can modify their expectations. Wishful thinking also seems to play more of a role in influencing children's predictions than in influencing their assessments of past performance (Pressley et al., 1987).

There seems to be no one reason for young children's consistent overestimation of their competencies. Rather, there appears to be a variety of factors that contribute to children's overly optimistic evaluations of their own abilities: cognitive limitations, with children performing in a sophisticated manner only under optimal conditions; different definitions of success and failure, with an emphasis on the role of effort; and wishful thinking. This combination of factors results in a self-enhancement bias in young children, which we believe contributes to a sense of self-efficacy.

The Advantages for Young Children of Overestimating Their Abilities

We propose that young children's poor metacognition, in terms of predicting and evaluating their own motor and intellectual abilities, provides some advantages. Being overly optimistic about one's abilities permits young children to practice cognitive and social skills without being acutely aware of negative feedback. Although good metacognition is generally associated with good cognition in older children, we believe that being in touch with one's aptitudes is not beneficial during the preschool years. The young child who is consistently accurate in evaluating feedback about his or her performance will be sure to experience many failures. Ignorance of their limitations allows children to try more diverse and complex behaviors that may be out of their grasp at the present time (see Bjorklund & Green, 1992).

The benefits of young children's limited awareness of their abilities and their expanded experience that results are twofold. First, it allows the child to practice, which may be a precursor to effective use of these abilities later in life. Second, it allows children to develop more positive self-images than would be the case if they were aware of their limited abilities. Bandura (1981, 1989a, 1989b) has noted that self-efficacy evaluations play an important role in self-concept, and exposure to consistent failures at an early age when these failures are due not to lack of effort but to lack of ability may encourage the development of a poor self-image. He has noted that it is *perceived* self-efficacy, rather than true self-efficacy, that determines the amount of time and effort one will expend on a given task. Likewise, perceived self-efficacy influences the situations and experiences that one will attempt; whether or not one actually has the ability to perform these functions is not as critical a factor.

Following our belief that there are benefits for children in overestimating their physical and cognitive abilities, we think that such overestimation would be particularly apparent in preschool children's imitation. Adults, with their enhanced knowledge base and greater abilities to profit from what they hear or read, infrequently imitate models overtly. In contrast, imitation of models, both live and televised, seems to be a common practice among preschoolers, who acquire much of what they know through watching and imitating.

Below we present three studies of children's evaluations of their imitative abilities. The first two studies document preschool children's overestimation of their imitative abilities in naturalistic settings. In the final study, we investigate age changes in meta-imitation and relate the accuracy of children's predictions and postdictions to a measure of verbal intelligence. This is a first attempt to demonstrate the potentially adaptive nature of young children's limited meta-imitation skills.

Study 1: A Diary Study of Preschool Children's Meta-Imitation

One source of information about children's knowledge of their imitative skills is their parents. When we first became interested in the development of meta-imitation and discussed it with friends, colleagues, and students, we were repeatedly told stories by parents of young children grossly (and humorously) overestimating their imitative abilities. We decided to take advantage of the expertise of parents and designed a diary study in which parents observed their preschool children's imitative attempts.

Twenty-one parents (19 mothers, 2 fathers) of preschoolers watched their children over a 2-week period and made evaluations of their children's attempts at imitating models. The socioeconomic background of the parents ranged from lower-middle to upper-middle class; the majority were upper-middle class families. To make developmental comparisons, we divided the children into younger and older groups. There were four girls and seven boys in the younger group (mean age = 3 years, 7 months) and six girls and four boys in the older group (mean age = 5 years, 2 months).

Parents were asked to record children's estimates of how well they thought they would be able to imitate the behavior in question (prediction), to describe children's imitative attempts, and to ask children how well they thought they had done (postdiction). The model was frequently a parent or an older sibling, but was sometimes a character on television. Children's pre- and postdictions were compared to parents' evaluations of how successful children had been, with each behavior (both prediction and postdiction) being classified (by the authors) as either *accurate*, an *overestimation*, or an *underestimation*. One hundred thirteen observations for predictions and 126 for postdictions were scored. Table 4.1 provides several sample observations taken from parents' diary sheets and examples of how they were scored.

The percentage of imitative attempts for each classification is presented in Table 4.2 by age (young vs. old) and task (prediction vs. postdiction). As can be seen, children rarely underestimated their imitative abilities, with only 5.1% of their predictions and 2.5% of their postdictions being underestimations. For predictions, both the older and younger children tended to overestimate their abilities, with overestimations accounting for 56.9% of all of their imitative attempts, whereas their attempts were described as accurate on only 37.8% of the time. Children were more accurate in their postdictions, with 57.9% of their evaluations being accurate, and only 39.6% being overestimations. These patterns were confirmed in a 2 (age: young vs. old) × 2 (sex) × 2 (task: prediction vs. postdiction) × 3 (classification: overestimation vs. accurate vs. underestimation) analysis of variance with repeated measures on the task and

TABLE 4.1 Some examples of parents' observations and how they were scored—Study 1.

Sample journal entry #1
1. *Date and time*: 3-2-89, 4 PM
2. *Task and model imitated*: Diving in pool; woman in early 20s, on a TV commercial for gum. Patrick said that he could dive into the pool as well as the girl on television "real easy." He took a few running steps and jumped head first in the pool, landing more on his stomach than anything else.
3. *Child's prediction*: He said he'd be able to do it "real easy".
4. *Child's evaluation*: I asked him how he thought he did and he said that he did a great job.
5. *Parent's review*: My impression was that Patrick did a perfect belly flop, but I'd give him an "A" for effort.

Score: Prediction: overestimation; Postdiction: overestimation

Sample journal entry # 2
1. *Date and time*: 3-4-89, 3:30 PM
2. *Task and model imitated*: We were at the zoo watching the chimpanzees swing from the trees. Michael was very impressed by the way the chimps could swing from one branch to another. The next day at home, Michael was on his gym set outdoors, and I asked him if he thought he could swing from bar to bar, like the chimps had done. He said that he couldn't, but I told him to try anyway, with me standing underneath him. He got the hang of it right away, and swung from one bar to another and then to a third, using just about the same movements that the chimps had.
3. *Child prediction*: Michael didn't think he could do it.
4. *Child evaluation*: Michael still thought he hadn't done it very well.
5. *Parent's review*: Although he wasn't in the trees, he actually did a very good job imitating the chimps' swings, even if he didn't think he did.

Score: Prediction: underestimation; Postdiction: underestimation

Sample journal entry # 3
1. *Date and time*: 3-5-89, 10 AM
2. *Task and model imitated*: Ryan imitated me diapering a baby. I was watching Ryan play with her dolls. I asked her if she could diaper her doll like she had seen me do with her baby brother. She answered, "Of course." She had many of the right moves, and did get the diaper on her doll so that it stayed, but that's about it. Ryan showed me her doll and I asked her how she thought she did. She said, 'It's not as good as yours, mommy. I can do better next time."
3. *Child's prediction*: Ryan thought that she could do it.
4. *Child's evaluation*: Ryan correctly observed that she hadn't done as good a job as I had done.
5. *Parent's review*: Ryan was right. She had actually done a pretty poor job, but her enthusiasm was wonderful.

Score: Prediction: overestimation; Postdiction: accurate

classification factors. The analysis yielded no significant effects of age or sex, but did produce significant effects of classification (accurate = overestimations > underestimations) and a task × classification interaction, $F(2, 26) = 9.05$, $p < 0.001$. Subsequent analysis (Newman-Keuls, $p < 0.01$) of the significant interaction revealed that, in predicting how successful children would be in imitating a model, they were significantly more likely to overestimate than to be accurate, and significantly more likely to be accurate than to underestimate. The pattern for postdic-

TABLE 4.2 Percentage of behaviors rated as overestimation, accurate, and underestimation by age (young vs. old) and task (prediction vs. postdiction)—Study 1.

	Prediction (%)			Postdiction (%)		
	Over-estimation	Accurate	Under-estimation	Over-estimation	Accurate	Under-estimation
Young (n = 11)	58.9	35.2	5.9	41.9	54.9	3.3
Old (n = 10)	54.8	40.9	4.2	37.1	61.3	1.6
Mean	56.9%	37.8%	5.1%	39.6%	57.9%	2.5%

tion was different, with children being most likely to be classified as accurate in their evaluations of how well they had done, followed by overestimations, with underestimations being infrequent.

Some examples of parents' reports of their children's behavior may be illustrative.

Parents reported that children tried to imitate adult tasks, such as washing dishes or putting on make-up. For instance, one mother wrote that she was awakened one morning by a crash from the bathroom, where she found her 5-year-old son standing over the broken pieces of his cereal bowl. He explained that he was washing his bowl, just like his mother usually did, but it was slippery and fell out of his hands. He insisted that he was quite capable of washing his own bowl, and that the slip that morning was just an accident. His mother was understanding, but asked him not to wash dishes by himself. The child not only did not understand about wet dishes being slippery, but he couldn't even reach the faucets!

Parents also reported to us that occasionally their children tried to imitate TV characters dancing or performing other physical feats, such as karate. Almost unanimously, the parents said that their children's attempts were little more than jumping up and down or relatively uncoordinated kicking. Yet that was not the way the children saw things, often professing pride in how well they mimicked the actions.

Below are some other typical examples of children's imitative attempts (from parents' diaries), their evaluations of their abilities, and their parents' comments.

I was putting on make-up and Tricia [age: 3 years, 3 months] said she wanted to put on "lickstick" too. I asked how well she thought she would do it and she answered, "pretty good."

She did get some on her lips, but also on her face and her hands.

I asked her to look in the mirror and tell me how well she did. She was very pleased. "Just like you, mommy!"

Cynda [age: 3 years, 7 months] had watched her father play basketball a lot and she wanted to play too. I asked her how well she thought she could do and she said she could make a basket. (The hoop was regulation height—10 feet high.)

She tried to make a basket, but she actually just threw the ball up in the air. When she saw how far she had missed, she told me that the ball was too heavy for her.

Cara [age: 3 years, 8 months] was watching her sister Megan (8 years) jump rope. I asked her if she could jump just like Megan. She replied that she could.

Cara did not actually jump the rope. She hopped up and down a few times while she shook the rope.

Afterward, she seemed very proud of her accomplishment.

In general, children tended to overestimate their imitative abilities but were more accurate in evaluating how well they had imitated the modeled behavior, although more than one third of the children continued to overestimate their actual performance. Underestimation was rare.

Study 2: Meta-Imitation in a Preschool Environment

In a second naturalistic study, we observed and interviewed 3-, 4-, and 5-year-old children in their preschool classrooms about their imitative abilities. Twelve 3-year-olds (5 girls, 7 boys), 23 4-year-olds (11 girls, 12 boys), and 17 5-year-olds (12 girls, 5 boys) served as subjects. Episodes of imitation, both immediate and delayed (i.e., of some behavior observed hours or days earlier) were identified by a teacher in the classroom who had been trained in naturalistic observation procedures. To make accurate evaluations of the imitative behaviors, only highly structured tasks with easily identifiable behaviors, demonstrated by teachers during school, were selected. For example, in the color mixing task, drops of colored water were mixed in small glass jars (from left to right), and then each color was soaked up with a paper towel. In the mirror polishing task, a cotton swab was dipped one time in polish and applied to a mirror by making small circles. Then the swab was thrown away, and the polish wiped off the mirror with a cotton ball.

Children were selected from separate classrooms of 3-, 4-, and 5-year-olds from a Montessori school. Most children were from upper-middle-class families. The observer watched a group of six to eight children for 30-min blocks in each classroom, looking for situations in which a child was imitating a behavior he or she had seen displayed in the classroom recently (e.g., paint mixing, mirror polishing). The information collected consisted of the time of the event, the model, the task imitated, and the child's performance. The performance was recorded in as much detail as possible, exactly as it occurred, and no judgments were made at this time. After children completed the task, the observer approached them and asked who had taught them the task, and if they thought they had performed it as well as the model. Children were not disturbed by the observer while performing the task and every effort was made to minimize the effects of the observer's presence on the children's behavior.

The observer and a second person later evaluated children's imitative attempts based on the written record. Children's evaluations of their imitative attempts were scored as either overestimations, accurate, or underestimations. Interrater agreement of children's imitative accuracy was 95%. For most children (8 3-year-olds, 14 4-year-olds, and 11 5-year-olds), a single imitative attempt was observed. For the remaining children, up to four imitative attempts were observed and evaluated. Eighty-seven imitative attempts were observed in all.

The percentage of observations that were classified as overestimations, accurate, and underestimations are shown in Tables 4.3A and 4.3B. The percentages reported in Table 4.3A reflect only the first observation per child. The percentages in Table 4.3B include all of the observations (i.e., the second through fourth datum points for those children observed more than once). As can be seen, the results are similar regardless of whether all the data or only one observation per child is considered. An inspection of the tables reveals that overestimation was high for the 3- and 4-year-olds, but declined sharply for the 5-year-olds, who evaluated their imitative attempts correctly more than three quarters of the time. As in the diary study, underestimation was extremely rare, with only one incidence being observed. Age differences in the distribution of first observations that were classified as accurate versus overestimations (from Table 4.3A) were confirmed by a significant chi-square test, $\chi^2(2) = 6.71, p < 0.05$.

In this study, only children's postdictions were obtained (i.e., how well they thought they had done), and the results are similar to those reported by parents in the diary study. Underestimation was nearly nonexistent,

TABLE 4.3 Percentage of observations rated as overestimation, accurate, and underestimation for each subject's first observation (3A) and for all the observations (3B)—Study 2.

3A (first observation per subject only)	Overestimation (%)	Accurate (%)	Underestimation (%)
3-year-olds	42	58	0
4-year-olds	61	35	4
5-year-olds	24	76	0
Mean	42	56	1

3B (all observations)	Overestimation (%)	Accurate (%)	Underestimation (%)
3-year-olds	55	45	0
4-year-olds	62	36	3
5-year-olds	21	79	0
Mean	46	53	1

with children tending to overestimate how well they had performed on slightly less than half of the observations. Unlike the diary study, older children (5-year-olds) were more likely to be accurate in their assessments of their imitative attempts than younger children. The failure to find an age difference in the diary study was likely related to the type of tasks parents observed their children doing or asked their children to perform. Parents generally reported more complex tasks for older children than for younger children in that study. The current study was more naturalistic, in that children were observed spontaneously imitating tasks they had witnessed earlier. Under these conditons, older children were better able to assess accurately how successful they had been relative to younger children. The greater accuracy of the older children may reflect improved monitoring abilities or perhaps the fact that they are better able to judge their performance in relation to an objective (i.e., adult-like) standard.

Study 3: An Experimental Assessment of the Development of Meta-Imitation

Our two naturalistic studies illustrate that preschool children generally overestimate their imitative abilities and are more accurate in assessing how well they have done (postdiction) than how well they will do (prediction). Their accuracy (at least postdiction) improves with age. Although naturalistic studies such as these are important, these questions can also be usefully addressed in controlled experiments. In this study, we showed 3-, 4-, and 5-year-old children videos of adults performing simple tasks (juggling and tossing a ball into a large, plastic trash can) at three different difficulty levels. After watching each episode, we asked children how well they thought they could imitate the model they had just seen and later gave them the opportunity to try the task themselves. We then asked them how well they thought they had done performing the task. We later compared children's estimates of their abilities to that of the experimenter, who rated the child's imitative attempts on a three-point scale. Children in this study were also administered the verbal subtest of the Wechsler Preschool and Primary Scale of Intelligence (WPPSI) as an indication of verbal intelligence. Metacognitive skills have been found to be related to intelligence in older children (Borkowski & Peck, 1986; Borkowski, Reid, & Kurtz, 1984; Schneider, Körkel, & Weinert, 1987), and we wished to investigate the relationship between preschool children's predictions and postdictions of their imitative abilities and intelligence here. However, we did not predict that WPPSI scores would correlate significantly with children's imitative accuracy, at least not for the youngest children. Previous research has found little relationship between intelligence or academic achievement and young children's perceived competency (see Stipek & Mac Iver, 1989), and we similarly predicted low correlations here, at least for the 3- and 4-year-olds.

Subjects in this study were 30 3-year-olds (11 girls and 19 boys), 35 4-year-olds (20 girls and 15 boys), and 33 5-year-olds (13 girls and 20 boys). Most of the children were white and from middle-income and upper-middle-income families and attended a private preschool in South Florida.

Each child was seen individually by a female experimenter in a single 15- to 20-min session. Children were told that they would be shown videos of people doing different things and would be asked if they thought they could "copy" the model. After a brief practice video in which children were introduced to the procedure, the actual testing began. Children were instructed to answer the questions in the form of (a) "Yes, I can do it just like the person on TV", (b) "I'm not sure if I can do it like the person on TV", or (c) "No, I couldn't do it like the person on TV." Children were shown two models (one male, one female) performing two different tasks (juggling tennis balls and tossing tennis balls into a large trash can) at three different levels of difficulty (simple, intermediate, and difficult). This resulted in children observing six different episodes. The first task consisted of juggling one, two, or three tennis balls; the second consisted of tossing a tennis ball into a large plastic trash can from a distance of $1\frac{1}{2}$, 3, or 7 feet. The order in which the two tasks and the three difficulty levels within each task were presented was conterbalanced across subjects.

The tasks used in this experiment were selected so that children would have some familiarity with the behaviors involved but would likely not have experienced the specific tasks in question. To increase the likelihood that children were not basing their performance expectations on previous experience, the experimenter specifically asked children, "Do you think you can toss (or juggle) the ball(s) *exactly like the person on TV?*," rather than simply asking them if they can perform the behavior. The emphasis was on copying the model exactly and not just their skill at performing a particular task.

After children had seen all the difficulty levels in the first task, they were provided with tennis balls (in the case of the juggling task) or tennis balls and a plastic trash can (in the case of the tossing task). The experimenter asked "Would you like to try to do this just like the person on TV?". The children then performed the task at each difficulty level, beginning wtih the simplest. After each attempt, they were asked "Do you think you did that just like the person on TV?" A three-point scale was used for making all evaluations. A score of 1 was assigned to positive answers (e.g., "Yes, I did it just like the person on TV . . ."), a score of 2 to the neutral answers (e.g., "I'm not sure . . ."), and a score of 3 to the negative answers (e.g., "No, I didn't do it like the person on TV . . ."). Children's answers were recorded, and the experimenter took care not to comment on the child's performance until after the completion of the entire experiment (at which time all children were told that they had done a very good job and performed as well as their peers). After completion of the first task, children were administered the vocabulary subtest of the WPPSI and then told they would view another person doing things on TV. The procedure was then repeated for the second task.

Mean prediction and postdiction accuracy scores were computed for each subject for each task (tossing, juggling) × difficulty level (simple, intermediate, difficult) by subtracting a child's estimate of his or her performance (range 1 to 3) from the corresponding evaluation of the

TABLE 4.4 Mean prediction and postdiction accuracy scores by age (3-, 4-, and 5-years), task (tossing and juggling), and difficulty level (simple, intermediate, and difficult)—Study 3.[a]

	Prediction			
	Simple	Intermediate	Difficult	Mean
3-year-olds				
Tossing	0.07	0.73	1.10	0.63
Juggling	0.73	1.03	0.97	0.91
	0.40	0.88	1.04	0.77
4-year-olds				
Tossing	0.03	0.43	0.63	0.36
Juggling	0.09	0.57	0.43	0.36
	0.06	0.50	0.53	0.36
5-year-olds				
Tossing	0.03	0.06	0.48	0.19
Juggling	0.15	0.42	0.36	0.31
	0.09	0.24	0.42	0.25

	Postdiction			
	Simple	Intermediate	Difficult	Mean
3-year-olds				
Tossing	0.27	0.90	0.47	0.55
Juggling	0.80	1.17	0.50	0.82
	0.54	1.04	0.49	0.69
4-year-olds				
Tossing	0.31	0.34	0.49	0.38
Juggling	0.43	0.63	0.31	0.46
	0.31	0.49	0.40	0.42
5-year-olds				
Tossing	−0.03	0.30	0.39	0.22
Juggling	0.21	0.55	0.21	0.32
	0.09	0.43	0.30	0.27

[a] Perfect accuracy = 0; positive scores reflect overestimation; negative scores reflect underestimation.

experimenter. Mean accuracy scores are presented in Table 4.4, separately for prediction and postdiction, by age, task, and difficulty level (perfect accuracy = 0; positive scores reflect overestimation; negative scores reflect underestimation).

An analysis of variance performed on these data produced a significant main effect of age, $F(2, 155) = 6.82$, $p < 0.01$, with the 3-year-olds overestimating significantly more ($M = 0.72$) than the 4-year-olds ($M = 0.39$) and 5-year-olds ($M = 0.26$), who did not differ from one another.[1] As can be seen from the table, this pattern was the same for both the prediction and postdiction scores. Also significant were the main effect of difficulty level and several interactions. Inspection of the significant task × difficulty level interaction, $F(2, 184) = 10.21$, $p < 0.001$, indicated that, for the tossing task, children were least accurate for the difficult level (0.59), followed by the intermediate level (0.45) and the simple level (0.11) (all differences significant, Newman-Keuls, $p < 0.05$). For the juggling task, children were least accurate at the intermediate level (0.71), where their accuracy scores were significantly different from those at the simple (0.39) and difficult (0.45) levels. Accuracy at the simple and difficult levels did not differ. Also significant was the difficulty level × prediction/postdiction interaction, $F(2, 184) = 18.7$, $p < 0.001$. Subsequent inspection of this effect indicated that prediction (0.17) was more accurate than postdiction (0.33) for the simple tasks, but that postdiction (0.39) was more accurate than prediction (0.65) for the difficult tasks. There was no difference between pre- and postdiction scores for the intermediate tasks (0.53 and 0.63, respectively).

Inspection of the significant age × difficulty level × prediction/postdiction interaction, $F(4, 184) = 3.95$, $p < 0.01$, showed that 4- and 5-year-old children were more accurate than 3-year-olds in all relevant contrasts except for the difficult level of postdiction, where performance was relatively good and undifferentiated among the age groups (mean accuracy scores = 0.48, 0.40, and 0.30 for 3-, 4-, and 5-year-olds, respectively). The 3- and 4-year-olds were also equal for the simple level, postdiction condition. Also, the difference between the 4- and 5-year-olds was nonsignificant in all but two comparisons: intermediate level prediction (means = 0.5 and 0.24 for 4- and 5-year-olds, respectively) and simple level postdictions (means = 0.37 and 0.09).

In general, regular age differences in children's abilities to evaluate their imitative abilities were observed in both prediction and postdiction. On average, children of all ages overestimated their imitative abilities, with overestimation being the greatest for the difficult tossing task and

---

[1] Two significant sex effects were found in the analysis. Boys overestimated the juggling task more so than girls and were also more inaccurate on the tasks of intermediate difficulty than girls.

TABLE 4.5 Correlations between scores on the vocabulary subtest of the WPPSI and prediction and postdiction accuracy scores at each age level—Study 3.

		Predictions	Postdictions
3-year-olds	(n = 30)	0.19	0.15
4-year-olds	(n = 35)	0.20	0.46[b]
5-year-olds	(n = 33)	−0.21	−0.39[a]

[a] $p < 0.05$.
[b] $p < 0.01$.

the intermediate juggling task. Children were equally likely to overestimate their performance on the prediction and postdiction tasks, with prediction being more accurate for the simple tasks and postdiction being more accurate for the difficult tasks.

As we mentioned earlier, each child was administered the vocabulary subtest of the WPPSI as an indication of verbal intelligence. Children's accuracy scores were summed across all conditions and correlated with the WPPSI scores to assess the relationship between intelligence and young children's meta-imitation. Because few children underestimated their performance, correlations between accuracy and WPPSI scores are a reflection of the relationship between children's overestimation of their imitative skills and verbal intelligence. Although for older children good (accurate) metacognition is associated with higher levels of intelligence, we hypothesized no such relationship for the youngest children in this study. Such a pattern would reflect the fact that consistently overestimating one's imitative abilities is not a sign of poor cognition per se for preschoolers, but rather reflects the adaptive value for young children of being out of touch with their limited imitative abilities. We also recognize the limits of the WPPSI as a measure of intelligence and introduce these data only as preliminary and suggestive findings.

The WPPSI scores were correlated separately with children's prediction and postdiction accuracy scores and are presented in Table 4.5.[2] As can be seen, for the prediction scores the correlations were not significant at any age level. The pattern, however, was in the predicted direction, with the correlations for the 3- and 4-year-olds being positive (i.e., high overestimation associated with high WPPSI scores), whereas the correlation was negative for the 5-year-olds (i.e., low overestimation associated

[2] A subset of children were also administered the Information subtest of the WPPSI. Patterns of correlations were similar whether accuracy scores were computed with the (a) information and (b) information plus vocabulary WPPSI scores, or (c) WPPSI vocabulary scores alone.

with high WPPSI scores). The magnitude of the differences between the correlations of the 5-year-olds and the younger children were significant or approached significance (one-tailed test) (5- vs. 4-year-olds, $z = 1.64$, $p = 0.05$; 5- vs. 3-year-olds, $z = 1.51$, $p = 0.07$).

The pattern of the postdiction scores was similar to that of prediction, except that the magnitude of the correlations was greater (and significant) for the 4- and 5-year-olds. Four-year-olds with higher WPPSI scores overestimated more than 4-year-olds with lower WPPSI scores. This relationship was reversed for the 5-year-olds, with children with higher WPPSI scores being more accurate in their estimates of their imitative performance than children with lower scores. The differences in the magnitude of the correlations between the 5-year-olds and the two groups of younger children were significant (one-tailed test) (5- vs. 4-year-olds, $z = 3.58$, $p < 0.001$; 5- vs. 3-year-olds, $z = 1.69$, $p = 0.05$).

The results of the correlational analysis are consistent with our hypothesis that, for young children, being out of touch with their limited imitative abilities is not a sign of poor cognition. For 5-year-olds, children who were more accurate in their estimations of their imitative abilities (particularly postdiction) had higher WPPSI scores, reflecting the not too startling fact that brighter children have better metacognitive awareness than less bright children (cf. Schneider et al., 1987). This was not the case for 3- and 4-year-olds, however, with the relationship between overestimation and WPPSI scores being positive, significantly so for the 4-year-olds' postdiction scores. Although the WPPSI vocabulary subtest is a highly limited indication of intelligence, the absence of a negative correlation between it and the 3- and 4-year-old children's overestimation of their imitative abilities suggests, at the least, that poor meta-imitative skills are not a sign of low intelligence in young children. Rather, we argue that young children's tendency to overestimate their imitative abilities serves an adaptive function by encouraging them to practice and attempt behaviors that they would not attempt if they were aware of their actual imitative limitations.

The Development of Meta-Imitation and the Adaptive Nature of Cognitive Immaturity

In this series of studies we have demonstrated something that is likely not too surprising to most readers. Preschool children consistently overestimate their imitative abilities, becoming more accurate between the ages of 3 and 5 years. The diary study indicated that children of all ages are better able to evaluate their performance than to predict it. Although we found no main effect of prediction versus postdiction in the third study, children's estimations for the difficult tasks (tossing a ball into a trash can from 7 feet and juggling three balls) were more accurate than their predictions, suggesting that children are better able to evaluate their imitative attempts than to predict them for tasks that are currently beyond their competencies (unlike the simple tasks). A final finding of the third study was the developmental relationship between extent of overestimation and a measure of verbal intelligence. As might be expected, good meta-imitation (i.e., accurate estimations) was associated with higher intelligence scores for the oldest children tested. The reverse was true for the 3- and 4-year-olds, however. Although only two of six correlations were significant, the magnitude of the difference between the correlations of the 5-year-olds and the young children reached or approached significance for both the prediction and postdiction scores. This reflects, we believe, the fact that overestimation of one's imitative skills is adaptive for young children. As children's imitative abilities improve over the preschool years, the expected negative relationship between overestimation and intelligence is found, consistent with research investigating other aspects of metacognition (e.g., Schneider et al., 1987). We will discuss briefly below some possible reasons for children's consistent overestimation of their imitative skills and the possibility that such overestimation has cognitive advantages (see also Bjorklund & Green, 1992).

Why Do Children Overestimate Their Imitative Abilities?

In the beginning of this chapter, we discussed metacognitive and achievement motivation research documenting young children's tendencies to overestimate their abilities. Age differences in children's general cognitive abilities, how they define success and failure, and wishful thinking have all been hypothesized to contribute to young children's overly optimistic opinions of their own skills. Our data do not permit us to differentiate among these alternatives and, moreover, we doubt whether any one explanation can account for children's consistent overestimations. We would, however, like to elaborate on the possibility that children have different definitions of success. More specifically, we propose that young children may be very lenient in evaluating how their performance compares with their internal standard.

Bandura (1981, 1986, 1989a) theorized that motivation based on aspirational standards is a cognitive process in which internal standards are compared to actual attainment. The resulting motivational effects in children include self-evaluation of their own attainment, how well they think they are able to meet their own standards (perceived self-efficacy), and adjustment of standards to keep them attainable. Our results are in keeping with the possibility that young children are quite lenient with themselves in terms of comparing their performance with internal standards, in that any approximation may be "close enough." Sometimes, it may be that they unconsciously set lower standards for themselves so that any effort will result in surpassing the standard.

This possibility is consistent with the theorizing of Siegler (1988, 1990; Siegler & Jenkins, 1989), who has developed a model that accounts for children's responses in identifying words and solving simple arithmetic problems. According to Siegler, in identifying words or retrieving an answer to an arithmetic problem, there is a criterion of activation level that must be reached before a child directly retrieves a response to a question. For example, if the activation criterion for the questions $3 + 5 = ?$ is 0.40, only those potential responses that are activated to that level or greater will be retrieved. If the associative strength between the problem and the answer meets or exceeds the criterion, that answer is immediately retrieved (fact retrieval). If, however, the associative strength falls short of the criterion, another, more laborious but accurate strategy is chosen. In arithmetic, that strategy may involve counting (e.g., "1, 2, 3 . . . 4, 5, 6, 7, 8") and in word identification the strategy may involving "sounding out" the word. Siegler found that some children set a very high criterion, decreasing the possibility that any single answer will be sufficiently strong to reach the criterion threshold; other children set a lower criterion threshold, increasing the possibility that an answer will be quickly retrieved. This model can be applied to children's evaluations of their imitative competencies. Young children may set a lower criterion for their imitative abilities, so that most attempts on their part surpass the criterion and are considered to be a success. Presumably, with age and experience the criterion is raised, becoming more adult-like. It is likely that children's criteria are domain-specific and are raised at differing rates depending on the task. Because children have more experience evaluating their actual performance than predicting their imitative abilities, they should have a more conservative criterion for postdiction than prediction tasks, a result that was found in Study 1.

The Advantages of Not Knowing How Poorly One Can Imitate

In the beginning of this chapter, we suggested that poor metacognitive abilities may be an advantage rather than a disadvantage to young children. Let us reiterate our views, specifically with respect to meta-imitation here.

An unrealistic optimism about their own abilities gives young children the opportunity to practice skills in situations where accurate metacognition might discourage them from doing so. As pointed out by Stipek (1984), learned helplessness, the belief that an individual has no control over a situation, is relatively rare among young children, who generally expect success in achievement situations and evaluate their competencies favorably. This optimistic attitude may encourage children to attempt behaviors they would not otherwise try if they had more realistic conceptions of their abilities. Ignorance of their limitations allows children to try more diverse and complex behaviors that may be currently beyond their abilities. This allows them to practice skills to a greater degree and may indeed foster long-term cognitive benefits. This seems especially true for imitation, which constitutes a substantial amount of preschool children's activities (e.g., Abramovitch & Grusec, 1978).

Another important aspect of young children's overly optimistic views of their own abilities is the confidence it gives them. Children who believe they are competent (even if they are not) develop feelings of positive self-efficacy. According to social cognitive theory (Bandura, 1986, 1989a, 1989b), self-percepts of efficacy, whether accurate or faulty, operate as cognitive mediators of action, and therefore exert their influence in a wide domain of behaviors. Some of the things influenced by a child's perceived self-efficacy are choice of environments, activities, duration, and amount of energy expended. Bandura has noted that when self-efficacy is poor, people tend to behave ineffectually regardless of their actual abilities, and that high self-efficacy facilitates development: "The stronger the belief [of individuals] in their capabilities, the greater and more persistent are their efforts. When they achieve substandard performances, people who have self-doubts about their cognitive capabilities slacken their efforts or abort their attempts prematurely, whereas those who have a strong belief in their capabilities exert greater effort to master the challenge" (Bandura, 1989b, p. 730).

It is perhaps young children's lack of self-doubt that produces the persistency needed if tasks are to be mastered and knowledge increased. In this sense, cognitive immaturity is an asset rather than a liability.

Conclusions

In this chapter, we have presented evidence that young children have overly optimistic opinions of their imitative abilities, with this optimism declining over the preschool years. More important than the demonstration of another cognitive "meta," however, is the counterintuitive demonstration that good meta-imitation is not associated with high levels of intelligence until the age of 5 years. For 3- and 4-year-old children, overestimation is actually positively related to intelligence (albeit to a moderate and usually nonsignificant degree). These results argue that young children's overly positive beliefs in their imitative abilities are actually adaptive. Such unrealistic optimism, of course, is not always a blessing, with young children requiring watchful adults to guide their endeavors and steer them away from dangerous situations (Bandura, 1989a). But there is a plus side to believing that one is more competent that one actually is. Young children's beliefs that they know more than they actually do and can do more than they actually can, provide them with positive perceptions of their own skills. This positive sense of self-efficacy encourages them to attempt things that they would not otherwise try if they had a more realistic idea of their abilities (see Bjorklund & Green, 1992).

Young children expect success, and, as far as they are concerned, they usually achieve it. Such unrealistic opinions of their own abilities are easily seen as examples of poor cognition, something children will outgrow. But their unrealistic optimism actually may be something to be cultivated. For example, Stipek (1984), discussing young children's over-estimations of their academic ability, argued that rather than trying to make young children's judgments of their abilities more accurate, we should "try harder to design educational environments which maintain their optimism and eagerness" (p. 53). Children who believe they are skillful and in control (even when they are not) are more apt to act that way. Rather than burdening them with too much reality, parents and teachers can take advantage of young children's poor metacognitive skills in general and their poor meta-imitation skills specifically, encouraging them to practice new skills and praising them for their "successes." And they are likely to feel successful, even though it may not look that way to an adult observer.

Acknowledgments. We would like to thank the staff and children of Addison Mizner Montessori School, Henderson University School, and Florence Fuller Day Care Center for their assistance in conducting this study. We thank Coleen Quinn, Janice Giangrande, and Kimberly Borden for help in collecting and scoring data, and Barbara Bjorklund for her many comments and suggestions in all parts of this research.

References

Abramovitch, R., & Grusec, J. (1978). Peer imitation in a natural setting. *Child Development*, *49*, 60–65.

Bandura, A. (1981). Self-referent thought: A developmental analysis of self-efficacy. In J.H. Flavell & L. Ross (Eds.), *Social cognitive development: Frontiers and possible futures*. Cambridge, England: Cambridge University Press.

Bandura, A. (1986). *Social foundations of thought and action*. Englewood Cliffs, NJ: Prentice-Hall.

Bandura, A. (1989a). Social cognitive theory. In R. Vasta (Ed.), *Annals of child development* (Vol. 6). Greenwich, CT: JAI Press.

Bandura, A. (1989b). Regulation of cognitive processes through perceived self-efficacy. *Developmental Psychology*, *25*, 729–735.

Bandura, A., & Walters, R.H. (1963). *Social learning and personality development*. New York: Holt, Rinehart, & Winston.

Bjorklund, D.F. (1989). *Children's thinking: Developmental function and individual differences*. Pacific Grove, CA: Brooks/Cole.

Bjorklund, D.F., & Green, B.L. (1992). The adaptive nature of cognitive immaturity. *American Psychologist, 47*, 46–54.

Borkowski, J.G., & Peck, V.A. (1986). Causes and consequences of metamemory in gifted children. In R.J. Sternberg & J.C. Davidson (Eds.), *Conceptions of giftedness*. Cambridge, England: Cambridge University Press.

Borkowski, J.G., Reid, M.K., & Kurtz, B.E. (1984). Metacognition and retardation: Pragmatic, theoretical, and applied perspectives. In P.H. Brooks, R. Sperber, & C. McCauley (Eds.), *Learning and cognition in the mentally retarded*. Hillsdale, NJ: Erlbaum.

Cavanaugh, J.C., & Perlmutter, M. (1982). Metamemory: A critical examination. *Child Development, 53*, 11–28.

Clifford, M.M. (1978). The effects of quantitative feedback on children's expectations of success. *British Journal of Educational Psychology, 48*, 220–226.

Dweck, C.S., & Elliott, E.S. (1983). Achievement motivation. In P. Mussen & M. Hetherington (Eds.), *Handbook of child psychology: Vol. 4 Socialization, personality, and social development*. New York: John Wiley & Sons.

Flavell, J.H. (1987). Metacognitive development. In J.M. Scandura & C.J. Brainerd (Eds.), *Structural/process theories of complex human behavior*. Alphen a. d. Rijn, The Netherlands: Sijthoff & Noordhoff.

Flavell, J., Friedrichs, A., & Hoyt, J. (1970). Developmental changes in memorization processes. *Cognitive Psychology, 1*, 324–340.

Flavell, J., & Wellman, H. (1977). Metamemory. In R.V. Kail, Jr. & J.W. Hagen (Eds.), *Perspectives on the development of memory and cognition*. Hillsdale, NJ: Erlbaum.

Garner, R. (1990). Children's use of strategies in reading. In D.F. Bjorklund (Ed.), *Children's strategies: Contemporary views of cognitive development*. Hillsdale, NJ: Erlbaum.

Grusec, J.E., & Abramovitch, R. (1982). Imitation of peers and adults in a natural setting: A functional analysis. *Child Development, 53*, 233–240.

Harter, S., & Pike, R. (1984). The pictorial scale of perceived competence and social acceptance for young children. *Child Development, 55*, 1969–1982.

Heckhausen, H. (1984). Emergent achievement behavior: Some early developments. In J.G. Nicholls (Ed.), *The development of achievement motivation*. Greenwich, CT: JAI Press.

Kuczynski, L., Zahn-Waxler, C., & Radke-Yarrow, M. (1987). Development and content of imitation in the second and third years of life: A socialization perspective. *Developmental Psychology, 23*, 276–282.

Levin, J.R., Yussen, S.R., De Rose, T.M., & Pressley, M. (1977). Developmental changes in assessing recall and recognition memory capacity. *Developmental Psychology, 13*, 608–615.

Miller, P.H. (1985). Metacognition and attention. In D.L. Forrest-Pressley, G.E. MacKinnon, & T.G. Waller (Eds.), *Metacognition, cognition, and human performance* (Vol. 2). New York: Academic Press.

Miller, D.J., & Thelen, M.H. (1986). Imitation in a naturalistic setting as a function of response uncertainty. *The Journal of Genetic Psychology, 147*, 113–121.

Money, J. (1988). *Gay, straight, and in between: The sexology of erotic orientation*. New York: Oxford University Press.
Moynahan, E.D. (1976). The development of the ability to assess recall performance. *Journal of Experimental Child Psychology*, *21*, 94–97.
Nicholls, J. (1978). The development of the concepts of effort and ability, perceptions of academic attainment and the understanding that difficult tasks require more ability. *Child Development*, *49*, 800–814.
Parsons, J.E., & Ruble, D.N. (1977). The development of achievement-related expectancies. *Child Development*, *48*, 1075–1079.
Pawlby, S.J. (1977). Imitative interaction. In H.R. Schaffer (Ed.), *Studies in mother-infant interaction*. Glasgow, Scotland: University of Strathclyde Press.
Phillips, B.N. (1963). Age changes in accuracy of self-perceptions. *Child Development*, *34*, 1041–1046.
Piaget, J. (1930). *The child's conception of physical causality*. London: Routledge & Kegan Paul.
Piaget, J. (1962). *Play, dreams, and imitation in childhood*. New York: Norton.
Pressley, M., Levin, J.R., Ghatala, E.S., & Ahmad, M. (1987). Test monitoring in young grade school children. *Journal of Experimental Child Psychology*, *43*, 96–111.
Schneider, W. (1985). Developmental trends in the metamemory-memory behavior relationship: An integrative review. In D.L. Forrest-Pressley, G.E. MacKinnon, & T.G. Waller (Eds.), *Cognition, metacognition, and human performance* (Vol. 1). New York: Academic Press.
Schneider, W. (1988, March). *Conceptual and methodological problems in doing self-report research*. Paper presented at the annual meetings of the American Educational Research Association, New Orleans, LA.
Schneider, W., Körkel, J., & Weinert, F.E. (1987). The effects of intelligence, self-concept, and attributional style on metamemory and memory behaviour. *International Journal of Behavioral Development*, *10*, 281–299.
Schneider, W., & Pressley, M. (1989). *Memory development between 2 and 20*. New York: Springer-Verlag.
Siegler, R.S. (1988). Individual differences in strategy choices: Good students, not-so-good students, and perfectionists. *Child Development*, *59*, 833–851.
Siegler, R.S. (1990). How content knowledge, strategies, and individual differences interact to produce strategy choice. In W. Schneider & F.E. Weinert (Eds.), *Interactions among aptitudes, strategies, and knowledge in cognitive performance*. New York: Springer-Verlag.
Siegler, R.S., & Jenkins, E. (1989). *How children discover new strategies*. Hillsdale, NJ: Erlbaum.
Stipek, D. (1981). Children's perceptions of their own and their classmates' ability. *Journal of Experimental Child Psychology*, *73*, 404–410.
Stipek, D. (1984). Young children's performance expectations: Logical analysis or wishful thinking? In J.G. Nicholls (Ed.), *Advances in motivation and achievement: Vol 3. The development of achievement motivation*. Greenwich, CT: JAI Press.
Stipek, D., & Daniels, D. (1988). Declining perceptions of competence: A consequence of changes in the child or the educational environment? *Journal of Educational Psychology*, *80*, 352–356.

Stipek, D., & Hoffman, J. (1980). Development of children's performance-related judgments. *Child Development*, *51*, 912–914.

Stipek, D., & Mac Iver, D. (1989). Developmental change in children's assessment of intellectual competence. *Child Development*, *60*, 521–538.

Stipek, D., Roberts, T., & Sanborn, M. (1984). Preschool-age children's performance expectations for themselves and another child as a function of the incentive value of success and the salience of past performance. *Child Development*, *55*, 1983–1989.

Thelen, M.H., Dolinger, S.J., & Roberts, M.D. (1975). On being imitated: Its affects on attention and reciprocal imitation. *Journal of Personality and Social Psychology*, *31*, 467–472.

Weinert, F.E. (1986). Developmental variations of memory performance and memory related knowledge across the life span. In A. Sorensen, F.E. Weinert, & L.R. Sherrod (Eds.), *Human development: Multidisciplinary perspectives*. Hillsdale, NJ: Erlbaum.

Wellman, H.M. (1985). A child's theory of mind: The development of conceptions of cognition. In S.R. Yussen (Ed.), *The growth of reflection*. New York: Academic Press.

Whitehurst, G.J., & Sonnenschein, S. (1985). The development of communication: A functional analysis. In G.J. Whitehurst (Ed.), *Annals of Child Development* (Vol. 2). Greenwich, CT: JAI Press.

Yussen, S., & Levy, V. (1975). Developmental changes in predicting one's own span of short-term memory. *Journal of Experimental Child Psychology*, *19*, 502–508.

5 Parental Influences on Children's Cognition

KARL S. ROSENGREN, DOUGLAS A. BEHREND, AND
MARION PERLMUTTER

In recent years there has been an increasing focus on the social influences on cognitive development. The notion that social interaction is important for a child's cognitive growth is not new. Many cognitive development theorists, including both Piaget and Vygotsky, believed that social interaction plays a crucial role in various aspects of cognitive development. The goal of this chapter is to examine the manner in which parents promote their children's cognitive development through social interaction. We first provide a background of the theoretical context on this issue, focused mainly on the writings of Piaget and Vygotsky. Then we briefly review current work on the role of social interaction on cognitive development. Finally, we suggest a model of how parents influence their children's cognitive development and report some of our own research in this area.

We focus on parental influences because, for most children, parents serve as the primary source of social influence during the child's first years of life, and because we believe that aspects of the early parent–child relationships are important for later cognitive development. We also believe that social interaction in the context of close relationships provides significant benefits for cognitive development over interaction in other contexts. These ideas are developed more fully in the pages that follow. In addition, we discuss various factors that we believe should be included in a model of social influences on children's cognition. These factors include parental style, parental warmth and supportiveness, task difficulty, and the age of the child. We believe that the data presented later in this chapter support the inclusion of these variables in models of parental influences on cognitive development. Before turning to these ideas, we first review both Vygotsky's and Piaget's ideas on social interactional influences, since these two theoreticians have had the most dramatic impact on present thinking and research on social influences on cognitive development.

Theoretical Background

Vygotsky

Since the translation of some of Vygotsky's writings in the 1960s and 1970s, his views on social influences on cognition have been incorporated in many investigations of cognitive development in social contexts. One of Vygotsky's (1962, 1978) main assumptions was that cognition originates in social interaction. He proposed that a key aspect of development is the internalization of cultural knowledge in the form of various tools, goals, and activities considered to be acceptable by the society in which a child is developing. The acquisition of cultural knowledge, which occurs when a child interacts with other members of his or her society, enables the child to become a functional member of that society. This developmental process, in Vygotsky's view, is driven by a dialectical process that involves three factors: individual maturation, personal experience, and experience with various cultural tools and activities (Wertsch, Minick, & Arns, 1985). The dialectic between these three factors serves to provide motivation for individuals to adapt to the demands and expectations of the culture in which they live.

Vygotsky proposed that children acquire the necessary cognitive skills to fit into society through interaction with more accomplished members of society. Most often adults or more competent peers serve this role. During interactive problem-solving situations, these individuals structure the task in a manner that allows the child to play a significant role in the task's completion. An important aspect of this structuring is passing on the skills and knowledge that will eventually allow the child to solve the problem on his or her own. Thus, Vygotsky argued that, at first, more competent individuals serve to regulate a child's behavior, gradually transferring the necessary skills and information to the child, so that the child may later independently regulate his or her own behavior. One might view this shift from other-regulation to self-regulation as involving two interrelated processes. On the one hand, the more competent individual at first might be viewed as a coach, then a teammate, and finally as a cheerleader. On the other hand, the child might be viewed as first being a member of the crowd, then watching from the bench, participating in minor aspects of the game, and finally becoming a key player in the game.

Vygotsky believed that both the child's own language and the language of others play a key role in the internalization process. First, the verbalizations of parents or more competent peers were assumed to regulate children's behavior. Then, as children were acquiring a skill, they would begin to regulate their own behavior via their own speech (often referred to as private speech), and finally to internalize these private utterances so that regulation was completely internalized and became thought or "inner speech." Much of the recent research inspired by Vygotsky has focused on parents' language to children (e.g., Ninio, 1983), and the role of the child's own language while performing a task (e.g., Behrend, Rosengren, & Perlmutter, 1989; Frauenglass & Diaz, 1985).

Another important concept in Vygotsky's (1978) model of social interactional influences was the concept of the *zone of proximal development* (ZPD). The zone of proximal development was defined as the difference between the level of performance achieved by a child while working independently on a problem and the level of performance achieved by the same child with the help of a more competent peer or adult. Vygotsky proposed that it is only within this range of performance that instruction would be effective in promoting cognitive change. In recent years the concept of the zone of proximal development has been more broadly viewed by researchers as a range of tasks or skills that a child is able to perform effectively with the aid of a more competent individual (Brown & Ferrara, 1985; Rogoff & Wertsch, 1984). Within this broader view of the ZPD, one could easily include such concepts as *readiness* or *sensitive area*. Thus, instruction that pushes children slightly beyond what they are capable of accomplishing by themselves should be most effective in promoting cognitive development and the acquisition of new skills.

Piaget

Piaget's views on the role of social interaction in cognitive development differed in a number of ways from those of Vygotsky. First, although Piaget (1932) considered social interaction to be one of the major factors in cognitive development, social interaction played a smaller role in Piaget's theoretical views than it did in Vygotsky's. Second, rather than believing, as Vygotsky did, that cognition originates from interaction with others, Piaget believed that certain cognitive structures must be in place in order for a child to benefit from social interaction. That is, if the requisite cognitive structures were not already possessed by a young child, Piaget believed that the child would be unable to assimilate the information provided by interaction with others. Thus, where Vygotsky saw cognition and its development originating through interaction with others, Piaget saw social interaction as completing, or fine-tuning, cognitive structures, and not truly playing a causal role in their development (Perret-Clermont & Brossard, 1985). Indeed, Piaget (1932, 1968) argued that social interaction increased in importance for cognitive development as a child moved from preoperational to concrete operational thought. He argued that with the decline of egocentrism, children become able to recognize how their ideas conflict with those of others. It is at this point, when a child can collaborate with others and consider alternative viewpoints, that a child can use conflicting information to restructure thought and advance to higher stages of cognition. Thus, whereas Vygotsky viewed social interaction as important to cognitive development from birth, Piaget argued that social interaction would not promote cognitive growth until late in the preoperational stage.

Another way in which Piaget and Vygotsky differed was that only Piaget (1932, 1968) argued that interaction among peers would be more conducive to advancing cognitive processes than interactions between children and adults. Piaget believed that children would play a much more active role in interactive problem solving when working with a peer than when working with an adult. Because adult–child relations tend to be characterized by the adult regulating and controlling the child, Piaget viewed the child as playing a much more passive role in adult–child interactions than in child–child interactions. He therefore argued that interactions among peers, or symmetrical relationships, were more likely to allow both members of the interaction to participate in a problem-solving activity than (asymmetric) interactions between children of different ages, or between children and adults. Symmetrical interactions would thus be most beneficial to cognitive development, since the child would have an easier time understanding when his or her own views differed from those of peers and would be more likely to understand how to resolve this conflict.

Thus, for Piaget the importance of social interaction lies in the sociocognitive conflict that arises as part of the normal process of discourse between two individuals. Conflict between a child's and another's perspectives stimulate a state of disequilibrium, which drives the child to resolve the conflict on his own.

Relationships and Social Interaction

Social interaction occurs most often in the context of established relationships. Hartup (1989) has argued that relationships may be categorized as being either horizontal or vertical. Horizontal relationships are those in which each of the participants are at an equivalent level on some dimension, such as social power, knowledge, or authority. Vertical relationships are those in which the participants are at very different levels of power, authority, or knowledge. These types of relationships also have been labeled as symmetric and asymmetric, respectively.

In general, Piaget emphasized the contributions of symmetric relationships to cognitive development, whereas Vygotsky emphasized the importance of asymmetric relationships. Recently, Azmitia and Perlmutter (1989) have suggested that the salience of these relationships is affected by a child's level of development and movement through societal institutions (e.g., segregation of individuals by age in the schools emphasizes symmetrical relationships).

Parent–child relationships are only one type of close relationship. Recently, Azmitia and Perlmutter (1989) argued that the strongest social influences on cognitive development are most likely to occur in the context of established relationships. Relationships with parents, peers, siblings, and teachers all play important and somewhat different roles in promoting cognitive development. In the following section we discuss why social interaction in the context of established relationships may play a central role in promoting cognitive development. We then briefly explore some of the most common relationships in which children are involved, and then more extensively consider the parent–child relationship.

Azmitia and Perlmutter (1989), elaborating on the ideas of Hartup (1985), have proposed that social interaction serves a number of functions in promoting cognitive development. First, skills emerge in the contexts provided by social interactions and relationships. Second, both general knowledge and information about appropriate behaviors are provided through social interactions and relationships. More specifically, close relationships provide the emotional support that is necessary for the child to explore new tasks and new environments confidently. Finally, early close relationships also serve as models for later ones. Thus, skills and interactional abilities developed in the context of early social interaction benefit a child during later social interactions.

Social interaction in the context of close relationships should provide greater benefits to the members of an interactive pair than social interaction among individuals who do not have a close relationship. A number of reasons for this pattern have been outlined by Azmitia and Perlmutter (1989). First, individuals who know each other well are more likely to be aware of one another's strengths and weaknesses. This knowledge allows the members of a relationship to tailor guidance and instruction on a given task to the most appropriate level. Second, individuals may feel more comfortable asking questions and offering guidance when they are working on a problem with someone they know well. Third, since the individuals have a shared history in the relationship, little attention or energy needs to be devoted to establishing and maintaining the social interaction that occurs in a collaborative problem-solving setting. Thus, individuals who know each other well should be able to devote more time and energy to solving the problem than to working out aspects of the relationship.

Sibling Relationships

The view outlined above does not imply that all close relationships provide the same opportunities for beneficial social interaction. For example, although siblings, especially older ones, play an important role in the early cognitive development of children, what little is known about social interaction between siblings suggests a very different pattern than that obtained in parent–child interaction. The few studies that have been conducted on sibling relationships show that older siblings tend to dominate the interaction with a younger sibling, initiating both more agonistic and prosocial behavior (Abramovitch, Corter, & Lando, 1979). Older siblings more often assume the role of teacher or manager of the interaction than younger siblings (Brody, Stoneman, & MacKinnon, 1982). On the surface, this finding does not seem that different from the finding that parents largely control the interactions with their young children (Youniss, 1980). However, the older sibling is likely to receive a much greater cognitive benefit from the interaction than would a parent. Although no research has directly addressed the issue of whether either party actually benefits from sibling interactions, research has shown that tutoring of younger peers leads to benefits for the tutor in terms of academic achievement (Feldman, Devin-Sheehan, & Allen, 1976). One would expect these benefits to carry over to tutoring situations in sibling relationships. In addition, first-born children who have younger siblings have been found to perform better than only children on intelligence tests and academic achievement (Zajonc, Markus, & Markus, 1979). The implication of this finding is that opportunities to instruct and tutor a younger child, whether they be a peer or sibling, provide some cognitive benefits for the tutor as well as for the learner.

These patterns of findings contrast with those found in parent–child relationships, where the most benefits are gained by the younger member of the interactive pair. Furthermore, in families with many children, there appear to be some negative consequences (e.g., lower scores on various cognitive measures) associated with being later born (Zajonc & Markus, 1975). Thus, whereas sibling relationships may play an important role in social cognitive development, little is known about the precise nature of these relationships, and what is known suggests that they operate in a much different manner than parent–child relationships.

Peer Relationships

As noted above, Piaget viewed peers as playing a significant role in promoting cognitive change. Research examining the social cognitive influences of peers suggests that they play a significant role in aspects of development in later childhood and adolescence, but play a rather limited role in promoting cognitive development in the preschool and early childhood years. For example, a number of studies that have examined preschoolers' performance on various tasks have failed to show that collaborative problem solving has significant cognitive benefits over individual activity (e.g., Bearison, Magazamen, & Filardo, 1986; Perlmutter, Behrend, Kuo, & Muller, 1989; Perret-Clermont, 1980). However, as Azmitia and Perlmutter (1989) and Perlmutter et al. (1989) have suggested, the peers' role at this age may be more that of encouraging task engagement, rather than one of promoting cognitive change. Even a best friend would most likely not play as great a role in the socialization of cognition as a child's parent until at least the early school years. This expectation is based in part on the nature of early peer relations, which have been characterized as being the outcome of proximity and shared activities (Mueller & Brenner, 1977), and as not very deep or very long lasting (Gottman & Parkhurst, 1980). Thus, it is unlikely that any of a child's early peer relations could match the history and investment of the early parent–child relationship.

It has been suggested by Azmitia and Perlmutter (1989) that since peer relations are more cooperative in nature, and parent–child relationships are more controlling in nature, the former type of relationships may allow children to be more active in the learning process. Support for this hypothesis has been provided by Ellis and Rogoff (1986). These researchers found that children tended to be more compliant and shy when working with an adult rather than a peer tutor. When these children worked with a peer they often sought guidance and clarification and were more active in the problem-solving process. In an earlier study, however, Ellis and Rogoff (1982) found that children tended to learn more from an adult tutor than from a slightly older peer. Thus, even though there may be a more balanced interaction in peer interactions, there may not be as much learning occurring as in parent–child interaction.

Azmitia and Perlmutter (1989) have also suggested that adult tutors other than parents may spontaneously involve children in the process of solving the problem and offer guidance and clarification when they feel the child needs it, rather than waiting for the child to ask for help. Since the adult is leading the interaction and providing support without the child requesting it, it may appear that the child is not playing an active role in the interaction. A different pattern of interaction may be obtained in peer interactions where one child has greater expertise than the other or when the members of an interactive pair have a close relationship.

Parent–Child Relationships

We suggest that parents (or other primary caregivers) play a privileged role in early cognitive development and that these early social influences serve to lay the foundation for future cognitive growth. This view in itself is not a new idea. Many investigators have examined how parents promote their child's cognitive development through interaction. Indeed, the work of Wertsch and his colleagues (Wertsch, 1978; Wertsch & Stone, 1985) suggests that mother–child learning dyads epitomize the developmental progression from other- to self-regulation described by Vygotsky. However, Brown and Ferrara (1985) have suggested that both the age and identity of the social agent are somewhat irrelevant. They argue that individuals in a variety of roles (i.e., teachers, tutors, and master craftsmen) can and often do serve to promote the development of self-regulation in others by gradually diminishing their own guidance and allowing the novice to develop their own abilities (Brown & French, 1979; Cole, 1985). We do not disagree with this position, but believe that parent–child interaction, and primarily the mother–child relationship in our culture, has a privileged status in the promotion of self-regulation in children. We also argue that the parent–child relationship, by its nature, influences a child's development in a more complex and lasting manner than social interaction in other contexts.

The parent–child relationship is the relationship that occurs earliest and is most likely to have the greatest impact on early aspects of cognitive development. There are a number of other reasons why parents may serve a more influential role in early aspects of cognitive development than peers or other adults. First, parents have a much greater level of investment in the cognitive development of their child as compared to peers, siblings, or other adults. Second, parents' shared history with their child should enable a parent to optimize any joint problem-solving situation, since they would not require any transitional period to establish interactional patterns. Although this advantage would also exist for siblings, parents are more likely than siblings to understand their child's basic abilities and limitations. A parent is also more likely to be able to read and effectively interpret signals provided by their child, especially those signals that indicate the child needs more or less assistance.

Relationships and Development

It is likely that the influence of various types of relationships varies over development. As Hartup (1989) has suggested, vertical relationships, in the form of parent–child relationships, emerge very early in development, whereas horizontal relationships do not emerge until the second or third year of life. Thus, in the first few years of life one would expect parents to be the primary social forces influencing cognitive development. Due to the history and nature of the relationship the importance of parents should continue, even as peer relationships emerge. While children are spending more and more time with peers, first perhaps in preschool, and more universally when they enter formal schooling, they are also achieving greater cognitive maturity. At this time, peers likely gain in importance as social agents influencing cognitive development. The relative importance of parents and peers may be difficult to assess in this period, but it may be that parents and peers influence cognitive development it different domains and in different ways. These types of influences are likely to change over the course of both an individual's development and the history of the relationships in which that individual is involved.

Paradigms to Investigate Parental Influences on Cognitive Development

There have been a number of different approaches to examining the manner in which parents influence a child's cognitive development. Traditionally, researchers have focused on aspects of the general input that parents provide for their children, emphasizing for the most part linguistic input. More recently, researchers have begun to investigate aspects of the interaction itself, focusing on the concept of parental scaffolding.

Vygotsky placed a special emphasis on the importance of language as a mediator of cognitive development. Following this idea, several researchers have examined the nature of speech directed toward children in various settings, including picture-book reading (Ninio, 1983; Goodsitt, Grady-Reitan, & Perlmutter, 1988), problem-solving (Wertsch, McNamee, McLane, & Budwig, 1980), and teaching tasks (Wood, 1980). These studies have validated the notion that others' speech plays an important role in the regulation of children's behavior and ultimately in the growth of self-regulation.

More recently, researchers have begun to focus on more interactive aspects of parent–child problem solving. In these investigations, researchers have examined how parents make a problem accessible to a child by sensitive and responsive instruction in the zone of proximal development. Much of this research has been concerned with the concept of *scaffolding*, which was first elaborated by Wood, Bruner, and Ross (1975) to capture the nature of parents' behavior in joint problem-solving situations.

Scaffolding

In recent years the concept of scaffolding has been an influential way of describing how parents adjust or modify the level of regulation they provide while their child is performing a task. This term was originally used by Wood, Bruner, and Ross (1975) to describe the interactive style of effective tutors. A parent (or other tutor) who scaffolds a task for their child modifies both the level of regulation and instruction that they provide as a function of a child's ability or success at solving a specific problem (Rogoff & Gardner, 1984).

Parental scaffolding is usually assessed following the methods developed by Wood, Bruner, and Ross (1975). In this approach, researchers have observed the interaction of tutors working with children on a task. The focus of the analysis is on individual bouts of instruction, which are scored in terms of the level of support (e.g., no intervention, general verbal start "now you do one," specific verbal instructions, identification of the next step, or demonstration of the task) and types of successful instruction employed by the tutor (e.g., corrections, directions, and reminders). This conceptualization of scaffolding has proven to be useful in demonstrating the manner in which parents and other tutors interact with and structure tasks for young children. Most of these studies, however, have focused on the joint problem-solving situation itself. These investigators have rarely attempted to assess the relation between parental scaffolding and subsequent performance by the child.

Beyond Scaffolding

We believe that it is important to look beyond the joint problem-solving session to understand the full scope of social cognitive influences. Scaffolding, especially that which occurs in the context of parent–child relationships, involves more than discrete instructional bouts defined by the level at which instruction has been given. It is true that this level of instruction is clearly a valid level at which to examine the role of parents in scaffolding a task. However, we believe that parental influences are more complex in nature and that the impact of parental influences should be studied not only in ongoing parent–child interactions, but also in terms of its effect on the subsequent behavior and performance of the child.

We believe that a model of parental influences on children's cognition must incorporate measures that reflect those more global aspects of the interaction that capture the important aspects of the interaction that are related to the history of the parent–child relationship. We suggest that this component of parental scaffolding involves a particular style or quality of interaction that may not be captured by purely quantitative, microanalytic investigations of parent–child interaction. In this vein, we conceptualize scaffolding similarly to Rogoff and Gardner (1984), who defined scaffolding as occurring when a more competent individual adjusts task conditions "to produce appropriate understanding of a particular problem for a learner at a particular level of ability" (p. 109). Although this definition encompasses discrete instructional episodes, it also conveys the more global characteristics of parent–child interaction that we believe are important to a complete description of the role of parents in children's cognitive development. In this view, a parent not only tutors and instructs the child, but does so in a way that is highly sensitive to the characteristics of the child and adaptive to the changing demands of a task. Thus, we suggest that more global measures of parental influences may serve to capture how the history of the relationship impacts the problem-solving situation.

Our view of the role of parents incorporates a more qualitative conceptualization of scaffolding, one that borrows from the literature on parental influences on early social–emotional development (e.g.,

Ainsworth, Blehar, Waters, & Wall, 1978; Sroufe & Waters, 1977). Specifically, we believe that parental responsiveness and sensitivity to the child should be examined in a broader manner than they have in traditional approaches to social effects on children's cognition.

Research on early social development has shown that the quality of caretaking and attachment classification has been correlated with problem-solving behavior at 2 years (Matas, Arend, & Sroufe, 1978; Frankel & Bates, 1990). Other research (Sroufe & Fleeson, 1986) has shown that the quality of attachment is related to exploration and problem solving. This work suggests that more global aspects of the parent–child relationship, especially aspects of maternal responsiveness, should be considered in any model of social cognitive influences.

This idea has been more fully examined by Bornstein and his colleagues (Bornstein, 1989; Bornstein & Tamis-LeMonda, 1989). Specifically, Bornstein (1989) has highlighted how two modes of parental influences, social interaction and didactic interactions, appear to promote cognitive growth. The social mode involves how parents express their feelings toward the child and engage them in interpersonal interaction through the use of physical and verbal strategies (e.g., physical comforting, face-to-face contact, smiling, nonverbal vocalizing). Although the primary goal of these behaviors is to engage the child in interpersonal exchange, these behaviors have been associated with promoting cognitive growth in the child (e.g., Bee, Barnard, Eyres, Gray, Hammond, Spietz, Snyder, & Clark, 1982; Olson, Bates, & Bayles, 1984).

Didactic exchanges are those that focus the child on important and relevant aspects of the environment (Bornstein, 1989). These interactions focus a child's attention on task-relevant dimensions, introduce the child to new areas or novel ideas, and help the child to interpret aspects of the environment or aspects of the task (Bornstein, 1989). These exchanges may occur either physically or verbally. Bornstein views scaffolding as one type of didactic exchange. In general, research has shown that didactic interactions and maternal responsiveness are relatively stable over short periods of time (i.e., for a week or a month) during the first year of life and are positively associated with information processing and linguistic abilities of children up to a year later (Bornstein, 1989; Bornstein & Tamis-LeMonda, 1988; Tamis-LeMonda & Bornstein, 1989). Thus, measures of parental style can be reliable indicators of some aspects of later cognitive development.

Implicit in the investigation of parental responsiveness is the notion that parents vary in how sensitive or responsive they are to their child's needs. However, few researchers examining parents' scaffolding have addressed the issue of individual differences in parents' interactional styles. There seems to be an implicit assumption that parents, by virtue of being parents, automatically and effectively scaffold. There is, however, ample evidence to suggest that not all parents are equally sensitive to their child's needs. Indeed, research by Wood and his colleagues (e.g., Wood, 1980; Wood & Middleton, 1975) suggests that there are differences in the sensitivity of mothers tutoring their children in a simple copying task. These differences were found to be predictive of the child's subsequent performance on the task. Extreme shifts in use of Wood's tutorial levels was found to be an ineffective teaching strategy (Wood, Wood, & Middleton, 1978).

More recently Pratt, Kerig, Cowan, and Cowan, (1988) have examined the relation between variations in parenting style and measures of scaffolding. These researchers employed a variety of tasks (block matrix, elicited stories, and matrix classification) to examine how parental characteristics relate to the effectiveness of the parent in scaffolding the tasks for their children. They found that parents who were categorized as authoritative, according to Baumrind's model of parenting styles (1967, 1973), provided more appropriate scaffolding, exhibited higher dyad success percentages, and, in terms of Wood's microlevels, appropriately shifted their instruction to meet the child's needs. This study represents an important step in linking microanalytic measures of aspects of the interaction to broader measures of parental style.

A Model of Parental Influences on Children's Cognition

Our view of parental influences on children's cognition incorporates a number of principles from each of the perspectives discussed previously. In particular, our view incorporates individual differences in parental characteristics, as well as timing of influences, and characteristics of the child into an overall model of parental influences.

Parent Characteristics

For the present purposes, we consider three parental style variables that may influence a child's performance in joint problem solving and in subsequent performance. The first of these variables is *responsiveness* (see Bornstein & Tamis-LeMonda, 1989; Sroufe, 1985). Responsiveness here refers primarily to the socioemotional support offered by the more competent other; that is, responsiveness taps the cognitive and didactic sensitivity shown by the parent. We believe that a didactic style that pays little attention to the child's emotional or motivational state is not a truly responsive style.

A second component of parental interactive style is referred to as *structuring*. Structuring is the component that is most closely related to the type of tutorial interactions that traditionally have been the focus of scaffolding studies (Pratt et al., 1988; Wood et al., 1976). Structuring refers to the manner in which the parent adjusts the task environment, either verbally or physically, to support the child's ongoing task activities. For example, if a parent and child were working together on a complicated jigsaw puzzle, the parent might physically structure the task for the child by separating all the edge pieces into a separate area for the child to work on, or by placing puzzle pieces adjacent to each other so the child might try to attach them. Structuring also can involve providing simple instructions that are most relevant to the task at hand. In our puzzle example, such structuring might involve an instruction to find a specific piece (e.g., "Let's find the piece with some blue on it that looks like it goes with this one"). Parents' use of more global strategies or instructions that are relevant to performance on similar tasks are also part of structuring the task. For example, a parents' suggestion to "First find the corner pieces, and then the edges," provides information about solving puzzles in general. Effective structuring includes both of these levels of instruction and involves adjusting the structure in response to the child's changing state over time.

The third variable we believe to be an important aspect of parental style is *control*. Implicit in the notion of scaffolding is that effective scaffolding allows the child to continue to be the primary regulator of his or her own behavior. An interactive style in which the parent takes over primary responsibility for task-related executive decisions is the antithesis of scaffolding because such a style provides little opportunity for the child to learn to regulate his or her own performance. Low or moderate levels of control that maintain a task within the child's zone of proximal development are indicative of effective scaffolding in our view. We also view control as containing verbal and physical aspects. In a joint puzzle-solving task (Rosengren, Behrend, & Perlmutter, in preparation), we found that a few parents exerted control physically by taking pieces from the child and placing the pieces themselves. Other parents controlled the task verbally, by issuing directives and commands. In our view, parents who exert high levels of control appear more interested in completing the task than in passing on skills and information to the child.

At this global level, we view effective scaffolding to refer to an interactive style that is both responsive and structuring without being overly controlling. We believe that this type of scaffolding should serve to improve a child's performance by making it more likely that a difficult task will fall within a child's zone of proximal development.

Timing of Parental Effects

We argue that the parental influences discussed in the previous section operate at different points in time within the interactive problem-solving context (see Table 5.1). That is, some aspects of parental influence will have their greatest influence during the joint problem-solving situation,

TABLE 5.1 Timing, method, and effect of parental characteristics on children's performance.

Parental characteristic	Timing of influence	Method of influence	Effect of influence
Responsiveness	Immediate and delayed	Provides confidence and motivation	Engages child so that child persists on task
Structure	Immediate	Brings task into ZPD	Makes performance effective and efficient
	Delayed	Passes on skills and information	Makes performance effective and efficient
Control	Immediate	Regulates behavior	Keeps child on task when parent is present
	Delayed	Failure to pass on skills and information	Ineffective and inefficient performance

whereas other influences may carry over to later situations when the child is working alone.

We suggest that parental responsiveness, by maintaining the child's engagement in the task, has a direct influence on a child's performance in the interactive problem situation. We argue here that responsiveness serves to reinforce and encourage a child, providing the child with motivation to continue the task. Thus, we expect parental responsiveness to correlate most highly with measures of the child's task persistence (e.g., time on task, attention, etc.) during the interactive session.

In addition, we argue that responsiveness should influence the child's later performance in a more indirect manner. We suggest that responsive parents promote confidence in their child, and that this confidence serves as motivation for the child to work on a task independent of parental support. This aspect of responsiveness is most likely influenced by the history of the relationship over time. That is, responsive parents provide their children with a secure emotional base that provides their children with the message that they are capable individuals who can function on their own. Thus, responsive parents should have children who are engaged and motivated to perform well when they are working independently. In this sense, we view the social influences on cognition as aggregating over time since this emotional base is something that develops gradually in the context of the relationship.

Parents who provide structure for their children help to bring the task into the child's zone of proximal development. During the joint problem-solving situation, this structure should translate into effective or efficient performance (e.g., performance measures of speed and accuracy). We expect that these effects would primarily impact performance in the interactive setting, but in addition, in certain circumstances would extend to the child to the child's independent performance (e.g., when a child is in a transitional period of development).

We suggest that a controlling style of interaction should have a more negative influence on a child's performance of a task both in interactive situations and when the child is working independently. A parent who controls his or her child is likely to alienate the child, leading to low levels of engagement and motivation. In addition, a controlling style will fail to allow the child to develop the skills and confidence to perform independently. There are some instances where control might in fact be beneficial, but we will explore these instances more fully in the section that follows.

Characteristics of the Child

One limitation of most work on parental influences on children's cognition is that it focuses primarily on what the parents do during the interaction, or qualities of the parents that might serve to promote the child's development. That is, the work focuses on what the parent enables the child to do during the joint problem-solving setting, and not on what the parent does during the session that actually enables the child to perform subsequently at a higher level on their own. Thus, the main focus has been on what parents do, not on the process by which what they do serves to transfer knowledge and skill to their children. In addition, research that has investigated parental responsiveness and the quality of the parent–child relationship has not systematically examined how these parental variables may interact with the age of the child and characteristics of the task that is the focus of the interaction.

We believe that what the child brings to the task situation (i.e., how the child's prior knowledge, skills, and developmental level influence the manner in which parents structure the task) should not be forgotten in studies of parent–child interaction. From this perspective it is important to focus on when a child might benefit most from interaction with another. If a child is already highly skilled at a task, then parental input should do little to aid that child's performance. In this situation, parental responsiveness may simply serve to maintain the child's engagement in the task. Such engagement might enable the child to continue to practice highly developed skills that might show declines without such practice. Conversely, if a child is faced with a task well beyond his or her abilities, then he or she may not exhibit any benefits on that task from parental guidance. Here, however, a sensitive parent may change the nature or goals of the task. One could view both of these instances as being situations where the child's zone of proximal development is relatively narrow. One would expect a child to benefit most from instruction when they exhibit a relatively large zone of proximal development. The implication here is that a child's ability to perform the task on his or her own without parental guidance needs to be assessed if the effects of parental guidance are to be isolated.

The age of the child is also an important variable to consider. Being responsive to the needs of the child means very different things for the parent of a 2-year-old and the parent of a 5-year-old. However, age-appropriate parental responsiveness should be effective at promoting problem solving regardless of the developmental level of the child. Likewise, children at different ages may require more or less structuring of a task. We must also consider how age of the child and familiarity or difficulty of a task interact. Thus, we expect structuring to be most strongly related to the performance of younger children, children who are relatively unfamiliar with a task, or children engaged in tasks that are beyond their independent abilities, regardless of their age. Although control often may have negative consequences on cognitive development, controlling parents actually may be better able to engage younger children in the task and help focus their attention on the task. In some ways, this speculation is similar to the notion that as children develop and learn to regulate their own behavior they require less external regulation. Before the maturation of self-regulatory processes, control on the part of the parent may allow the child to remain engaged in a task and thus benefit from the interaction. However, control in this situation should have negligible effects on the performance of children who are working independently, because the children have not yet developed the necessary skills to regulate their own behavior in the absence of some outside help.

Research on Parental Style and Performance

How does the interactive style of the parents in an interactive setting influence children's task performance both with their parent and independently? We set out to investigate these questions in a study of preschool children solving puzzles both alone and with their mothers. We included puzzles of varying levels of difficulty and examined children's performance both with and without their mothers during an initial session (Time 1) and then a week later (Time 2). We included 72 mother–child pairs, with equal numbers of boys and girls at three ages (2, 3, and 5 years).

We assessed parental interactive style using three seven-point Likert scales that assessed: *Responsiveness*—the emotional and cognitive support by provided by the parent; *Structure*—the physical and verbal adjustment of the task; and *Control*—the degree to which the parent took primary responsibility for completing the task and set limits on the child's behavior. (The complete scales are available from the authors upon request.) Parents were rated according to these scales by two independent coders; interrater reliability was at least 0.80 for each scale.

It is important to note that the three scales were not (and were not intended to be) completely orthogonal. The responsiveness and structure scales both were designed to assess parents' sensitivity to the child's changing needs over the task situation. The responsiveness scale tended to tap more affective sensitivity, whereas the structure scale tapped aspects of the parents' cognitive sensitivity. We did not expect any relationship between these two scales and the control scale, although a negative relationship might be expected between responsiveness and control. Interscale correlations confirmed these expectations. Scores on the responsiveness and structuring scales were positively correlated ($r = 0.67$, $p < 0.01$), but the control scale was not correlated with either the responsiveness ($r = -0.01$) or structure scales ($r = 0.12$). This pattern of intermeasure correlations is consistent with our general conceptualization of parental scaffolding.

We examined three measures of the child's performance: the number of attempts at placing puzzle pieces (a measure of persistence), the number of successful placements of puzzle pieces (a measure of effectiveness), and a ratio of successful placements to overall attempts (a measure of efficiency). We examined these measures for the children both when they were working alone and with their mothers. We also calculated a difference score for each performance measure based on the difference between the child's performance alone and the child's performance while working with their mother. These difference scores may be thought of as assessments of the child's zone of proximal development.

To examine the relationship between our measures of parental style and children's performance, Pearson correlations between the measures described above were calculated for each age group separately for performance at both Time 1 and Time 2. (Note that whereas the parental style measures were only assessed at Time 1, if, as we believe, these variables capture aspects of the relationship that are stable over time, they should be consistent from session to session.)

The pattern of results obtained was quite different for each of the three age groups (see Table 5.2). For the 2-year-olds, parental style was most highly correlated with the child's number of attempts in the joint puzzle-solving situation at both Time 1 ($r_{\text{responsiveness}} = 0.40$, $p < 0.01$, $r_{\text{structure}} = 0.59$, $p < 0.01$, $r_{\text{verbal control}} = 0.54$, $p < 0.01$) and Time 2 ($r_{\text{structure}} = 0.44$, $p < 0.01$, $r_{\text{verbal control}} = 0.40$, $p < 0.01$). At Time 1, structure was also found to relate to the 2-year-olds' success and efficiency in the alone session ($r = 0.44$, $p < 0.01$ for each), but these relations did not hold up at Time 2. In fact, at Time 2 a negative relationship was observed between the child's attempts in the alone situation and measures of

TABLE 5.2 Correlations between maternal ratings and children's performance.

Parental Style	Attempts Alone	Attempts With	Attempts Diff	Successes Alone	Successes With	Successes Diff	Percent Alone	Percent With	Percent Diff
Time 1									
2-year-olds' performance									
Responsiveness	0.44	0.40	—	—	0.40	—	—	0.39	—
Structure	—	0.59	0.42	0.44	—	—	0.44	—	—
Verbal	—	0.57	0.48	—	—	—	—	—	—
Physical	0.48	0.49	—	0.47	—	—	0.46	—	—
Control	—	—	0.40	—	—	—	—	0.40	0.45
Verbal	—	0.54	0.47	—	0.42	—	—	0.42	0.38
Physical	—	—	—	—	—	—	—	—	0.45
3-year-olds' performance									
Responsiveness	—	—	—	—	0.39	0.40	—	0.40	0.42
Structure	—	—	—	—	—	—	—	0.38	0.39
Verbal	—	—	—	—	—	—	—	0.41	0.41
Physical	—	—	—	—	—	—	—	0.34	—
Control	—	—	—	—	—	—	—	—	—
5-year-olds' performance									
Responsiveness	—	—	—	—	—	—	—	0.52	—
Structure	—	—	—	—	0.45	—	—	0.46	0.48
Verbal	—	—	—	—	0.48	—	—	0.42	0.47
Physical	—	—	—	—	0.39	—	—	0.47	0.44
Control	—	—	0.41	—	0.43	—	−0.41	0.37	0.55
Verbal	—	—	—	—	0.47	—	—	0.63	0.68
Time 2									
2-year-olds' performance									
Responsiveness	−0.43	—	0.55	—	0.42	0.42	—	—	—
Structure	−0.42	0.44	0.64	—	—	—	—	—	—
Verbal	—	0.42	0.56	—	—	—	—	—	—
Physical	−0.48	0.43	0.65	0.47	—	—	0.46	—	—
Control	—	0.41	0.50	—	0.51	0.51	—	0.43	0.43
Verbal	—	0.40	0.56	—	0.42	0.42	—	—	—
Physical	—	—	0.40	—	0.51	0.51	—	0.45	0.45
3-year-olds' performance									
Control	—	−0.61	−0.61	—	—	—	—	—	—
Verbal	—	−0.58	−0.52	—	—	—	—	—	—
Physical	—	−0.57	−0.60	—	—	—	—	—	—
5-year-olds' performance									
Responsiveness	—	—	—	—	—	—	—	—	—
Structure	—	—	—	—	—	—	—	—	—
Control	—	—	—	—	—	—	—	—	—

maternal responsiveness ($r = -0.43$, $p < 0.01$) and maternal structure ($r = -0.42$, $p < 0.01$). Thus, for the 2-year-olds, parental behavior seemed most strongly related to the child's current task performance, with little carryover to sessions alone either on that day or 1 week later. It is interesting that all of the parental measures obtained at Time 1 were correlated with the difference in attempts made in the alone and with mother situations at Time 2. This result, and the negative correlations between performance in the alone condition at Time 2 and parental measures obtained at Time 1, suggest that for 2-year-olds, the mother may provide regulation that enables the child to be persistent on the task; however, few skills or abilities may actually be passed on to the child that will enable him or her to succeed at the task on his or her own.

For 3-year-olds a slightly different pattern was observed. At Time 1, parental measures were most highly correlated with measures of efficiency when the child was working together with his or her mother ($r_{responsiveness} = 0.40$, $p < 0.01$, $r_{structure} = 0.38$, $p < 0.01$). These correlations were not obtained at Time 2. Instead, measures of control were found to be negatively related to the number of attempts at Time 2 while working with the mother. These results suggest that mothers tend to improve the efficiency of their 3-year-olds during an ongoing task. However, the results also suggest that whereas parental control has little if any influence during performance of the current task for 3-year-olds, it tends to have a negative influence on performance on a similar task a week later.

The relation between parental style and 5-year-olds' performance at Time 1 was similar to that obtained for the 3-year-olds. At Time 1, parental style was most highly correlated with children's efficiency when working with his or her mother ($r_{responsiveness} = 0.52$, $p < 0.01$, $r_{structure} = 0.46$, $p < 0.01$). However, parental control was positively correlated with both successful attempts ($r = 0.43$, $p < 0.01$) and efficiency ($r = 0.37$, $p < 0.01$), and negatively correlated to the child's efficiency alone ($r = -0.41$, $p < 0.01$). No significant correlations were found between parental style and performance at Time 2 for the 5-year-olds. These results suggest that parental style serves to increase both effectiveness and efficiency of 5-year-olds, primarily when the child is working with his or her mother.

We take these results as an indication that it is important to examine multiple parent and child characteristics in order to understand the role of parents in promoting cognitive development in their children. The failure to find many relationships between parental style and children's performance while the child was working alone suggests that this finding was perhaps because our parental measures were based on a relatively small window of parental behavior (a 10-min interaction) obtained in only the first session. It also may be that the familiarity of the task (puzzles were used in all sessions, although different puzzles were used in each session) may have decreased motivation and interest of the child at Time 2.

Conclusions and Suggestions for Further Research

We suggest that a model of social influences on cognitive development must incorporate measures of individual differences of both child and tutor. Not all parents (siblings, teachers, or peers) respond the same way, or even in effective ways. We believe that we must consider the "goodness of fit" between the child's needs and the tutor's style. Few investigators have systematically considered the multiple levels at which social influences may occur, yet these levels may have distinct influences on a child's learning and cognitive development. Finally, the timing of the effects of social influences must be considered. Most studies investigate the relation between interaction and performance during the task situation or performance shortly after the interaction. We believe that there is a need for examination of longer term influences, especially when considering social influences in close relationships.

Traditional scaffolding measures, like those developed by Wood (e.g., Wood, 1980; Wood & Middleton, 1975) that examine the "region of sensitivity of instruction" or use of "contingent-shift" rules, have been found to predict children's subsequent performance shortly after the interactive session. However, these effects would not be expected to be long lasting, unless the child was in a transitional period of development or if the ZPD was relatively large. It is not yet clear whether optimal learning occurs when the ZPD is large or relatively small. It would seem that greater learning should occur when the ZPD is large and that if the ZPD is small the individual would benefit little from instruction. Thus, we suggest that the greatest impact of interaction would exist when a child exhibits a relatively large ZPD. Although this prediction is inherent in the definition of the zone of proximal development, for the most part it remains untested.

A first step in investigating social influences on children's cognition is to examine how others' behaviors vary as a function of the attributes of the child. The attribute of the child that has thus far received the most attention is age (e.g., many studies have shown age-related differences in how parents respond to their children). Other variables that are also important to consider are the child's intelligence, experience with the task, motivation to perform the task, and ability to perform the task alone. This last variable is important because it provides an indication of a child's skill before the interaction. This knowledge is essential for understanding the influence the interaction has on the child. Surprisingly, few studies addressing how social interactions in the zone of proximal development promote self-regulation have included assessments of the skills a child brings to the problem (Azmitia & Perlmutter, 1989). Without this prior assessment, it is impossible to determine to what degree the child is benefitting from the interaction.

It is also important to consider aspects of the tasks used to examine social influences. Specifically, researchers should consider how task difficulty or novelty interact with tutors' behaviors. If tutors are sensitive to the child's needs, dramatic differences in the tutors' behavior should be observed when the tasks vary. These differences could be seen in two ways. First, differences in tutor guidance might exist when the tasks are from different domains. On the one hand, this pattern may be due to the nature of the problems associated with the various domains. On the other hand, it may be due to tutors perceiving certain domains of problems to be more difficult for the child and modify their instruction accordingly. Another approach could involve variations of task difficulty or novelty within a domain to determine if tutors modify their level of intervention as a function of task difficulty or novelty.

It is also clear that longitudinal research is needed to investigate more fully the changing role of others as regulators of children's cognitive development. One would expect that as a child acquires the necessary skills to perform a task adequately a sensitive tutor would gradually decrease their role from one of structuring and regulating the child's performance to one of being more supportive of the child's own accomplishments. This shift might be viewed as a change from the role of coach to cheerleader. Many social influences on cognition may aggregate over time. What this means is that it may be difficult to assess social influences in single sessions. Consider, for example, a parent reading a book to his or her child. Although many parents do develop specific routines for reading a particular book, it is also the case that there is a lot of variation in the reading and information provided over multiple reading trials. Thus, looking at a single session may not provide a truly accurate portrayal of the information being passed onto children.

It is also true that there exist multiple levels of social influences. Azmitia and Perlmutter (1989) make the distinction between molar and molecular levels of social influences. At the molar level are those social influences that function as part of larger institutions within a culture, such as the influences of schools on cognitive development. Although this level is important, the focus of the present chapter is on social influences occurring at the molecular level, or the level of individual interaction. We have suggested that even within the molecular level, there are a variety of levels in which social influences impact cognitive development. We envision a hierarchy of levels of social influences at the molecular level that involve different processes and influences on cognitive development over different time courses. That is, some social influences on cognitive development tend to have an immediate impact on a child's performance on a given task and others operate to aid a child's performance on later attempts at solving a given task.

Learning is often facilitated in social contexts by partners providing knowledge, strategies, and methods for making a problem more manageable. However, the presence of others can also serve as a motivator, either by their mere presence (Zajonc, 1965), by providing emotional support and encouragement, or by making the task more enjoyable (Azmitia & Perlmutter, 1989; Perlmutter et al., 1989). To date, most of the studies of social influences on cognitive development have examined the immediate or synchronic effects on a child's performance of a task. However, we believe that many of the most important influences of social interaction work over time, and therefore may not be indicative of performance on the immediate task.

References

Abramovitch, R., Corter, C., & Lando, B. (1979). Sibling interaction in the home. *Child Development, 50*, 997–1003.

Ainsworth, M.D.S., Blehar, M.C., Waters, E., & Wall, S. (1978). *Patterns of attachment: A psychological study of the strange situation*. Hillsdale, NJ: Erlbaum.

Azmitia, M., & Perlmutter, M.A. (1989). Social influences on children's cognition: State of the art and future directions. In H.W. Reese (Ed.), *Advances in child development and behavior* (Vol. 22, pp. 89–144). New York: Academic Press.

Baumrind, D. (1967). Child care practices anteceding three patterns of preschool behavior. *Genetic Psychology Monographs, 75*, 43–88.

Baumrind, D. (1973). The development of instrumental competence through socialization. In A.D. Pick (Ed.), *Minnesota Symposium on Child Psychology* (Vol. 7, pp. 3–46). Minneapolis: University of Minnesota Press.

Bearison, D.J., Magazamen, S., & Filardo, E.K. (1986). Socio-cognitive conflict and cognitive growth in young children. *Merrill-Palmer Quarterly, 32*, 51–72.

Bee, H.L., Barnard, K.E., Eyres, S.J., Gray, C.A., Hammond, M.A., Spietz, A.L., Snyder, C., & Clark, B. (1982). Prediction of IQ and language skill from perinatal status, child performance, family characteristics, and mother-infant interaction. *Child Development, 53*, 1134–1156.

Behrend, D.A., Rosengren, K.S., & Perlmutter, M.A. (1989). A new look at children's private speech: The effects of age, task difficulty, and parent presence. *International Journal of Behavioral Development, 12*, 305–320.

Bornstein, M.H. (1989). Between caretakers and their young: Two modes of interaction and their consequences for cognitive growth. In M.H. Bornstein & J.S. Bruner (Eds.), *Interaction in human development* (pp. 197–214). Hillsdale, NJ: Erlbaum.

Bornstein, M.H., & Tamis-LeMonda, C.S. (1989). Maternal responsiveness and cognitive development in children. In M.H. Bornstein (Ed.), *Maternal responsiveness: Characteristics and consequence* (pp. 49–61). San Francisco: Jossey-Bass.

Brody, G.H., Stoneman, Z., & MacKinnon, C.E. (1982). Role asymmetries in interactions among school-aged children, their younger siblings, and friends. *Child Development, 53*, 1364–1370.

Brown, A.L., & Ferrara, R.A. (1985). Diagnosing zones of proximal development. In J.V. Wertsch (Ed.), *Culture, communication and cognition: Vygotskian perspectives* (pp. 273–305). London & New York: Cambridge University Press.

Brown, A.L., & French, L.A. (1979). The zone of proximal development: Implications for intelligence testing in the year 2000. *Intelligence, 3*, 255–277.

Cole, M. (1985). The zone of proximal development: Where culture and cognition create each other. In J.V. Wertsch (Ed.), *Culture, communication and cognition: Vygotskian perspectives* (pp. 146–161). London & New York: Cambridge University Press.

Ellis, S., & Rogoff, B. (1982). The strategies and efficacy of child versus adult teachers. *Child Development*, *53*, 730–735.

Ellis, S., & Rogoff, B. (1986). Problem solving in children's management of instruction. In E.C. Mueller & C.R. Cooper (Eds.), *Process and outcome in peer relationships* (pp. 301–325). Orlando, FL: Academic Press.

Feldman, R.S., Devin-Sheehan, L., & Allen, V.L. (1976). Children tutoring children: A critical review of research. In V.L. Allen (Ed.), *Children as teachers: Theory and research on tutoring*. Orlando, FL: Academic Press.

Frankel, K.A., & Bates, J.E. (1990). Mother-toddler problem solving: Antecedents in attachment, home behavior, and temperament. *Child Development*, *61*, 810–819.

Frauenglass, M.H., & Diaz, R.M. (1985). Self-regulatory functions of children's private speech: A critical analysis of recent challenges to Vygotsky's theory. *Developmental Psychology*, *21*, 357–364.

Goodsitt, J., Grady-Reitan, J., & Perlmutter, M. (1988). Interaction between mothers and preschool children when reading novel and familiar books. *International Journal of Behavioral Development*, *11*, 489–506.

Gottman, J.M., & Parkhurst, J.T. (1980). A developmental theory of friendship and aquaintanceship processes. In W.A. Collins (Ed.), *Development of cognition, affect, and social relations, The Minnesota Symposia on Child Psychology* (Vol. 13, pp. 197–254). Hillsdale, NJ: Erlbaum.

Hartup, W.W. (1985). Relationships and their significance in cognitive development. In R.A. Hinde, A.-N. Perret-Clermont, & J. Stevenson-Hinde (Eds.), *Relationships and cognitive development* (pp. 66–82). London & New York: Oxford University Press.

Hartup, W.W. (1989). Social relationships and their developmental significance. *American Psychologist*, *44*, 283–292.

Matas, L., Arend, R.A., & Sroufe, L.A. (1978). Continuity of adaptation in the second year: The relationship between quality of attachment and later competence. *Child Development*, *49*, 547–556.

Mueller, E., & Brenner, J. (1977). The origins of social skills and interaction among playgroup toddlers. *Child Development*, *48*, 854–861.

Ninio, A. (1983). Joint book reading as a multiple vocabulary acquisition device. *Developmental Psychology*, *19*, 445–451.

Olson, S.L., Bates, J.E., & Bayles, K. (1984). Mother-infant interaction and the development of individual differences in children's cognitive competence. *Development Psychology*, *20*, 166–179.

Perlmutter, M., Behrend, S., Kuo, F., & Muller, A. (1989). Social influences in children's problem solving. *Developmental Psychology*, *25*, 744–754.

Perret-Clermont, A.-N. (1980). *Social interaction and cognitive development in children*. London: Academic Press.

Perret-Clermont, A.-N., & Brossard, A. (1985). On the interdigitation of social and cognitive processes. In R.A. Hinde, A.N. Perret-Clermont, & J. Stevenson-Hinde (Eds.), *Relationships and cognitive development* (pp. 309–327). London & New York: Oxford University Press.

Piaget, J. (1932). *The moral judgment of the child*. Glencoe, IL: Free Press.

Piaget, J. (1968). *Six psychological studies*. New York: Vintage Press.

Pratt, M.W., Kerig, P., Cowan, P.A., & Cowan, C.P. (1988). Mothers and fathers teaching 3-year-olds: Authoritative parenting and adult scaffolding of young children's learning. *Development Psychology*, *24*, 832–839.

Rogoff, B., & Gardner, W. (1984). Adult guidance of cognitive development. In B. Rogoff & J. Lave (Eds.), *Everyday cognition: Its development in social context*. Cambridge, MA: Harvard University Press.

Rogoff, B., & Wertsch, J.V. (Eds.). (1984). *Children's learning in the zone of proximal development*. San Francisco: Jossey-Bass.

Sroufe, L.A. (1985). Attachment classification from the perspective of infant-caregiver relationships and infant temperament. *Child Development*, *56*, 1–14.

Sroufe, L.A., & Fleeson, J. (1986). Attachment and the construction of relationships. In W. Hartup & Z. Rubin (Eds.), *Relationships and Development*. Hillsdale, NJ: Erlbaum.

Sroufe, L.A., & Waters, E. (1977). Attachment as an organizational construct. *Child Development*, *48*, 1184–1199.

Tamis-LeMonda, C.S., & Bornstein, M.H. (1989). Habituation and maternal encouragement of attention in infancy as predictors of toddler language, play, and representational competence. *Child Development*, *60*, 738–751.

Vygotsky, L.S. (1962). *Thought and language*. Cambridge, MA: Harvard University Press.

Vygotsky, L.S. (1978). *Mind in society*. Cambridge, MA: Harvard University Press.

Wertsch, J.V. (1978). Adult-child interaction and the roots of metacognition. *Quarterly Newsletter of the Institute for Comparative Human Development*, *1*, 15–18.

Wertsch, J.V., McNamee, G.D., McLane, J., & Budwig, N.A. (1980). The adult–child dyad as problem-solving system. *Child Development*, *51*, 1215–1221.

Wertsch, J.V., Minick, N., & Arns, F. (1985). The creation of context in joint problem solving. In B. Rogoff & J. Lave (Eds.), *Everyday cognition: Its development in social context* (pp. 151–171). Cambridge, MA: Harvard University Press.

Wertsch, J.V., & Stone, C.A. (1985). The concept of internalization in Vygotsky's account of the genesis of higher mental functions. In J.V. Wertsch (Ed.), *Culture, communication and cognition: Vygotskian perspectives* (pp. 162–182). London & New York: Cambridge University Press.

Wood, D. (1980). Teaching the young child: Some relationships between social interaction, language, and thought. In D. Olson (Ed.), *The social foundations of language and thought* (pp. 280–296). New York: Norton.

Wood, D., Bruner, J., & Ross, G. (1976). The role of tutoring in problem solving. *Journal of Child Psychology and Child Psychiatry*, *17*, 89–100.

Wood, D., & Middleton, D. (1975). A study of assisted problem solving. *British Journal of Psychology*, *66*, 181–191.

Wood, W., Wood, H., & Middleton, D. (1978). An experimental evaluation of four face-to-face teaching strategies. *International Journal of Behavioral Development*, *1*, 131–147.

Youniss, J. (1980). *Parents and peers in social development: A Sullivan–Piaget perspective*. Chicago, IL: University of Chicago Press.
Zajonc, R.B. (1965). Social facilitation. *Science*, 269–274.
Zajonc, R.B., & Markus, G.B. (1975). Birth order and intellectual development. *Psychological Review*, *82*, 74–88.
Zajonc, R.B., Markus, H., & Markus, G.B. (1979). The birth order puzzle. *Journal of Personality and Social Psychology*, *37*, 1325–1341.

6
Memory Strategies: Natural Development and Use Following Instruction

MICHAEL PRESSLEY AND PEGGY VAN METER

This chapter is about the development of competent use of memory strategies. There are two fundamental topics covered here. One is natural development of strategies. The second is strategy development by instruction.

One of the difficulties in writing this chapter is that current models of mind and efficient mental functioning are substantially different from the models that were prevalent when much of the best-known memory strategies research was conducted. The work on memory development conducted in the middle to late 1960s (e.g., see Flavell, 1970) was motivated by the hypothesis that use of strategies accounted for much, if not all, of the developmental variation in memory abilities. This position yielded in the 1970s as it became understood that what one knows about memory and memorizing (i.e., metamemory; Kreutzer, Leonard, & Flavell, 1975) contributes to use of strategies. For instance, understanding that a strategy promotes a particular type of memory performance increases the likelihood that the strategy will be elected to mediate that performance (see Pressley, Borkowski, & O'Sullivan, 1984, 1985, for reviews; also, Schneider & Pressley, 1989, chapter 5). The focus on strategies decreased more in the late 1970s with the emergence (Chi, 1978) of the hypothesis that the nonstrategic knowledge base could and often did mediate performances long believed to be strategically determined (for overview, see Bjorklund, 1987). During the 1980s, there also was increasing awareness that motivation can be a critical determinant of memory performance (Borkowski, Carr, Rellinger, & Pressley, 1990). As the 1980s progressed, interest in basic processes and structures in cognition increased. Discussions of traces, connections, and neurophysiological architecture were common, especially during the second half of the decade (Brainerd & Reyna, 1990; Churchland, 1986; Pinker & Mehler, 1988; Rabinowitz & McAuley, 1990). Even the most adamant of the advocates for basic factors as critical determinants of memory discuss them in relation to higher order components, however (e.g., Brainerd, Reyna, Howe, & Kingma, 1990, pp. 82-84).

In short, at the beginning of the 1990s, it is accepted that sophisticated cognition involves complex interactions and interdependencies between strategies, metacognition, knowledge, motivation, and basic capacities (e.g., Pressley, Borkowski, & Schneider, 1989; see Schneider & Weinert, 1990, for perspectives on how these components might interact). Those identifying more with any one of these components than with others were obliged, at least at a theoretical level, to establish how their preferred component was functionally related to other factors. Thus, in this chapter there is much discussion of how our preferred component, strategies, functions in relation to metacognition, nonstrategic knowledge, motivation, and basic capacities.

A second difficulty in constructing this chapter was the striking shift in methodologies over the 25-year modern history of memory development (see Schneider & Pressley, 1989, chapter 1, for the history dating back to Ebbinghaus). In general, the more dated the research in this era (i.e., the closer to the middle 1960s), the more likely it was conducted with traditional laboratory tasks such as list or paired-associate learning. Much of the more recent work (albeit not all, especially the emerging work on basic representational capacities and structures; e.g., Brainerd et al., 1990) has been conducted with more naturalistic materials and tasks. Some recent research, for example, is qualitative and inductive rather than quantitative and deductive, a methodological direction that has great promise for opening new theoretical conceptions of strategy use and strategy instruction. In fact, a number of researchers who once used laboratory tasks moved on to the study of text memory (Pressley, Johnson, Symons, McGoldrick, & Kurita, 1989) and teaching of strategies in classrooms (Harris & Pressley, 1991; Pressley, Goodchild, Fleet, Zajchowski, & Evans, 1989). To cover both historically prominent and contemporary issues in the development of memory strategy capabilities, the continuum of extremely basic to ecologically valid research must be covered. A complication, however, is that the development of strategy use has been studied in considerably greater detail in basic tasks, such as list or associative learning, than it has in more complicated situations, such as text learning in classrooms. (This is partially an artifact of the longer history of research with the more basic tasks.) Thus, when natural development of strategy use is discussed, it makes most sense to focus on extremely basic research. Memory strategy use following instruction can be covered with respect to many more types of materials.

Entire volumes have been written about memory development (e.g., Schneider & Pressley, 1989). Thus, a third challenge is devising a format that permits distillation of the most important messages of this literature without patronizing the readership by presenting only a series of very general claims. The approach we adopt is to present a number of questions about the development of memory strategies and their instruction that we encounter frequently, both in the general psychological literatures and in interactions with other professionals. Most of these questions tap issues driving the field today.

There Isn't an Agreed Upon Definition of Strategy, Is There?

This question is presented to us with surprising frequency, especially since one of us (M.P.) offered a definition of a strategy at a conference in 1984, later published as part of Pressley, Forrest-Pressley, Elliott-Faust, and Miller (1985, p. 4) and, in modified form, in Pressley, Forrest-Pressley, and Elliott-Faust (1988, p. 102). The 1985 statement of it is especially appropriate here:

> [strategies] . . . are composed of cognitive operations over and above the processes that are a natural consequence of carrying out [a] task, ranging from one such operation to a sequence of interdependent operations. Strategies achieve cognitive purposes (e.g., memorizing) and are potentially conscious and controllable activities.

Pressley and his colleagues had been trying to construct a definition that captured (a) consciously controlled processes, (b) processes that are automaticized and automatically used in task situations where once they were controlled and used only with conscious intention, and (c) processes that are driven by materials so compatible with the strategic process that doing the task obligates the process (e.g., when a highly associated word pair is studied, such as *pin-balloon*, adults often automatically produce linking images, such as a *pin* popping a *balloon*). Howe and O'Sullivan (1990) referred to this third possibility as *semantic capture* by a strategy because processing the to-be-learned content induces elaborations, extensions, and reorganizations regardless of learner intentions to do so. Because Pressley et al.'s definition conflicted with claims made by others that strategies are always conscious and controlled (e.g., Bjorklund & Harnishfeger, 1990; Paris, Lipson, & Wixson, 1983), it was controversial. Pressley and his associates took the position they did on intentionality because automatic and controlled versions of similar processes generally serve the same function and often produce comparable outcomes (Hasher & Zacks, 1979; Naus & Halasz, 1979; Schneider & Shiffrin, 1977; Shiffrin & Schneider, 1977). Moreover, the long-term goal of strategy instruction often is automatic use of processes. In addition, many automatic processes are considered to be strategies by the scientists studying them most closely. Lundeberg's (1987) work on strategies used by lawyers as they read cases is an example. In contrast, critics of the Pressley et al. (1985) definition viewed automatized and automatically occurring processes as skills, efficient processes that could and should be distinguished from their controlled, less efficient brethren, the strategies. Such thinking reflects that most studies of strategic functioning and strategy instruction in particular have been concerned with intentional use of strategies.

The debate continued over the criticality of intentionality as a determinant of strategic processing in a recent volume edited by Bjorklund (1990) with some of the contributions in that volume favoring the Pressley et al. (1985) position. Consider, for example, Mark Ashcraft's views about what comprises a strategy (1990, p. 186):

> Nowadays . . . the term strategy has a considerably broader connotation, loosely "how some task is performed mentally." Though some current research preserves the notion that a strategy is a deliberate and conscious mental procedure, an equally valid case can be made that strategies need not be deliberate or conscious in order for the term to be applied meaningfully. Indeed, this change in connotation is almost literally forced upon us by the evidence that formerly conscious or controlled mental processes could achieve a substantial degree of automaticity with practice (Posner & Snyder, 1975; Shiffrin & Schneider, 1977). Thus, in order to accommodate the far broader range of behavior and mental processing now being investigated in the area of cognitive development, and to accomodate empirical effects such as the growth of automaticity, the term strategy must be redefined. It must also be liberalized to include not only the deliberate and conscious but also the nondeliberate and automatic processes and procedures by which various mental events take place.

One of the main motivations of Pressley and his colleagues for deemphasizing intentionality was the effective reduction of the number of cognitive animals that need explaining when intentionality is dismissed as a critical feature differentiating strategic from nonstrategic behaviors. Thus, for every strategy specified by Pressley et al. (1985), a controlled strategy and an automatic skill is supposed by their critics. Howe and O'Sullivan (1990) elegantly summarized how potentially counterproductive this situation is:

> . . . the extent to which processing is effortful is more a matter of degree, with different processes or processing components lying on a continuum ranging from *predominantly automatic* to *predominantly controlled*. When aspects of memory development are dissected in an all-or-none manner, rather than viewed as variations on a continuum, we effectively isolate (both empirically and theoretically) what are integral components of the behavior under study. In order to understand how an individual "solves" a memory problem, we must take into account those processes that are executed effortfully, and the way in which processes that vary in degree of effortfulness conjoin to produce organized (strategic) behavior. By simply focussing on one set of processes at a time, we may tend to ignore the emergent properties inherent in strategy use. (p. 132)

Although these analyses in Bjorklund (1990) encourage an even stronger commitment to an intention-free definition of strategy use than was presented previously, we are not certain that it really makes any practical difference which viewpoint on intentionality is adopted. In attempting to identify even a single piece of research or research direction affected by this debate, we came up empty handed. Given that there seems to be little of research consequence that follows from the debate over the definition of strategy, we will not be returning to it in what follows, for there are many more important issues to cover here.

Don't Strategies Develop Naturally During the Elementary School Years?

This question is grounded in some of the oldest and most prominent work in memory development, work that is still featured in literature summaries, especially those intended for general audiences (e.g., Kail, 1988). There is a great deal of evidence that children's rehearsal of lists increases during the elementary years.

Rehearsal

Consider a typical serial recall task: Children are presented a list of items, one at a time in a particular order. One popular methodology is to present a series of picture cards arranged in a left-to-right array, with the left-most item first turned face up for a brief exposure, then the adjacent card is turned, continuing until the right-most card is turned (e.g., Flavell, Beach, & Chinsky, 1966).

Consider also a potent strategy that can be applied to this task, referred to as *cumulative-rehearsal, fast-finish* by those who have investigated it (Barclay, 1979; Butterfield & Belmont, 1977). This involves rehearsal of the early- and middle-list items in order as they are revealed. Thus, if items are *dog*, *apple*, *car*, *basket*, *radio*, *cup*, and *pencil*, when the *dog* is revealed, rehearsal involves saying, "Dog, dog, dog." When the *apple* is revealed, both items are included, "Dog, apple, dog, apple . . ." This rehearsal continues until near the end of the list, so that when radio is shown, the subject repeats, "Dog, apple, car, basket, radio, dog, apple . . ." Rather than generating more rehearsals when the next-to-last item, *cup*, is revealed, however, the subject might move on quickly to uncover the final item, *pencil*, then quickly cover the *pencil* and proceed to recall the list. After quickly stating the last two items, *cup* and *pencil*, the first five items might then be recalled in their order of presentation. That is, the last two items are dumped from short-term memory whereas the first five items are retrieved from longer term traces that were established via cumulative rehearsal. The longer term memories contain both item and position information. Two types of items are recalled at especially high levels using this approach: (a) information near the end of the list (recency effect), reflecting material that was dumped from short-term memory, and (b) information near the beginning of the list (primacy effect), presumably because earlier list items are rehearsed more than middle-list items.

Do young children use such an elaborate strategy? No. In fact, coordinated use of the cumulative rehearsal and fast-finish components is not observed at all until late adolesence (Barclay, 1979). Normally achieving middle-elementary-grade children rely mostly on cumulative rehearsal alone. Furthermore, if they rehearse at all, preschoolers and early-elementary-grades children do not use cumulative rehearsal extensively, but rather are more likely to repeat only the item currently presented (see Schneider & Pressley, 1989, chapter 3, for a detailed review of the relevant literature).

To be certain, this account is simplified. For instance, if the list includes items saliently compatible with strategies other than rehearsal, such strategies are sometimes observed. For example, McGilly and Siegler (1989, 1990) asked children to learn lists of digits in order. Some of the strings presented for study consisted of digits in their naturally occurring order (e.g., 3-4-5-6-7) and other strings were in random order (e.g., 5-4-6-3-7). Strings in natural order were more likely to be recoded by the subject during study (e.g., the learner saying, "3 to 7"), whereas random strings were more likely to be cumulatively rehearsed. Even young grade school children's rehearsal included both recoding and some cumulative rehearsal, with these two approaches applied differentially to ordered sequences and random sequences, respectively.

Even so, there is substantial growth in rehearsal skills and propensities to use rehearsal during the elementary school years, with cumulative rehearsal well established by the late elementary years. With advancing age, slightly longer and more complex strings of items are cumulatively rehearsed (e.g., Ornstein, Naus, & Liberty, 1975). The fast-finish component is added during adolesence (Barclay, 1979).

Developmental Change or Effect of Experience?

An important question about rehearsal was whether the progression identified in the rehearsal-list learning studies represented a developmental change, and hence one that was somehow organically determined and universal, or whether it is a shift mediated by experience. So long as the work was being produced only in the Western and industrialized countries, it was impossible to disentangle developmental from experiential-cultural effects, especially effects of formal education: In the West, the number of years of schooling is almost entirely confounded with age in child samples, at least those available to researchers in large numbers.

Cross-cultural researchers, however, were able to identify cultures in which age and education confoundings were much less certain, societies in which only some of the children attended school. Western-schooled students in these cultures were compared to others in the culture. When tested on classical memory tasks, as well as other cognitive tasks, there was generally a consistent effect of schooling. That is, students who experienced at least several years of Western-style schooling were more likely to process materials like Western students than were those without such educational experience (e.g., Sharp, Cole, & Lave, 1979; Stevenson, Parker, Wilkinson, Bonnevaux, & Gonzales, 1978; Wagner, 1974, 1978).

Recent cross-cultural evidence about the effects of education on use of "Western" strategies is even more striking. Not all Western, industrialized cultures encourage to the same extent the use of the strategies commonly studied by American researchers, with differences between countries in the amount of environmental support for memory strategies relating to children's use of strategies. Specifically, Carr, Kurtz, Schneider, Turner, and Borkowski (1989) found that German parents reported more at-home instruction of memory strategies to their children than did American parents. In addition, they determined that German children are much more likely to sort categorizable items into semantic categories in preparation for a recall test than are American children, replicating the finding of Schneider, Borkowski, Kurtz, and Kerwin (1986). These correlational patterns are consistent with the conclusion that parental instruction affected both understanding of strategies (i.e., metacognition about the strategies) and use of them. In short, the research of Carr et al. (1989) provides much more compelling support for the conclusion that strategy use was related to instruction of strategies than to development per se. (For complementary data from this same research group, see Kurtz, Carr, & Schneider, 1988; Kurtz, Borkowski, & Deshmukh, 1988; Kurtz, Schneider Carr, Borkowski, & Rellinger, 1990; Deshmukh, Turner, Kurtz, & Borkowski, 1989.)

Bebko and McKinnon (1990) also provided dramatic evidence of experiential effects on use of rehearsal strategies. Bebko (1979, 1984) reported previously that elementary-age deaf children were less likely to rehearse during list learning than normal same-age (elementary age) peers. Bebko and McKinnon (1990) replicated that finding and also demonstrated that when number of years of language experience was considered, the age differences in use of rehearsal during list learning evaporated. Thus, a normal 7-year-old would have 7 years of language experience; so, for instance, might a deaf 11-year-old who was the child of deaf parents and had been enrolled in sign language instruction since age 4. Bebko and MacKinnon showed that children with 7 years of language experience rehearsed about the same amount regardless of hearing status, adding dramatic new evidence about the importance of experience to the natural development of strategy use. As strategy researchers have examined more and more populations and situations, it has proven necessary to modify the portrait of memory development that emerged from the earlier studies of list learning.

Strategy Use During the Preschool Years

Preschoolers are much more strategic than was evident in the early studies of list rehearsal. Consider the findings of one of the most frequently cited series of studies relevant to this point (DeLoache, Cassidy, & Brown, 1985). If a familiar object is hidden in a living room in full view of a child (i.e., the child is allowed to see where the object is placed) and the child is aware that she or he will later be required to retrieve the object, even 2-year-olds manifest strategic behaviors during the retention interval. Specifically, as they go about other activities, they frequently look at the spot where the item was hidden, point at the location, and say the name of the object. Very importantly, this research has made it possible to specify that such behaviors are in fact memory strategies. For instance, if everything is held constant except that the toy is hidden (e.g., under a couch pillow) rather than placed in a position where it is visible in the room (e.g., on top of the couch pillow), there is an increase in looking at the object's location, pointing, or saying the object's name in the hidden condition only (i.e., in the condition with the memory demand).

Baker-Ward, Ornstein, and Holden (1984) also provided a compelling demonstration that preschoolers do something when asked to memorize that they do not do when pursuing other goals. They provided children in two conditions with a set of toys. In both conditions, the children were permitted to play with these toys. In one, the instructions only specified play as the goal of the activity; in the other (i.e., memory) condition, the children were given a goal of remembering a subset of the toys. The latter children in general played less with the toys. Instead, the memory condition participants were more likely to look intensely at and name the to-be-remembered items during the "play" period than were the play condition subjects. That children engaged in strategic behaviors in the memory condition was unambiguous. Interestingly, however, these strategic processing differences did not translate into different recall levels for 4-year-olds in the two conditions, although corresponding strategic differences at the 6-year-old level did so translate. The 4-year-olds had memory strategies, but they were not useful to them yet.

It may be even worse than Baker-Ward et al. (1984) thought. In a similar memory situation, Newman (1990) reported that 4-year-olds who attempted to remember items (and employed strategies similar to the ones used by Baker-Ward et al.'s participants) actually remembered less than children who played with to-be-learned objects. This was a sensible outcome, since play often resulted in the creation of meaningful interactions between items that increased memorability (i.e., children created their own verbal and physical elaborations of to-be-learned materials; e.g., Levin, 1976; Rohwer, 1973). Newman's (1990) outcome complements well analyses by Rogoff and Mistry (e.g., 1990; based in part on

Kagan, Klein, Finley, Rogoff, & Nolan, 1979) that young children can overgeneralize rehearsal strategies that mediate learning of material lacking inherent organization. In doing so, they may neglect to process fully the meaningful aspects of to-be-learned content that could facilitate memory. The result is depressed performance. More optimistically, see Rabinowitz (in press) and Rabinowitz and McCauley (1990) for data suggesting that older students' memories may be positively affected by inherent organizational properties of to-be-learned materials even when they execute a strategy that does not exploit the meaningful properties of the materials. That is, older students may be more likely to process the meaning of to-be-learned materials even as they waste effort on a strategy not well matched to the demands of the task.

Even the most optimistic appraisal of the effectiveness of 4-year-olds' self-elected strategies is not that sanguine. Consider Lange, MacKinnon, and Nida (1989), who observed a number of strategies when 3- to 4-year-olds were attempting to remember a list of to-be-learned items. Correlations between recall and use of individual strategies were low; the highest correlation was between the amount of visual examination of to-be-learned items and recall level, $r = 0.27$, $p < 0.05$. The only other statistically significant correlation between recall and use of any single strategy was when the child named the object, $r = 0.25$, $p < 0.05$. Even when children were coded either as strategic (i.e., using any one of several possible strategies) or nonstrategic (i.e., not manifesting use of any strategies), the correlation between strategy use and recall was modest, $r = 0.41$, $p < 0.01$.

In summary, it is certainly not accurate to characterize preschoolers as nonstrategic. Nonetheless, there is great situational specificity in whether they deploy strategies. For example, although retrieval strategies occur in the setting studied by DeLoache et al. (1985), they often fail to occur when the retrieval task is a less familiar one in a less familiar setting. Examples include Ritter (1978), in which the retrieval problem involved styrofoam cups mounted on a turntable, and Sodian and Schneider (1990), in which preschoolers neither prepared good retrieval cues when they wanted an object found nor poor ones when they did not want an object located by another child. In addition, at least for some strategies in some situations, strategy use may have little effect on the performance of preschoolers (e.g., Baker-Ward et al., 1984).

We close this subsection with an illustration of how even a powerful encoding procedure can have little or no effect on young children's memory. In asking preschoolers and kindergarten children to learn paired associates, Pressley and MacFadyen (1983) used a procedure analytical enough to determine the locus of memory breakdown. Control participants were presented the pairs as separate pictures and, at testing, were given one pair member with the request to provide its mate. In a second condition, the paired items were presented in interactive pictures, a procedure that almost always improves paired-associate memory during the elementary school years. At testing, the participants in this interactive picture condition were given one of the pairmates and requested to recall the other. Performance in this condition was better than control performance only for the kindergarten children. A third condition made the preschooler's difficulty clear. This condition was identical to the interactive picture only condition at study. At testing, however, subjects were presented pictures of single objects and were instructed to think back to the picture they had seen at study to recall the pairmate. That is, they were given an explicit retrieval plan directing access of the visual mediator they had presumably stored during study. Consistent with the hypothesis that the preschoolers in the interactive picture only condition had stored an interactive image at study but were not using it at testing, recall in the interactive picture + retrieval condition was much better than in either of the other conditions. Adding the retrieval cue did not improve performance over memory in the interactive picture only condition at the kindergarten level, however. The preschool data in this study make clear that young children's memory failures can be failures to use representations they have encoded previously (see also Pressley & Levin, 1980); by kindergarten, stored images are used to retrieve pairmates even in the absence of an instruction to do so. The ability of 4- to 5-year-olds to remember scenes depicted in interactive pictures, however, is not complemented by the ability to create their own internal interactive images (i.e., in the absence of a picture depicting the interaction), as will be obvious in the next subsection.

Prolonged Development of Strategic Competence, When It Develops at All

The dramatic increase in the use of rehearsal strategies to mediate list learning during the elementary years is not paralleled by developments with respect to some other memory strategies. A favorite example for us, perhaps because of personal research experiences with it (see Pressley, 1982, for a review), is the development of the use of elaboration strategies to mediate associative learning tasks. Take the simple case of paired-associate learning. A pair such as "turkey-rock" can be learned rather easily by imagining a turkey sitting on a rock or making up a simple story about a turkey getting hit by a rock: These would be imagery and verbal elaborations, respectively (Rohwer, 1973). Such strategies are not used routinely and spontaneously during the grade-school years (e.g., Pressley & Levin, 1977a); moreover, even many young adults need to be prompted to use elaboration procedures (Bower, 1972; Kliegl, Smith, & Baltes, 1990; Rohwer, 1980; Rohwer & Litrownik, 1983; Rohwer, Raines, Eoff, & Wagner, 1977).

Some might expect that the situation would be better if more meaningful and familiar tasks were employed by researchers examining the development of strategies. In recent years Pressley and his colleagues have investigated learning of facts, a more ecologically valid associative task than paired-associate learning (see Pressley, Wood, & Woloshyn, 1990, for a review). Rather than producing a portrait of the competent adult learner, this program of research has instead opened a window on the many ways that adults can be incompetent. One conclusion that Pressley's group has reached is that there are many occasions when adults do not make use of prior knowledge they possess when they are trying to learn factual material, prior knowledge that improves memory when activated in the service of comprehension and coding of facts.

For example, Woloshyn, Willoughby, Wood, and Pressley (1990, Study 2) asked Canadian university students to learn information about universities in Canada, with the materials presented in factually dense text. Each student was presented a paragraph about each of five universities. Two of the instructional conditions in the study are particularly relevant here. In one, the reading control condition, the participants read the material aloud under an instruction to make certain they understood what was being read. In the second, the elaborative interrogation condition, participants were encouraged to relate the facts in the passages to their prior knowledge about the universities and the places where the universities were located. That is, they were asked to try to figure out why it made sense that the fact would be true of the university in question. (Because elaborations are generated as responses to such "why" questions, this procedure has become known as elaborative interrogation.) Knowledge of which schools went with which facts was much better in the elaborative interrogation condition than in the reading control condition, regardless of whether learning was incidental or intentional (which was systematically manipulated within the instructional conditions).

If the information in the text had been related spontaneously to the students' prior knowledge of Canada (i.e., in the reading control condition), no effect of elaborative interrogation should have been obtained. The to-be-learned facts were not fully related to relevant prior knowledge without a prompt to do so. Of course, not using prior knowledge as completely as possible in this fact-learning task contrasts explicitly with other tasks in which prior knowledge is accessed automatically as suggested by Bjorklund (1987; discussed later) and Siegler and Jenkins (1989). Determining when prior knowledge is accessed and used automatically to mediate memory and when it will be accessed and used only with special efforts to do so should be a priority as research on strategies and prior knowledge interactions continue—is it that some tasks are more complex than others? or that only very complete and very well organized knowledge is automatically tapped when attempting to learn "new" related material?

The conclusion that emerges from the work on elaborative strategies in particular is that adults may require instruction if they are to be as strategic as they might be. This is consistent with a recurrent theme in the literature on higher education throughout the 20th century. University students often do not study effectively (see Mathews, 1966, chapter 7, for a review). In fact, almost all university campuses now have study skills programs that are in high demand. Much of the instruction in these programs is of learning strategies, with memory strategies featured prominently alongside comprehension, writing, and problem-solving procedures. For instance, Devine (1987), one of the most sophisticated of the texts devoted to study skills instruction, has an entire chapter on memory, including instruction about representational imagery strategies, verbal mnemonic techniques, and prediction strategies, among others. There are also entire volumes summarizing strategies that have been demonstrated in research to improve adult memory of realistic academic content. Flippo and Caverly (1991) is one that is especially noteworthy because it spells out in detail what is known and what remains to be discovered about teaching strategies to adults.

Thus, there are many strategies, including memory strategies, that adults fail to use routinely, failures apparent to many professionals working with these students. What is extremely interesting is that many cognitive psychologists studying memory development believe otherwise. Consider, for example, Kail's (1984, p. 38) summary of the development of strategic competence:

> . . . a developmental progression was identified consisting of (1) infrequent use of strategies among 6-year-olds, (2) a transition stage from 6 to 9 years, and (3) reasonably mature, sophisticated use of strategies beginning at about age 10, which becomes increasingly "fine-tuned" during adolescence.

By the 1988 edition of his text, Kail (1988, p. 41) modified his view in light of the impressive work during the middle 1980s on use of strategies by preschoolers. Nonetheless, consistent with the perspective of many child researchers, Kail did not revise his views regarding development of strategic competence after age 10 years.

How could it be that cognitive psychologists overlooked the memory strategy deficiencies in adults? One reason may be that cognitive developmental psychologists have historically placed much greater emphasis on competence than performance. Thus, questions of strategic competence were reduced to questions about whether and when people used a strategy at all. Moreover, processes that adults execute certainly and efficiently (e.g., rehearsal during list learning) commanded a great deal of attention from the cognitive developmental research community.

In addition, some of the designs used by memory development researchers probably contributed to a false portrait of competence. For example, consider the Brown and Smiley (1977, 1978; Brown, Smiley, & Lawton, 1978) studies of strategy use during learning of text. These were conducted across a broad age range. Since participants at all developmental levels in these studies processed the same materials, there were confoundings of task difficulty and developmental level. That is, the to-be-learned materials were easier for the older than the younger participants. Adult participants might have been less strategically competent than they seemed in these studies if they had been given more difficult tasks. (For data strongly suggestive of this possibility, see Christopoulos, Rohwer, & Thomas, 1987, and Strage, Tyler, Rohwer, & Thomas, 1987.) Redoing some of the classic work with important confoundings eliminated seems absolutely necessary if a detailed understanding of the development of strategic competence is to be produced. Of course, this will require accepting other confoundings, such as different materials at different developmental levels. Resources for such research seem justified, especially with respect to learning in task situations that are ecologically valid and important, such as learning from text.

Summary

The form, rate, and schedule of age-related progressions in natural strategic competence will vary from strategy to strategy. Some simple strategies, such as attending to a place where a to-be-retrieved object has been hidden, can be detected during early childhood. Familiar settings, tasks, and materials often permit strategy use that would not occur in less familiar settings with novel tasks and foreign materials. Other strategies, including some very effective ones, are not commonly observed even among fairly bright and mature subjects, such as university students. And, of course, there are possibilities in between, which include strategies that seem to develop by the end of adolesence in some students but not others. There is a real variety here that cannot be captured by simple summaries.

The complexity increases when cross-cultural data are considered. In the early 1990s it is clear that many of the memory strategies studied by Western cognitive psychologists are stimulated in part by formal education and other effects of modern industrialized enculturation (Wagner, 1978). What strategies a person uses and when they use them is tied to their personal sociocultural history. (For an elegant short summary of this point, see Kurtz, 1990.) From this perspective, attempting to specify universal age-related strategic competencies makes no sense. It makes little sense from other perspectives either. This will become more apparent as the discussion continues: Whether strategy use occurs often depends on possessing prior knowledge that supports strategy use, metacognition about strategies, and supportive motivational beliefs.

Are Failures to Use Strategies Production Deficiencies?

In the 1960s, Flavell and his colleagues observed that children in the early grade-school years often failed to use cumulative rehearsal strategies. Nonetheless, with brief instruction, these same children could be taught how to apply these strategies in list-learning situations (e.g., Keeney, Cannizzo, & Flavell, 1967), with substantial gains in learning. Similarly, Moely, Olson, Hawles, and Flavell (1969) observed that children in kindergarten through grade 3 often failed to use a sorting-clustering strategy to learn lists containing categorizable items. Just as was the case with rehearsal, training these students to sort and cluster during study improved their list-learning performance dramatically. Outcomes like these provided inspiration for the hypothesis that many of children's memory failures were due to a lack of strategy production and that such deficiencies could be overcome by instruction, the production deficiency hypothesis.

Research Consistent with the Production Deficiency Hypothesis

By the early 1970s, several strands of evidence supported the position that people often fail to produce strategies they could execute if taught how to do so. Three lines of research were particularly relevant: First, many of the failures by non-Westerners to use strategies spontaneously were explained as failures to receive academic instruction in Western-type school settings (Cole & Scribner, 1977; Wagner, 1978). Second, cognitive acquisitions that long had been theorized as impenetrable to instruction (e.g., conservation and other concepts identified in Piagetian theory) proved to be quite teachable. For instance, Rosenthal and Zimmerman (1978) produced a book-length summary of research demonstrating that children's Piagetian conceptual development can be accelerated via instruction, especially through observational learning. Third, there were many studies in which memory strategy instruction had proven successful (see Pressley, Heisel, McCormick, & Nakamura, 1982, for an overview of the massive literature on this topic produced in the 1960s and 1970s). Nonetheless, not all failures to use strategies are simple production deficiencies.

Individual Differences in Susceptibility to Some Forms of Strategy Instruction

Not all strategies that students failed to produce on their own could be taught. For example, imagery generation was shown to be difficult for many children (see Pressley, 1977, 1982, for reviews). In a series of studies, Levin and Pressley and their colleagues produced a substantial body of evidence demonstrating that imagery instructional effects were, at least, limited for preschoolers and children in the early elementary grades. Some of this work was done with paired associates, some with vocabulary and definition pairings, and some with simple prose. With paired associates, the children were instructed to determine a linking relationship for pairs of items (e.g., for apple-arrow, an arrow piercing an apple) and then to make an internal image depicting the relationship (e.g., a mental picture of an arrow piercing an apple). The vocabulary research focussed on the keyword method (Atkinson, 1975; see Pressley, Levin, & Delaney, 1982, for a comprehensive review of research), which involves generating interactional images between definition referents and the referents of words that sound like part of the to-be-learned vocabulary item (i.e., the keyword). Thus, to learn the English word carlin, which means old woman, the learner could construct an image of an old woman driving a car. Imagery instructions for prose learning often consisted of teaching students to construct images representing the content of each sentence in a short story (Guttmann, Levin, & Pressley, 1978).

The results converged for the paired-associate, keyword method, and prose studies. For 3- to 8-year-olds, imagery instructional effects were either not obtained or were obtained only in situations supportive of imagery formation. Thus, second-grade students could generate images to mediate learning of paired associates that involved strong associations between the paired items (e.g., needle-balloon). If the paired items were not so obviously related (e.g., turkey-rock), then imagery instructions were useful only with a fairly slow rate of presentation (i.e., 10 sec per pair; Pressley & Levin, 1977b). Further, Pressley and Levin (1978) found that second-grade students could use the keyword method, but only if they were provided concrete pictures of keyword and definition referents. That is, the method was effective for 7-year-olds only when they were required to do no more than construct an internal linking image. Additionally, Guttmann et al. (1977) demonstrated that 5- to 8-year-old children could not generate representational images of simple prose from scratch but could do so if provided pictures that partially specified the relationships in the text. A number of follow-up studies confirmed these results (Digdon, Pressley, & Levin, 1985; Purkel & Bornstein, 1980; Ruch & Levin, 1979). See Pressley, Borkowski, and Johnson (1987) for an up-to-date review of relevant studies and Kosslyn, Margolis, Barrett, Goldknopf, and Daly (1990) for complementary evidence of imagery generation and manipulation deficiences in 5- to 8-year-olds compared to older children.

What might account for the age-related improvements in the ability to profit from imagery strategy instruction? Pressley and Levin (1978), influenced in part by the theorizing of Pascual-Leone (e.g., 1970), proposed that functional short-term memory capacity might be critical. For instance, their analysis of the keyword strategy was that it required substantial short-term memory to execute: Given a word like carlin and a keyword for it (e.g., car), the learner had to access images of an old woman and a car and a plausible interaction between them, a multiple-component, short-term capacity demanding process. Support for this position comes from observations of better keyword method performance by second-grade children under conditions reducing the short-term capacity demands (i.e., when external pictures of keyword and definition referents were provided).

Almost a decade later, Pressley, Cariglia-Bull, Deane, and Schneider (1987) tested the short-term memory capacity hypothesis again. This study was more analytical and the resulting data more telling. Children in grades 1 through 6 heard complicated sentences specifying relations between concrete elements (e.g., The fat boy ran with the gray balloon). In one condition, participants were instructed to try hard to remember the sentences, since a memory test would follow presentation of all of the sentences. In the second condition, children were instructed to construct images depicting the meaning of the sentence. As in previous research, the imagery versus control difference was significant for students in grades 4, 5, and 6, but not for the younger participants. Much more interesting, however, was that short-term memory capacity differences between students were much more predictive of performances in the imagery instructional condition than in the control condition. In fact, short-term memory was the best predictor of performance in the imagery condition and remained a significant predictor even after age and general ability factors were taken into account. In contrast, short-term memory was of little value in predicting the performances of control children.

Cariglia-Bull and Pressley (1990) replicated the procedures in Pressley, Cariglia-Bull, et al. (1987), except that in this second study the subjects read the sentences rather than heard them. In addition, the study included only children in the last three elementary years (grades 4, 5, and 6). The results obtained in Pressley, Cariglia-Bull, et al.'s (1987) listening situation were replicated with the reading version of the task. Indeed, when the Pressley, Cariglia-Bull, et al. (1987) data were reanalyzed after removing the grade 1, 2, and 3 participants, the correlations in Pressley, Cariglia-Bull, et al. (1987) were practically identical with the correlations in Cariglia-Bull and Pressley (1990). In both of these studies, short-term capacity was an important predictor in the imagery instructional condition but not in the control condition.

Case's (1985) analysis of cognitive developmental progression advanced the idea that age-related increases in cognitive competence are often due to age-related increases in functional short-term capacity. Our guess, based partially on Case's theory, is that short-term capacity differences between learners may predict successful use of a number of strategies.

Unfortunately, this hypothesis has not been evaluated vigorously for any memory strategy except for imagery. (See, however, Guttentag, 1984; Guttentag, Ornstein, & Siemens, 1987; and Kee & Davies, 1988, 1990, 1991, for demonstrations linking spontaneous increased use of capacity-demanding strategies with increases in developmental level [and hence, functional capacity].) The methods developed in Cariglia-Bull and Pressley's research on imagery could be adapted easily in order to evaluate how individual differences in short-term memory capacity affect use of other strategies.

Summary

Learners often fail to use a memory strategy on their own, although they may be able to execute it with good results when prompted to do so. There are many studies in the literature in which one group is taught a strategy and a control group is not, with subsequent differences in performance favoring the instructed group. Nonetheless, such effects are not always obtained. There is great value in understanding individual differences that permit some learners to use particular strategies profitably given little prompting and preclude others from realizing strategy instructional benefits at all. In the best of all possible instructional worlds, strategy teaching would be tailored to student abilities (e.g., Cronbach & Snow, 1977). Before that could be possible, however, it is necessary to know which abilities count with respect to which strategies. Short-term memory capacity is one that does matter, at least with some strategies. That it does provides support for theories positing capacity as a critical determinant of cognitive competence. Memory development researchers should be stimulated more than they have been in the past to pay attention to lower order competencies and structures as determinants of higher order functioning.

Improved Strategic Competence or Increases in Accessible Knowledge?

David Bjorklund (1985, 1987) is the most research-productive proponent of the position that at least some age-related improvements in memory performance are due to changes in the extent and accessibility of the knowledge base. This is consistent with the general perspective that many developmental improvements in performance are mediated by an increasingly complete, organized, and accessible knowledge base (e.g., see Siegler & Jenkins, 1989, for one of the most empirically defensible and complete of these models). Bjorklund's research on this problem has primarily involved learning of categorizable lists of items. The classic finding is that the amount recalled increases with increasing age but, more critically, the organization of recall also improves. Better organization means that older students are more likely to recall items from the same category together than are younger children, even when same-category items are not blocked together at the time of study. The traditional interpretation of this finding was that the more organized recall of older students reflects the segregation of items into their categories as an approach to study (Moely, 1977). An alternative hypothesis, first advanced by Lange (1973, 1978), is that if reorganization at study does increase with development, it has little to do with the development of strategies. Rather, developmental increases in recall and organization of categorizable lists may occur because of age-related increases in the size and organization of the knowledge base (see especially Rabinowitz & McAuley, 1990). The increases in the knowledge base increase the likelihood of learners making associations between category members on study lists. Another possibility is that the developmental increases in recall organization are produced by developmental improvements in retrieval processes, ones mediated by the expanding knowledge base. That is, as each item is recalled, there is the possibility of automatic association to other items in the category. Items from the study list that are in the same category are especially likely to be cued, since they were activated in the learner's consciousness during the study trial.

Bjorklund's work (and that of others) on recall of categorizable lists is not (and could not be) definitively informative about questions of strategic versus automatic knowledge-base mediation. With this task, there is no pattern of outcomes that would unambiguously pinpoint memory improvements as caused by use of intentional associational and organizational strategy use rather than automatic knowledge-mediated associations and reorganizations, a point Bjorklund concedes (Bjorklund & Buchanen, 1989, p. 453). (See the earlier discussion of Bjorklund and Harnishfeger, 1990, for their view of the criticality of intentional rather than automatic use if strategies.)

Nonetheless, there are some patterns that Bjorklund believes more likely reflect intentional strategy use than automatic mediation of learning. One is the following: After study of a randomly organized list of categorizable items, words from the same category are recalled together with shorter latencies between recall of same-category items and longer latencies between recall of different-category items. Thus, suppose a study list was composed of four items from each of categories A, B, C. . . . Recall might be as follows: B1, B3, B4, B2, A4, A3, A2, A1, C4, C2 . . . with much shorter latencies between recall of B1 and B3, B3 and B4, A4 and A3, A3 and A2, and so on than between recall of B2 and A4, A1 and C4. But what if there was automatic reorganization at study because of automatic associations between same-category items rather than deliberate strategic reorganization? Would that not produce category-clustered recall with rapid recall once a category was entered?

And also produce lower within-category latencies than between-category latencies? The classic ad hoc explanatory dilemma here should be obvious. Many patterns of clustering/latency outcomes could be explained either by intentional strategy use or by automatic knowledge-base mediation.

Even so, Bjorklund's general conclusion that good memory is often due to automatic, knowledge-related processing rather than more deliberate processing of to-be-learned materials is consistent with important theoretical positions, such as variations of schema theory (Anderson & Pearson, 1984; Schank, 1982), and is undoubtedly correct. No reasonable memory researcher could fail to be impressed with the correlations between prior knowledge and performance, associations with performance that are greater than those produced by other variables including ones long held in high regard as predictors of cognitive performance (e.g., IQ; see Schneider & Körkel, 1989; Schneider, Körkel, & Weinert, 1989, 1990). Automatic knowledge-base mediation can explain a number of findings in the memory literature better than intentional strategic processing, including the following examples: (a) Associations that are highly meaningful (ranch-cowboy) are easier to learn than more arbitrary associations (ranch-floor) as shown by Kee and Davies (1988, 1990, 1991) and Rohwer, Rabinowitz, and Dronkers (1982). This is true even when equal attention is given to easy-to-relate and hard-to-relate items, as when young grade-school children, who do not differentially study easy- and hard-to-learn associations, are the subjects (DuFresne & Kobasigawa, 1989); (b) People learn more new content from domains with which they are familiar (Chiesi, Spilich, & Voss, 1979; Schneider, Körkel, & Weinert, 1987); (c) Prior knowledge related to to-be-learned information is often reported to have been presented as part of to-be-learned materials (e.g., Brown, Smiley, Day, Townsend, & Lawton, 1977); (d) Scenes comprising elements in meaningful relation to one another are much easier to remember than disorganized scenes comprising the same elements (see Mandler, 1984, for a review).

Given that relating new content to prior knowledge can facilitate acquisition, some argue (Hirsch, 1987; Ravitch & Finn, 1987) that improving the knowledge base should be the focus of educational interventions. One problem with these positions, however, is that the knowledge base is not always used to maximum advantage in the absence of instructions about how to exploit it. For instance, without elaborative interrogation instructions (discussed earlier; e.g., Woloshyn et al., 1990), adults often fail to use their knowledge to full advantage to mediate their learning. Thus, even though development of the knowledge base is a sensible way to increase future learning, it may not maximize future learning unless learners are also taught how this can mediate their academic performances.

In short, whether the knowledge base automatically mediates learning depends on what is being learned. For some tasks and materials that are strongly related to prior knowledge, there is no need for strategy instruction, for there will be automatic associations to the knowledge base that will produce good memory of to-be-learned materials. On other occasions, relations between the knowledge base and to-be-learned materials will exist but the learners will not autonomously exploit those relationships. Strategies, such as the elaborative interrogation procedure, that encourage relating the to-be-learned information to the knowledge base are useful on those occasions. When associations between the knowledge base and to-be-learned content are nonexistent or less obvious, other strategies can be helpful, strategies that depend less on prior knowledge related to the to-be-learned content.

If all of this seems vague, it is. Fifteen years of research on knowledge by strategy interactions has produced incomplete understanding of knowledge and strategy relationships. This is largely because the structure of prior knowledge is so poorly understood (see Ornstein, 1990, for commentary) but also because so much of the effort has been expended on a task (categorizable list learning) that cannot produce unambiguous conclusions about knowledge and strategy relationships.

More positively, different paradigms and materials have provided a clearer understanding of strategy versus knowledge effects as well as strategy-knowledge trade-offs and coordinations. For instance, researchers like Siegler (e.g., 1988, 1990) are making progress in mapping out some simple knowledge bases. From the perspective of this chapter, what is most impressive about his work is that it has proven possible to specify when the knowledge base will mediate performance and when strategies will do so. For example, if a young child is presented an addition problem (e.g., 9 + 7), he or she will normally rely on the knowledge base if the math fact is overlearned and hence readily retrievable from long-term memory. Children use problem-solving strategies, such as counting on fingers, counting up, or using external manipulatives, only if the math fact is not in long-term memory. (The only exceptions to this generalization are extreme perfectionists who rely on strategies too much [Siegler, 1988].)

Research on strategy use during the study of text is also beginning to focus on differential strategy use as a function of the relation of text to prior knowledge. Pritchard (1990) offered an important study of this problem. Sixty grade-11 students, 30 from the U. S. and 30 from a South Pacific island (Palau), read two types of texts, ones containing cultural schema appropriate for the U. S. and ones including Paluan cultural schema. The readers thought aloud as they read, with the think alouds subsequently scored for strategy reports. Although the results were far too complicated to report in detail here (e.g., 22 different types of strategies were reported as used by the participants), there were some key differences in strategy use as a function of familiarity with the cultural schema in the text. Both rereadings and paraphrasings occurred more often with the culturally unfamiliar texts. In contrast, with culturally familiar texts, readers were more likely to relate what they were reading to previous text and to previous experiences, more likely to extrapolate from and speculate beyond the information presented in the text, and more likely to use their understanding of the prose format to interpret the text. In short, strategic processing was very different when the text content was related to prior knowledge.

Because Pressley and his associates view the theoretical issues being explored by Bjorklund and others as so critical to understanding the nature of sophisticated cognition, they are devoting considerable resources to this problem. Their initial study suggests that nonstrategic, automatic, and strategic use of knowledge can be separated. Woloshyn, Pressley, and Schneider (1992) presented Canadian and German adults with lists of facts about 11 Canadian provinces and 11 German states. In the elaborative interrogation condition, participants were required to answer "why" questions about each fact when it was presented for study (e.g., Why is Prince Edward Island the province with the highest percentage of its population of British ancestry? Why is Berlin the state with the highest percentage of Turkish workers?). Participants in a reading-to-understand condition read the facts with the goal of understanding each one. Both elaborative interrogation and reading-to-understand subjects subsequently took a test requiring them to match facts to the states or provinces to which they pertained. The most critical outcomes to consider here were that elaborative interrogation consistently facilitated performance. Even so, elaborative interrogation in the absence of prior knowledge (e.g., when Canadians processed German facts, when Germans processed Canadian facts) did not produce learning that was anywhere near the level of performance of reading-to-understand participants who possessed prior knowledge. Thus, when Canadian subjects used elaborative interrogation to learn German facts, they remembered 7.05 of them out of 66 on the test, which was significantly better than when Canadians read the German facts (mean in that condition = 4.60 remembered). Nonetheless, when Germans merely read the German facts, they remembered 17.20 on the posttest. Germans studying German facts in the elaborative interrogation condition remembered 23.40 items. The corresponding pattern with Canadian facts was identical: Reading-to-understand Germans studying Canadian facts remembered 5.80 items; elaborative interrogation Germans remembered 11.10 Canadian facts; Canadians reading Canadian facts remembered 17.10 of them; elaborative interrogation Canadians remembered 26.25 items. In short, there were unambiguous effects of automatic use of prior knowledge in this study and unambiguous effects of use of the elaborative interrogation strategy, with the effects of automatic knowledge mediation and strategic mediation fully separable.

More work like Pritchard's (1990) study, Siegler's research program (1988, 1990), and Woloshyn et al.'s (1992) analysis of automatic knowledge versus instructed strategic mediation is required if strategy by knowledge base interactions and strategy and knowledge trade-offs are to be understood completely. The importance of both automatic knowledge mediation and strategic processes in contemporary models of cognition provides great motivation for more such work.

What About the Durability of Strategy Instruction Effects?

Isn't that the rub, that strategies that are taught often are not maintained and are rarely generalized? Teaching students how to execute the processes that comprise a strategy in no way guarantees that they will use these processes when it is appropriate to do so. Learners sometimes fail to use strategies in situations and with materials similar to those present when they were taught the procedure originally. That is, there are sometimes maintenance failures. Transfer failures occur when learners sometimes do not apply the strategies they know to new situations and materials even when their use could be helpful.

Why are maintenance and transfer so uncertain? Sometimes students simply do not recognize that a procedure they know could be applicable in another situation. If this is the case, they can sometimes apply the procedure given gentle hints to do so (Gick & Holyoak, 1980, 1983; Ross, 1984). Sometimes apparent maintenance and transfer failures actually reflect student transformation of a strategy to the point that it is no longer recognizable or effective (see Harris, 1988, for elaboration of this point). Sometimes students do not continue to use a strategy because they do not like it, either not valuing the gains it produces or feeling the gains are not worth the effort required to carry out the procedure (e.g., Rabinowitz, Friedman, & Cohen, 1991). This list of reasons could go on and on.

Although we now recognize the many possible reasons for maintenance and transfer failure, it was not always so. In fact, much effort in the 1980s was in pursuit of magic bullets, one or a few potent elements that, when added to instruction, would dramatically increase maintenance and/or transfer. Much of this effort was stimulated by the general hypothesis that maintenance and transfer failures were due largely to incomplete metacognitive understanding of strategies (e.g., Borkowski, 1985; Brown, Bransford, Ferrara, & Campione, 1983). Thus, it was hypothesized that maintenance failures reflected lack of understanding of a strategy's effects, especially how its execution promoted performance. This stimulated experiments in a number of laboratories (see Pressley, Borkowski, & O'Sullivan, 1984, 1985, for reviews) that included at least two types of conditions, one in which a strategy was taught and one in which it was taught with some metacognitive embellishment—specifically, the value of the strategy was emphasized during instruction. The result was always the same. Maintenance was more likely when instruction included information about the value of the strategy. Thus, these studies produced evidence favoring the metacognitive hypothesis.

It was assumed, however, that more was needed to achieve transfer. Knowledge of how to self-regulate use of strategies and awareness of when and where trained strategies might be applicable (Brown et al., 1983) were considered important. Thus, interventions (e.g., reciprocal teaching; Palincsar & Brown, 1984) were devised that included a great deal of emphasis on self-instruction and self-monitoring (Meichenbaum, 1977) with transfer gains produced by these treatments attributed to the self-regulative components (Brown et al., 1983). Studies like O'Sullivan and Pressley (1984) appeared in which a strategy was trained and information about when and where to use it was either included or omitted from instruction. Receiving such information proved critical to transfer.

Despite success in producing controlled studies testing hypotheses about transfer, we did not learn how to teach strategies so that transfer was long-term and robust. The time seemed right for trying an alternative research tactic. Pressley and his colleagues have done that by identifying elementary schools in which strategy instruction leads to discernible achievement gains. Memory strategies are taught in these schools, although always as part of a repertoire of methods for enhancing chomprehension, composition, and problem solving. Using a number of qualitative approaches, including traditional case studies (Pressley, Gaskins, Wile, Cunicelli, & Sheridan, 1991), analyses based on Strauss's (1987) method of constant comparison (El-Dinary, Brown, Pressley, Schuder, & Bergman, 1992), discourse analyses (Gaskins, Anderson, Pressley, Cunicelli, & Satlow, 1992), and extensive and intensive interviews (Pressley, Gaskins, Cunicelli, et al., 1991), Pressley's group has been building a data-driven theory of teaching for transfer (see Pressley, El-Dinary, Gaskins et al., 1992; Strauss, 1987).

The emerging theory is that effective strategy teaching is long term, with strategy curricula presented over the course of at least several school years. Teachers model strategies and encourage students to model them also. Strategy instruction is not an add-on but rather is an integral part of the ongoing curriculum. Strategies are used to facilitate learning of regular content and completion of tasks that occur in all elementary classrooms (e.g., reading of content-area texts, such as those used for social studies and science). In these schools, strategies are fully explained, with reexplanations offered on an as-needed basis while students practice the processes they are learning. The advantages of using strategies and the learning gains they produce are reiterated often and made as obvious as possible (e.g., by encouraging students to compare their performances before and after starting to use strategies). Instruction and practice occur with a variety of materials and often across content areas. There is a lot of positive reinforcement for using strategies and explicit attempts to promote high academic self-esteem when students do well (especially when they do well using strategies; see Clifford, 1984). Students are encouraged to try to generalize the procedures they are learning (El-Dinary et al., 1992). And perhaps most salient of all, students and teachers interact cooperatively and respectfully at all times as they construct an understanding of strategies and the content covered in the curriculum (see Harris & Pressley, 1991, for an analysis).

In sum, we are coming to a more complete theory of how to promote strategy generalization than the ones predominating in the 1980s (although see Deshler, Alley, Warner, & Schumaker, 1981, for a model of special education that shares many features with the emerging theory). Memory theorists who emphasize the socialization of cognition (see Fivush & Hudson, 1990, for a variety of examples) will undoubtedly be impressed by the highly social, interactive nature of the effective strategy instruction we have observed. Consistent with direct explanation theories of instruction (e.g., Duffy & Roehler, 1987), good strategy teachers directly explain powerful strategies to their students and provide extensive reexplanations as students practice strategies, commentary that touches on all of the metacognitive and motivational elements of good strategy instruction overviewed here. Good intellectual socialization is extremely complicated, involving the development of repertoires of effective strategies that can be used in coordination with the knowledge base (see Pressley, Borkowski, & Schneider, 1989). There is scaffolding and guided discovery (Vygotsky, 1978; Wood, Bruner, & Ross, 1976). As our work and that of others on the nature of effective real-world strategy instruction continues in the 1990s, the many dimensions of good strategy instruction will become clearer.

Once a grounded theory is achieved, it will be time to return to experimental work to evaluate the theory. Any experimental test of such teaching must take place over a long period of time, for the evolving model explicitly specifies that sophisticated understanding of strategies and use of a repertoire of strategic techniques requires years of instruction. That means that even one or two true experimental tests of the approach will require enormous resources. Such experiments are critical if we are to know definitively whether self-regulated use of memory strategies can be taught so that children and adults use the strategies consistently to meet their memory needs.

Isn't A Lot of It Motivation?

Even if a person knows a strategy, that doesn't mean they will have the motivation to use it. That strategy use is very much dependent on motivation is reflected by the inclusion of motivation in most contemporary models of strategy use. Even more important, research on motivational contributions to strategy use has begun in earnest. For instance, although it has been known for some time that some children are more mastery oriented than others (e.g., see Nicholls, 1989), whether such individual differences are related to use of memory strategies per se has been investigated in Garrett Lange's laboratory in recent years. His studies, conducted with preschoolers and children up to 7 years of age, have involved studying lists of objects for subsequent recall. Unfortunately, there has been little support in this research for the hypothesis that academic mastery motivation is linked to strategy use. The correlations between preschoolers' academic mastery and strategy use were very low in Lange, MacKinnon, and Nida (1989) and academic mastery did not predict strategy use in Lange, Guttentag, and Nida (1990) once other potential predictors, such as metacognition about strategies, had been considered.

Other examinations of motivational effects on strategy use have provided more support for the role of motivation in strategy regulation. For instance, we provided earlier discussion of the many experiments in which information about the utility of a strategy has either been included or omitted in instruction. The consistent finding was that providing information about utility increased continued use of the instructed strategies. An obvious interpretation is that knowing a strategy improves task performance increases the motivation to use the strategy.

Pressley, Borkowski, and O'Sullivan (1984, 1985) argued that a crucial part of instruction is getting students to attribute whatever benefits accrue from instruction to use of strategies they are learning (cf. Clifford, 1984). That is, rather than following Weiner's (e.g., 1979) framework and encouraging students to attribute improved performance to effort alone, students should be encouraged to attribute success to effort expended in particular ways, effort expended through strategies well matched to task requirements. Borkowski and his associates (e.g., Borkowski, Weyhing, & Carr, 1988; Reid & Borkowski, 1987) have been engaged in research specifically aimed at evaluating this hypothesis. They have been conducting experiments in which students are taught a strategy or set of strategies and information about how strategic effort improves performance either provided or omitted. (For a description of a modal study, see Borkowski et al., 1990, pp. 74–76; Borkowski & Turner, 1990, also provides an informative summary). Maintenance and/or generalization is then tested. To date, such studies have yielded support for the hypothesis that durable use of strategies is produced by encouraging students to attribute their successes to the use of strategies matched to task requirements.

We are optimistic that the prominence of motivation and strategies in today's most important models of self-regulated learning will continue to stimulate a great deal of additional research on the ways motivation and strategy use are related. See Borkowski et al. (1990) for a review of the many potential relationships between motivation and strategy use.

Summing Up: What We Now Believe About Natural Development of Memory Strategies and Development of Strategic Competence via Instruction

There is some debate about the nature of cognitive strategies, particularly whether they must be used intentionally or can be deployed and executed automatically and out of consciousness. These definitional debates may be merely rhetorical, however, having little effect on the study of natural strategy use and strategy instruction, which continue to be the two most prominent general directions in the study of strategies.

Natural Use of Strategies

Some popular summaries once provided a simplified developmental summary of natural strategy use. It went like this: Preschoolers do not use strategies or use rudimentary versions of them, perhaps inconsistently at that. Use of strategies increases during the grade-school years, with the progression mostly completed by age 10 or 11 years. Adolescence to adulthood involves fine-tuning of strategies rather than a qualitative shift.

Simplified is a charitable evaluation of such summaries. They were mostly informed by developmental research on rehearsal strategies conducted between 1966 and 1975. More recent research on other strategies makes clear that the situation is much more complex. Some strategies can be observed in very young children; others are never used by anyone in the absence of explicit instruction. Some are used increasingly during the grade-school years; some are used increasingly between ages 5 and 17 years. Whether a person naturally uses strategies varies with their socioeducational background as well, with use of many strategies identified in Western cultures only appearing in people who have experienced Western-style education.

In recent years, some of the age-related improvements in memory that were once attributed to development of strategic competence are now understood as mediated by age-related increases in the extent, organization, and accessibility of the knowledge base. Although there are very good reasons to do all possible to enrich the knowledge base in general, we do not believe that this will maximize cognitive performance, for it has proven easy to demonstrate that people often do not use the prior knowledge they possess to mediate cognitive tasks. Thus, one class of strategies that students should be taught involves consistent use of their prior knowledge.

Strategy Instruction

The production deficiency hypothesis specified that failure to use strategies is an executive problem; that is, people can execute many strategies that they do not deploy on their own. Although this claim is far from universally true, many times it holds.

Given that some people cannot execute some strategies profitably, understanding who can execute what is an important direction in strategy instruction research. One effort to do so involves determining when basic capacity differences between learners predict differences in susceptibility to strategy instruction. This research is critical given theories of general cognitive functioning based on individual differences in basic and functional capacities (e.g., neo-Piagetian theory; Case, 1985).

Teaching a person how to carry out a process is one thing; teaching them how to carry out a process so that they know when, where, and how to deploy it and are motivated to do so is quite another. We learned a lot during the last decade about why maintenance/generalization failures occur and how to increase the likelihood of continued use of strategies. See, for example, Ghatala, Levin, Pressley, and Goodwin (1986) for an example of how young children's continued use of strategies depends on them noting the effects of the strategy, making the attribution that the effects were due to use of the strategy, and realizing that this attribution should be used in making future strategy choices (for related work, see Ghatala, Levin, Pressley, & Lodico, 1985; Lodico, Ghatala, Levin, Pressley, & Bell, 1983).

Our current work and that of our colleagues is aimed at developing a theory of teaching for transfer from the ground up (Glaser & Strauss, 1967). Extended, multicomponent instruction is the approach we have observed in schools deploying strategy instruction. We hope for a long-term experimental evaluation of the impact of such instruction on acquisition and use of a variety of memory strategies.

Closing Comments

Many who identify with nonstrategic factors in cognition have tried to make the case that strategies are not as important to maximally efficient cognition as strategy researchers have proposed; others have tried to make the case that strategy instruction will not make much of an impact on long-term cognitive functioning. The former point is supported, for instance, by demonstrations of good memory that are certainly mediated more by the knowledge base than by strategies (e.g., memory of meaningful chess positions by child chess experts; Chi, 1978). The latter point is sometimes defended by pointing to strategy transfer failures.

Even so, there are many strategies, memory and otherwise, that do improve a variety of performances when people either use them on their own or are taught to employ them (see Pressley & Associates, 1990). Our understanding of how to teach these strategies so they are used generally and appropriately is improving, with strategy instruction increasingly taking capacity, metacognition, world knowledge, and motivational factors into account. Since our view is that these four factors combine with strategies to determine much of cognitive competence, studying interrelations between these components should continue to be a high priority for researchers. For theoretical elaboration of this point, see Pressley, Borkowski, and Schneider (1989).

We recognize, of course, the challenge for quantitatively oriented researchers to design studies that are sensitive to so many factors. The approach to date usually has been to study two factors at a time (e.g., strategies vs. prior knowledge, strategy use as determined by capacity), for more ambitious designs are simply unwieldy. Of course, this is not a completely satisfactory approach in that comprehensive discussions of the effects of these components can only be made by collapsing over diverse studies with much guesswork required in the process. There is a methodological option, however, that permits simultaneous consideration of many factors, an option that we have elected in our recent research on teaching of strategies in classrooms. That is, qualitative methods can be used, a particularly apt tactic when attempting to develop a theory of how multiple determinants of behavior combine to produce performance (see Lincoln & Guba, 1985; Strauss, 1987). Our gauge is that the time is right to supplement the quantitative, deductive literature on memory strategies with qualitative, inductive studies. We are enthusiastic about these qualitative methods in light of our recent successes in identifying a framework about how to teach for generalization, a framework that eluded us (and others) who had evaluated hupotheses about generalization using traditional experimental methods. (For descriptions of our qualitative research that was sensitive to multiple potential determinants of generalization following instruction, see Pressley, El-Dinary, Gaskins, Schuder, Bergman, Almasi, & Brown, 1992). Qualitative work has a high potential for identifying new hypotheses about strategy development and strategy instruction that can subsequently be tested in quantitative deductive research. Although we in no way eschew the quantitative, experimental tactics with which we have so long identified, there is a growing understanding on our part that rigorous qualitative analyses might go a long way in moving forward the study of strategy development.

Acknowledgment. Writing of this chapter was supported by a grant to the first author from the General Research Board of the University of Maryland and by a University of Maryland Graduate School Fellowship to the second author.

References

Anderson, R.C., & Pearson, P.D. (1984). A schema-theoretic view of basic processes in reading comprehension. In P.D. Pearson, M. Kamil, R. Barr, & P. Mosenthal (Eds.), *Handbook of reading research* (pp. 255–291). New York: Longman.

Ashcraft, M.H. (1990). Strategic processing in children's mental arithmetic: A review and proposal. In D.F. Bjorklund (Ed.), *Children's strategies: Contemporary views of cognitive development* (pp. 185–211). Hillsdale, NJ: Erlbaum.

Atkinson, R.C. (1975). Mnemotechnics in second-language learning. *American Psychologist*, *30*, 821–828.

Baker-Ward, L., Ornstein, P.A., & Holden, D.J. (1984). The expression of memorization in early childhood. *Journal of Experimental Child Psychology*, *37*, 555–575.

Barclay, C.R. (1979). The executive control of mnemonic activity. *Journal of Experimental Child Psychology*, *27*, 262–276.

Bebko, J. (1979). Can recall differences among children be attributed to rehearsal effects? *Canadian Journal of Psychology*, *33*, 96–105.

Bebko, J. (1984). Memory and rehearsal characteristics of profoundly deaf children. *Journal of Experimental Child Psychology*, *38*, 415–428.

Bebko, J.M., & McKinnon, E.E. (1990). The language experience of deaf children: The relation to spontaneous rehearsal in a memory task. *Child Development*, *61*, 1744–1752.

Bjorklund, D.F. (1985). The role of conceptual knowledge in the development of organization in children's memory. In C.J. Brainerd & M. Pressley (Eds.), *Basic processes in memory development: Progress in cognitive development research* (pp. 103–142). New York: Springer-Verlag.

Bjorklund, D.F. (1987). How age changes in knowledge base contribute to the development of children's memory: An interpretive review. *Developmental Review*, *7*, 93–130.

Bjorklund, D.F. (Ed.) (1990). *Children's strategies: Contemporary views of cognitive development*. Hillsdale, NJ: Erlbaum.

Bjorklund, D.F., & Buchanen, J.J. (1989). Developmental and knowledge base differences in the acquisition and extension of a memory strategy. *Journal of Experimental Child Psychology*, *48*, 451–471.

Bjorklund, D.F., & Harnishfeger, K.K. (1990). Children's strategies: Their definition and origins. In D.F. Bjorklund (Ed.), *Children's strategies: Contemporary views of cognitive development* (pp. 309–323). Hillsdale, NJ: Erlbaum.

Borkowski, J.G. (1985). Signs of intelligence: Strategy, generalization, and metacognition. In S.R. Yussen (Ed.), *The growth of reflection in children* (pp. 105–144). Orlando, FL: Academic Press.

Borkowski, J.G., Carr, M., Rellinger, E.A., & Pressley, M. (1990). Self-regulated strategy use: Interdependence of metacognition, attributions, and self-esteem. In B.F. Jones (Ed.), *Dimensions of thinking: Review of research* (pp. 53–92). Hillsdale, NJ: Erlbaum.

Borkowski, J.G., & Turner, L.A. (1990). Transituational characteristics of metacognition. In W. Schneider & F.E. Weinert (Eds.), *Interactions among aptitudes, strategies, and knowledge in cognitive performance* (pp. 159–176). New York: Springer-Verlag.

Borkowski, J.G., Weyhing, R.S., & Carr, M. (1988). Effects of attributional retraining on strategy based reading comprehension in LD children. *Journal of Educational Psychology*, *80*, 46–53.

Bower, G.H. (1972). Mental imagery and associative learning. In L.Gregg (Ed.), *Cognition in learning and memory* (pp. 51–87). New York: Wiley.

Brainerd, C.J., & Reyna, V.F. (1990). Gist is the grist: Fuzzy-trace theory and the new intuitionism. *Developmental Review*, *10*, 3–47.

Brainerd, C.J., Reyna, V.F., Howe, M.L., & Kingma, J. (1990). The development of forgetting and reminiscence. *Monographs of the Society for Research in Child Development*, *55* (Nos. 3–4).

Brown, A.L., Bransford, J.D., Ferrara, R.A., & Campione, J.C. (1983). Learning, remembering, and understanding. In J.H. Flavell & E.M. Markman (Eds.), *Handbook of child psychology, Vol. III, Cognitive development* (pp. 77–166). New York: Wiley.

Brown, A.L., & Smiley, S.S. (1977). Rating the importance of structural units of prose passages: A problem of metacognitive development. *Child Development*, *48*, 1–8.

Brown, A.L., & Smiley, S.S. (1978). The development of strategies for studying texts. *Child Development*, *49*, 1076–1088.

Brown, A.L., Smiley, S.S., Day, J.D., Townsend, M.A.R., & Lawton, S.C. (1977). Intrusion of a thematic idea in children's comprehension and retention of stories. *Child Development*, *48*, 1454–1466.

Brown, A.L., Smiley, S.S., & Lawton, S.C. (1978). The effects of experience on the selection of suitable retrieval cues for studying texts. *Child Development*, *49*, 829–835.

Butterfield, E.C., & Belmont, J.M. (1977). Assessing and improving the executive cognitive functions of mentally retarded people. In I. Bialar & M. Sternlicht (Eds.), *Psychological issues in mental retardation* (pp. 277–318). New York: Psychological Dimensions.

Cariglia-Bull, T., & Pressley, M. (1990). Short-term memory differences between children predict imagery effects when sentences are read. *Journal of Experimental Child Psychology*, *49*, 384–398.

Carr, M., Kurtz, B.E., Schneider, W., Turner, L.A., & Borkowski, J.G. (1989). Strategy acquisition and transfer: Environmental influences on metacognitive development. *Developmental Psychology*, *25*, 765–771.

Case, R. (1985). *Intellectual development. Birth to adulthood.* Orlando, FL: Academic Press.

Chi, M.T.H. (1978). Knowledge structure and memory development. In R.S. Siegler (Ed.), *Children's thinking: What develops?* (pp. 73–96). Hillsdale, NJ: Erlbaum.

Chiesi, L., Spilich, G.J., & Voss, J.F. (1979). Acquisition of domain-related information in relation to high and low domain knowledge. *Journal of Verbal Learning and Verbal Behavior*, *18*, 257–273.

Christopoulos, J.P., Rohwer, W.D., Jr., & Thomas, J.W. (1987). Grade level differences in students' study activities as a function of course characteristics. *Contemporary Educational Psychology*, *12*, 303–323.

Churchland, P.S. (1986). *Neurophilosophy: Toward a unified science of the mind/brain.* Cambridge, MA: MIT Press.

Clifford, M.M. (1984). Thoughts on a theory of constructive failure. *Educational Psychologist*, *19*, 108–120.

Cole, M., & Scribner, S. (1977). Cross-cultural studies of memory and cognition. In R.V. Kail & J.W. Hagen (Eds.), *Perspectives on the development of memory and cognition* (pp. 239–271). Hillsdale, NJ: Erlbaum.

Cronbach, L.J., & Snow, R.E. (1977). *Aptitudes and instructional methods: A handbook for research on interactions*. New York: Irvington.

Deloache, J.S., Cassidy, D.J., & Brown, A.L. (1985). Precursors of mnemonic strategies in very young children's memory. *Child Development*, *56*, 125–137.

Deshler, D.D., Alley, G.R., Warner, M.M., & Schumaker, J.B. (1981). Instuctional practices for promoting skill acquisition and generalization in severely learning disabled adolescents. *Learning Disability Quarterly*, *4*, 415–421.

Deshmukh, K., Turner, L., Kurtz, B., & Borkowski, J.G. (1989, March). *Cognitive and metacognitive development in Maharashtrian children: The impact of schooling*. Presented at the annual meeting of the American Educational Research Association, San Francisco.

Devine, T.G. (1987). *Teaching study skills: A guide for teachers*. New York: Allyn & Bacon.

Digdon, N., Pressley, M., & Levin, J.R. (1985). Preschoolers' learning when pictures do not tell the whole story. *Educational Communication and Technology Journal*, *33*, 139–145.

Duffy, G.G., & Roehler, L.R. (1987). Improving reading instruction through the use of responsive elaboration. *The Reading Teacher*, *40*, 514–521.

Dufresne, A., & Kobasigawa, A. (1989). Children's spontaneous allocation of study time: Differential and sufficient aspects. *Journal of Experimental Child Psychology*, *47*, 274–296.

El-Dinary, P.B., Brown, R., Pressley, M., Schuder, T., & Bergman, J.L., et al. (1992). *A descriptive study of transactional strategies instruction*. College Park, MD: University of Maryland, College of Education.

Fivush, R., & Hudson, J.A. (Eds.) (1990). *Knowing and remembering in young children*. Cambridge, England: Cambridge University Press.

Flavell, J.H. (1970). Developmental studies of mediated memory. In H.W. Reese & L.P. Lipsitt (Eds.), *Advances in child development and behavior* (pp. 181–211). New York: Academic Press.

Flavell, J.H., Beach, D.H., & Chinsky, J.M. (1966). Spontaneous verbal rehearsal in a memory task as a function of age. *Child Development*, *37*, 283–299.

Flippo, R.F., & Caverly, D.C. (1991). *Teaching reading and study strategies*. Newark, DE: International Reading Association.

Gaskins, I.W., Anderson, R.C., Pressley, M., Cunicelli, E.A., & Satlow, E. (1992). The moves and cycles of cognitive process instruction. *Elementary School Journal*, *93*.

Ghatala, E.S., Levin, J.R., Pressley, M., & Goodwin, D. (1986). A componential analysis of the effects of derived and supplied strategy-utility information on children's strategy selections. *Journal of Experimental Child Psychology*, *41*, 76–92.

Ghatala, E.S., Levin, J.R., Pressley, M., & Lodico, M.G. (1985). Training cognitive strategy monitoring in children. *American Educational Research Journal*, *22*, 199–216.

Gick, M.L., & Holyoak, K.J. (1980). Analogical problem solving. *Cognitive Psychology*, *12*, 306–355.
Gick, M.L., & Holyoak, K.J. (1983). Schema induction and analogical transfer. *Cognitive Psychology*, *15*, 1–38.
Glaser, B.G., & Strauss, A.L. (1967). *The discovery of grounded theory: Strategies for qualitative research*. Chicago: Aldine.
Guttentag, R.E. (1984). The mental effort requirement of cumulative rehearsal: A developmental study. *Journal of Experimental Child Psychology*, *37*, 92–106.
Guttentag, R.E., Ornstein, P.A., & Siemens, L. (1987). Children's spontaneous rehearsal: Transitions in strategy acquisition. *Cognitive Development*, *2*, 307–326.
Guttmann, J., Levin, J.R., & Pressley, M. (1977). Pictures, partial pictures, and young children's oral prose learning. *Journal of Educational Psychology*, *69*, 473–480.
Harris, K.R. (1988, April). *What's wrong with strategy intervention research: Intervention integrity*. Presented at the annual meeting of the American Educational Research Association, New Orleans.
Harris, K.R., & Pressley, M. (1991). The constructivistic nature of cognitive strategy instruction. *Exceptional Children*, *57*, 392–404.
Hasher, L., & Zacks, R.T. (1979). Automatic and effortful processes in memory. *Journal of Experimental Psychology: General*, *108*, 356–388.
Hirsch, E.D. (1987). *Cultural literacy: What every American needs to know*. Boston: Houghton Mifflin.
Howe, M.L., & O'Sullivan, J.T. (1990). The development of strategic memory: Coordinating knowledge, metamemory, and resources. In D.F. Bjorklund (Ed.), *Children's strategies: Contemporary views of cognitive development* (pp. 129–155). Hillsdale, MJ: Erlbaum.
Kagan, J., Klein, R.E., Finley, G.E., Rogoff, B., & Nolan, E. (1979). A cross-cultural study of cognitive development. *Monographs of the Society for Research in Child Development*, *44*, (5, Serial No. 180).
Kail, R.V. (1984). *The development of memory in children* (2nd ed.). San Francisco: Freeman.
Kail, R.V. (1988). *The development of memory in children* (3rd ed.). San Francisco: Freeman.
Kee, D.W., & Davies, L. (1988). Mental effort and elaboration: A developmental analysis. *Contemporary Educational Psychology*, *13*, 221–228.
Kee, D.W., & Davies, L. (1990). Mental effort and elaboration: Effects of accessibility and instruction. *Journal of Experimental Child Psychology*, *49*, 264–274.
Kee, D.W., & Davies, L. (1991). Mental effort and elaboration: A developmental analysis of accessibility effects. *Journal of Experimental Child Psychology SZ*, 1–10.
Keeney, F.J., Cannizzo, S.R., & Flavell, J.H. (1967). Spontanous and induced verbal rehearsal in a recall task. *Child Development*, *38*, 953–966.
Kliegl, R., Smith, J., & Baltes, P.B. (1990). One the locus and process of magnification of age differences during mnemonic training. *Developmental Psychology*, *26*, 894–904.
Kosslyn, S.M., Margolis, J.A., Barrett, A.M., Goldknopf, E.J., & Daly, P.F. (1990). Age differences in imagery abilities. *Child Development*, *61*, 995–1010.

Kreutzer, M.A., Leonard, C., & Flavell, J.H. (1975). An interview study of children's knowledge about memory. *Monographs of the Society for Research in Child Development*, *40*, (1, Serial No., 159).

Kurtz, B.E. (1990). Cultural influences on children's cognitive and metacognitive development. In W. Schneider & F.E. Weinert (Eds.), *Interactions among aptitudes, strategies, and knowledge in cognitive performance* (pp. 177–199). New York: Springer-Verlag.

Kurtz, B.E., Borkowski, J.G., & Deshmukh, K. (1988). Metamemory development in Maharashtrian children: Influences from home and school. *Journal of Genetic Psychology*, *149*, 363–376.

Kurtz, B.E. Carr, M., & Schneider, W. (1988, April). *Development of attributional beliefs and self-concept in German and American children*. Presented at the annual meeting of the American Educational Research Association, New Orleans.

Kurtz, B.E., Schneider, W., Carr, M., Borkowski, J.G., & Rellinger, E. (1990). Strategy instruction and attributional beliefs in West Germany and the United States: Do teachers foster metacognitive development? *Contemporary Educational Psychology*, *15*, 268–283.

Lange, G. (1973). The development of conceptual and rote recall skills among school age children. *Journal of Experimental Child Psychology*, *15*, 394–406.

Lange, G. (1978). Organization-related processes in children's recall. In P.A. Ornstein (Ed.), *Memory organization in children* (pp. 101–128). Nillsdale, NJ: Erlbaum.

Lange, G., Guttentag, R.E., & Nida, R.E. (1990). Relationships between study organization, retrieval organization, and general and strategy-specific memory knowledge in young children. *Journal of Experimental Psychology*, *49*, 126–146.

Lange, G., MacKinnon, C.E., & Nida, R.E. (1989). Knowledge, strategy, and motivational contributions to preschool children's object recall. *Developmental Psychology*, *25*, 772–779.

Levin, J.R. (1976). What have we learned about maximizing what children can learn? In J.R. Levin & V.L. Allen (Eds.), *Cognitive learning in children*. New York: Academic Press.

Lincoln, Y.S., & Guba, E.G. (1985). *Naturalistic inquiry*. Beverly Hills: Sage.

Lodico, M.G., Ghatala, E.S., Levin, J.R., Pressley, M., & Bell, J.A. (1983). The effects of strategy monitoring on children's selection of effective memory strategies. *Journal of Experimental Child Psychology*, *35*, 263–277.

Lundeberg, M.A. (1987). Metacognitive aspects of reading comprehension: Studying understanding in legal case analysis. *Reading Research Quarterly*, *22*, 407–432.

Mandler, J.M. (1984). *Stories, scripts, and scenes: Aspects of schema theory*. Hillsdale, NJ: Erlbaum.

Mathews, M.M. (1966). *Teaching to read: Historically considered*. Chicago: University of Chicago Press.

McGilly, K., & Siegler, R.S. (1989). How children choose among serial recall strategies. *Child Development*, *60*, 172–182.

McGilly, K., & Siegler, R.S. (1990). The influence of encoding and strategic knowledge on children's choices among serial recall strategies. *Developmental Psychology*, *26*, 931–941.

Meichenbaum, D.M. (1977). *Cognitive behavior modification: An integrative approach*. New York: Plenum Press.
Moely, B.E. (1977). Organizational factors in the development of memory. In R.V. Kail & J.W. Hagen (Eds.), *Perspectives on the development of memory and cognition* (pp. 203–236). Hillsdale, NJ: Erlbaum.
Moely, B.E., Olson, F.A., Halwes, T.G., & Flavell, J.H. (1969). Production deficiency in young children's clustered recall. *Developmental Psychology*, *1*, 26–34.
Naus, M.J., & Halasz, F.G. (1979). Developmental perspectives on cognitive processing and semantic memory structure. In L.S. Cermak & F.I.M. Craik (Eds.), *Levels of processing in human memory* (pp. 259–288). Hillsdale, NJ: Erlbaum.
Newman, L.S. (1990). Intentional and unintentional memory in young children: Remembering vs. playing. *Journal of Experimental Child Psychology*, *50*, 243–258.
Nicholls, J.G. (1989). *The competitive ethos and democratic education*. Cambridge, MA: Harvard University Press.
Ornstein, P.A. (1990). Knowledge and strategies: A discussion. In W. Schneider & F.E. Weinert (Eds.), *Interactions among aptitudes, strategies, and knowledge in cognitive performance* (pp. 147–156). New York: Springer-Verlag.
Ornstein, P.A., Naus, M.J., & Liberty, C. (1975). Rehearsal and organizational processes in children's memory. *Child Development*, *46*, 818–830.
O'Sullivan, J.T., & Pressley, M. (1984). Completeness of instruction and strategy transfer. *Journal of Experimental Child Psychology*, *38*, 275–288.
Palincsar, A.S., & Brown, A.L. (1984). Reciprocal teaching of comprehension-fostering and comprehension-monitoring activities. *Cognition and Instruction*, *1*, 117–175.
Paris, S.G., Lipson, M.Y., & Wixson, K.K. (1983). Becoming a strategic reader. *Contemporary Educational Psychology*, *8*, 293–316.
Pascual-Leone, J. (1970). A mathematical model for the transition rule in Piaget's developmental stages. *Acta Psychologica*, *32*, 301–345.
Pinker, S., & Mehler, J. (Eds.) (1988). *Connections and symbols: A Cognition special issue*. Cambridge, MA: MIT Press.
Posner, M.I., & Snyder, C.R.R. (1975). Facilitation and inhibition in the processing of signals. In P.M.A. Rabbitt & S. Dornic (Eds.), *Attention and Performance V* (pp. 669–682). New York: Academic Press.
Pressley, M. (1977). Imagery and children's learning: Putting the picture in developmental perspective. *Review of Educational Research*, *47*, 586–622.
Pressley, M. (1982). Elaboration and memory development. *Child Development*, *53*, 296–309.
Pressley, M., & Associates (1990). *Cognitive strategy instruction that really improves children's academic performance*. Cambridge, MA: Brookline Books.
Pressley, M., Borkowski, J.G., & Johnson, C.J. (1987). The development of good strategy use: Imagery and related mnemonic processes. In M.A. McDaniel & M. Pressley (Eds.), *Imagery and related mnemonic processes: Theories, individual differences, and applications* (pp. 274–301). New York: Springer-Verlag.
Pressley, M., Borkowski, J.G., & O'Sullivan, J.T. (1984). Memory strategy instruction is made of this: Metamemory and durable strategy use. *Educational Psychology*, *19*, 94–107.

Pressley, M., Borkowski, J.G., & O'Sullivan, J.T. (1985). Children's metamemory and the teaching of memory strategies. In D.L. Forrest-Pressley, G.E. Mackinnon, & T.G. Waller (Eds.), *Metacognition, cognition, and human performance* (pp. 111–153). Orlando, FL: Academic Press.

Pressley, M., Borkowski, J.G., & Schneider, W. (1989). Good information processing: What it is and what education can do to promote it. *International Journal of Educational Research, 13*, 668–678.

Pressley, M., Cariglia-Bull, T., Deane, S., & Schneider, W. (1987). Short-term memory, verbal competence, and age as predictors of imagery instructional effectiveness. *Journal of Experimental Child Psychology, 43*, 194–211.

Pressley, M., El-Dinary, P.B., Gaskins, I.W., Schuder, T., Bergman, J., Almasi, J., & Brown, R. (1992). *Beyond direct explanation: Transactional instruction of reading comprehension strategies. Elementary School Journal, 92*, 513–555.

Pressley, M., Forrest-Pressley, D.L., & Elliott-Faust, D. (1988). What is strategy instructional enrichment and how to study it?: Illustrations from research on children's memory and comprehension. In F. Weinert & M. Perlmutter (Eds.), *Memory development: Universal changes and individual development* (pp. 101–130). Hillsdale, NJ: Erlbaum.

Pressley, M., Forrest-Pressley, D.L., Elliott-Faust, D.J., & Miller, G.E. (1985). Children's use of cognitive strategies, how to teach strategies, and what to do if they can't be taught. In M. Pressley & C.J. Brainerd (Eds.), *Cognitive learning and memory in children* (pp. 1–47). New York: Springer.

Pressley, M., Gaskins, I.W., Cunicelli, E.A., Burdick, N.J., Schaub-Matt, M., Lee, D.S., & Powell, N. (1991). Strategy instruction at Benchmark School: A faculty interview study. *Learning Disability Quarterly, 14*, 19–48.

Pressley, M., Gaskins, I.M., Wile, D., Cunicelli, B., & Sheridan, J. (1991). Teaching literacy strategies across the curriculum: A case study at Benchmark School. *Yearbook* of the National Reading Conference, *40*, 219–228.

Pressley, M., Goodchild, F., Fleet, J., Zajchowski, R., & Evans, E.D. (1989). The challenge of classroom strategy instruction. *Elementary School Journal, 89*, 301–342.

Pressley, M., Heisel, B.E., McCormick, C.G., & Nakamura, G.V. (1982). Memory strategy instruction with children. In C.J. Brainerd & M. Pressley (Eds.), *Progress in cognitive development research, Vol, 2, Verbal processes in children* (pp. 125–159). New York: Springer-Verlag.

Pressley, M., Johnson, G.J., Symons, S., McGoldrick, J.A., & Kurita, J.A. (1989). Strategies that improve memory and comprehension of what is read. *Elementary School Journal, 90*, 3–32.

Pressley, M., & Levin, J.R. (1977a). Developmental differences in subjects' associative learning strategies and performance: Assessing a hypothesis. *Journal of Experimental Child Psychology, 24*, 431–439.

Pressley, M., & Levin, J.R. (1977b). Task parameters affecting the efficacy of a visual imagery learning strategy in younger and older children. *Journal of Experimental Child Psychology, 24*, 53–59.

Pressley, M., & Levin, J.R. (1978). Developmental constraints associated with children's use of the keyword method for foreign language vocabulary learning. *Journal of Experimental Child Psychology, 26*, 359–372.

Pressley, M., & Levin, J.R. (1980). The development of mental imagery retrieval. *Child Development, 51*, 558–560.

Pressley, M., Levin, J.R., & Delaney, H.D. (1982). the mnemonic keyword method. *Review of Educational Research, 56*, 61–92.
Pressley, M., & MacFadyen, J. (1983). Mnemonic mediator retrieval at testing by preschool and kindergarten children. *Child Development, 54*, 474–479.
Pressley, M., Wood, E., & Woloshyn, V. (1990). Elaborative interrogation and facilitation of fact learning: Why having a knowledge base is one thing and using it is quite another. In W. Schneider & F.E. Weinert (Eds.), *Interactions among aptitudes, strategies, and knowledge in cognitive performance* (pp. 200–221). New York: Springer-Verlag.
Pritchard, R. (1990). The effects of cultural schemata on reading processing strategies. *Reading Research Quarterly, 25*, 273–295.
Purkel, W., & Bornstein, M.H. (1980). Pictures and imagery both enhance children's short-term and long-term recall. *Developmental Psychology, 16*, 153–154.
Rabinowitz, M. (in press). Semantic and strategic processing: Independent roles in determining memory performance. *American Journal of Psychology.*
Rabinowitz, M., Friedman, K., & Cohen, S. (1991). *On using and maintaining use of strategies: The influence of accessibility to knowledge.* Unpublished manuscript. New York: Fordham University, Department of Educational Psychology.
Rabinowitz, M., & McAuley, R. (1990). Conceptual knowledge processing: An oxymoron? In W. Schneider & F.E. Weinert (Eds.), *Interactions among aptitudes, strategies, and knowledge in cognitive performance* (pp. 117–133). New York: Springer-Verlag.
Ravitch, D., & Finn, C.E., Jr. (1987). *What do our 17-year-olds know? A report of the first national assessment of history and literature.* New York: Harper & Row.
Reid, M., & Borkowski, J.G. (1987). Causal attributions of hyperactive children: Implications for training strategies and self-control. *Journal of Educational Psychology, 79*, 296–307.
Ritter, K. (1978). The development of knowledge of an external retrieval cue strategy. *Child Development, 49*, 1227–1230.
Rogoff, B., & Mistry, J. (1990). The social and functional context of children's remembering. In R. Fivush & J.A. Hudson (Eds.), *Knowing and remembering in young children* (pp. 197–222). Cambridge, England: Cambridge University Press.
Rohwer, W.D., Jr. (1973). Elaboration and learning in childhood and adolescence. In H.W. Reese (Ed.), *Advances in child development and behavior* (Vol. 8, pp. 1–57). New York: Academic Press.
Rohwer, W.D., Jr. (1980). An elaborative conception of learner differences. In R.E. Snow, P.A. Federico, & W.E. Montague (Eds.), *Aptitude, learning, and instruction, Vol. 2, Cognitive process analysis of learning and problem solving* (pp. 23–46). Hillsdale, NJ: Erlbaum.
Rohwer, W.D, Jr., & Litrownik, J. (1983). Age and individual differences in the learning of a memorization procedure. *Journal of Educational Psychology, 75*, 799–810.
Rohwer, W.D., Jr., Rabinowitz, M., & Dronkers, N.F. (1982). Event knowledge, elaborative propensity, and the development of learning proficiency. *Journal of Experimental Child Psychology, 33*, 492–503.

Rohwer, W.D., Jr., Raines, J.M., Eoff, J., & Wagner, M. (1977). The development of elaborative propensity during adolescence. *Journal of Experimental Child Psychology*, *23*, 472–492.

Rosenthal, T.L., & Zimmerman, B.J. (1978). *Social learning and cognition.* New York: Academic Press.

Ross, B.H. (1984). Remindings and their effects in learning a cognitive skill. *Cognitive Psychology*, *16*, 371–416.

Ruch, M.D., & Levin, J.R. (1979). Partial pictures as imagery-retrieval cues in young children's prose recall. *Journal of Experimental Child Psychology*, *28*, 268–279.

Schank, R.C. (1982). *Dynamic memory: A theory of reminding and learning in computers and people*. New York: Cambridge University Press.

Schneider, Wa., & Shiffrin, R.M. (1977). Controlled and automatic human information processing: I. Direction, search, and attention. *Psychological Review*, *84*, 1–66.

Schneider, Wo., Borkowski, J.G., Kurtz, B.E., & Kerwin, K. (1986). Metamemory and motivation: A comparison of strategy use and performance in German and American children. *Journal of Cross-Cultural Psychology*, *17*, 315–336.

Schneider, Wo., & Körkel, J. (1989). The knowledge base and text recall: Evidence from a short-term longitudinal study. *Contemporary Educational Psychology*, *14*, 382–393.

Schneider, Wo., Körkel, J., & Weinert, F.E. (1987). The effects of intelligence, self-concept, and attributional style on metamemory and memory behavior. *International Journal of Behavioral Development*, *10*, 281–299.

Schneider, Wo., Körkel, J., & Weinert, F.E. (1989). Domain-specific knowledge and memory performance: A comparison of high- and low-aptitude children. *Journal of Educational Psychology*, *81*, 306–312.

Schneider, Wo., Körkel, J., & Weinert, F.E. (1990). Expert knowledge, general abilities, and text processing. In W. Schneider & F.E. Weinert (Eds.), *Interactions among aptitudes, strategies, and knowledge in cognitive performance* (pp. 235–251). New York: Springer-Verlag.

Schneider, Wo., & Pressley, M. (1989). *Memory development between two and twenty.* New York: Springer-Verlag.

Schneider, Wo., & Weinert, F.E. (Eds.) (1990). *Interactions among aptitudes, strategies, and knowledge in cognitive performance.* New York: Springer-Verlag.

Sharp, D., Cole, M., & Lave, C. (1979). Education and cognitive development: The evidence from experimental research. *Monographs of the Society for Research in Child Development*, *44* (Serial No. 170).

Shiffrin, R.M., & Schneider, Wa. (1977). Controlled and automatic human information processing: II. Perceptual learning, automatic attending, and a general theory. *Psychological Review*, *84*, 127–190.

Siegler, R.S. (1988). Individual differences in strategy choices: Good students, not-so-good students, and perfectionists. *Child Development*, *59*, 833–851.

Siegler, R.S. (1990). How content knowledge, strategies, and individual differences interact to produce strategy choices. In W. Schneider & F.E. Weinert (Eds.), *Interactions among aptitudes, strategies, and knowledge in cognitive performance* (pp. 74–89). New York: Springer-Verlag.

Siegler, R.S., & Jenkins, E. (1989). *How children discover new strategies.* Hillsdale, NJ: Erlbaum.
Sodian, B., & Schneider, W. (1990). Children's understanding of cognitive cuing: How to manipulate cues to fool a competitor. *Child Development, 61*, 697–704.
Stevenson, H.W., Parker, T., Wilkinson, A., Bonnevaux, B., & Gonzalez, M. (1978). Schooling, environment, and cognitive development: A cross-cultural study. *Monographs of the Society for Research in Child Development, 43* (Serial No. 175).
Strage, A., Tyler, A.B., Rohwer, W.D., Jr., & Thomas, J.W. (1987). An analytic framework for assessing distinctive course features with and across grade levels. *Contemporary Educational Psychology, 12*, 280–302.
Strauss, A.L. (1987). *Qualitative analysis for social scientists.* New York: Cambridge University Press.
Vygotsky, L.S. (1978). *Mind in society*. Cambridge, MA: Harvard University Press.
Wagner, D.A. (1974). The development of short-term and incidental memory: A cross-cultural study. *Child Development, 45*, 389–396.
Wagner, D.A. (1978). Memories of Morocco: The influence of age, schooling, and environment on memory. *Cognitive Psychology, 10*, 1–28.
Weiner, B. (1979). A theory of motivation for some classroom experiences. *Journal of Educational Psychology, 71*, 3–25.
Woloshyn, V.E., Pressley, M., & Schneider (1992). Elaborative interrogation and prior knowledge effects on learning of facts. *Journal of Educational Psychology, 84*, 115–124.
Woloshyn, V.E., Willoughby, T., Wood, E., & Pressley, M. (1990). Elaborative interrogation facilitates adult learning of factual paragraphs. *Journal of Educational Psychology, 82*, 513–524.
Wood, D.J., Bruner, J.S., & Ross, G. (1976). The role of tutoring in problem solving. *Journal of Child Psychology and Psychiatry, 17*, 89–100.

7
Applying Cognitive Developmental Principles in Classrooms

JULIA T. O'SULLIVAN

In the school system, what is taught and the way instruction is delivered is driven by educators' conceptualizations about how students learn. But conceptualizations of learning in school and instructional practices associated with these conceptualizations often stand in sharp contrast to current knowledge about cognitive development. Why? It is not because educators are unconcerned with the educational implications of psychological research. Indeed, educators and educational practice have always been influenced by psychology. Instead, the problem lies more with the translation of psychological research findings into educational models and the application of those models in classrooms. Sometimes the educational implications of research findings do not get translated into classroom practice at all. This often happens when research findings conflict with the prevailing philosophy of education. Such conflicts are typically resolved in favor of the philosophy. The continuing debate about the inclusion of phonological processing in early reading programs is a good example of this (Stanovich, 1991). When psychological research findings are translated into educational practice the translation is not always timely. For example, current instructional practices are more closely related to the behavioral psychology of the 1960s than to contemporary cognitive developmental models. Nor, in the translation process, do educational applications always keep faith with the underlying psychological theory and data. Psychologists, concerned with building psychological theory and models, do not always address the educational implications of their work. Often, this task is taken up by others less knowledgeable about the principles involved. For example, the instructional implications of operant psychology were often poorly understood and applications were quickly divorced from the parent theory.

Today, cognitive developmentalists are producing the type of knowledge that can be useful in schools, especially knowledge about those cognitive processes that can be taught and about the instructional procedures and conditions that promote them. In this chapter I examine how instructional practices driven by cognitive developmental principles would differ from current approaches. I outline some of the potential challenges and benefits, for both educational practice and cognitive developmental theory and research, that could accrue from actively pursuing such changes in education. To begin, the historic links between scientific psychology and education are reviewed and related to current educational conceptualizations of learning and their attendant instructional practices. Next, focusing on reading and memory, a select review of contemporary research on cognitive development is brought to bear on the questions of what should be taught and how that instruction should be delivered. Throughout, the emphasis is on mainstream elementary education (i.e., kindergarten to grade 6) in North America.

Historical Links Between Scientific Psychology and Education

Educational practice has always been influenced by psychology, although both the strength and directness of that influence has varied over the years. In his review of the historical links between scientific psychology and educational practice, Glaser (1982) pointed out that early in this century there were strong connections between the two enterprises. At that time, psychologists like Thorndike, for example, were convinced that the development of a science of human behavior was fundamental to the growth of the education profession. In the 1920s and 1930s, under Thorndike's leadership, educational subject matter was described as collections of to-be-learned associations and practice emphasized as the route to learning (Resnick, 1985). The drill and practice instructional routines so common in the schools today are rooted in these early models of learning.

Strong connections between scientific psychology and education did not last long after Thorndike. Glaser (1982) attributed this to the fact that each field turned its attention to building its own discipline and saw little need for maintaining a relationship with the other. Psychology concentrated on establishing itself as a scientific enterprise and psychology departments were housed in faculties of arts and sciences where educational applications were not prestigious activities. Had psychologists been a little more concerned with problems of learning and development in the school context, theory and research might have been influenced significantly (Glaser, 1982). Indeed, current cognitive developmental theory is remarkable in that it all but ignores the influence of variables associated with formal schooling. Education, meanwhile, particularly educational psychology and the psychometrics of educational testing, found its challenges primarily with practitioners and with practical problems of teacher training, curriculum development, and testing for the schools.

Concerned with building their profession, educators devoted less effort to nurturing the scientific and disciplinary roots of educational practice (Glaser, 1982).

During the 1950s connections between psychology and instructional technology were strengthened, with considerable impetus provided by military-sponsored research on problems of training (this "human factors" research contributed to the development of information processing models [Newell & Simon, 1972]) and by the influence of Skinner's operant psychology on education. At that time, models of learning had a decided behavioral and task-analytic flavor and, when applied to the school context, contributed to the development of methods and programs like mastery learning, behavior modification, and programmed instruction (Resnick, 1985). These applications continue to influence educational practice in almost every subject area in contemporary schooling. For example, the reading comprehension curriculum used in North American schools today was built on the behavioral and task-analytic models of learning that prevailed in the middle of the century (Dole, Duffy, Roehler, & Pearson, 1991). During this period, however, educational applications were not always faithful to the underlying theory and research. The instructional implications of Skinner's operant psychology were often poorly understood and applications too quickly separated from the parent theory. (See Dweck, 1986, for an interesting discussion of how instructional practices designed to increase students' motivation were based on an incomplete understanding of reinforcement principles.)

Since the 1960s the cognitive perspective has become the major theoretical force in psychology and cognitive-based models the dominant perspective on learning. Also, concern with the processes of learning educational subject matter, and with interventions that promote that learning, has become part of the mainstream of research on cognition, learning, and development (Resnick, 1985). Although much is written about educational applications of cognitive developmental research, instructional practice remains, for the most part, firmly rooted in applications of behavioral psychology. One reason for this is that the conceptualizations of learning that drive these instructional practices have more in common with the behavioral models of the 1950s and 1960s than with contemporary cognitive developmental perspectives. These conceptualizations and their related instructional models are outlined in the next section.

Models Driving Current Educational Practice

Conceptualizations of Academic Learning

Two critical assumptions are believed to govern learning in school (Iran-Nejad, 1990; Resnick, 1987). These are that learning (a) represents the internalization of external knowledge and (b) is intentional, occurring under conscious, executive control. The first assumption implies that information found in books or classroom lectures is the one and only source of academic learning. Accordingly, an author places his or her meaning in text and a good student can excise and reproduce that meaning in its original and invariant form. Consequently, there is one correct solution for each problem situation and the goal for the student is to get the right answer by applying an excise-absorb-reproduce algorithm to externally presented knowledge. The second assumption about learning in school implies that the only way students can regulate their learning is by deliberately allocating attentional and memory resources in a slow and inherently sequential manner (Iran-Nejad, 1990). Accordingly, teachers must share in this regulation by directing the students' attention to what should be learned, determining the amount of time available for learning, and so on.

Together, these two assumptions about the nature of learning in school emphasize external control (externally situated knowledge and teacher regulation). They paint a picture of the student as a passive recipient of knowledge and the teacher as a director and manager of time. Individual differences in achievement are primarily attributed to differential amounts of time and attention devoted to learning. This picture is clearly more reminiscent of behavioral perspectives on learning than recent cognitive conceptions. Worse, these assumptions severely constrain the role and contribution of variables demonstrated to be important in knowledge acquisition, including background knowledge (Bransford, Sherwood, Vye, & Rieser, 1986), automatic processing (Bjorklund, 1987), metacognition (Pressley, Borkowski, & Schneider, 1987), and the context surrounding learning, including its social nature (Vygotsky, 1978).

Models of Effective Instruction

Educational research on effective instruction is predicated on the conceptualization of learning outlined above. Consequently, in effective instruction research, factors under the control of the teacher such as the allocation and efficient use of time, the structure of classroom management, the nature of teacher feedback and reinforcement for students, and the relationship between what is taught and what is tested are highlighted. Little attention is paid to the role of the student or the context surrounding learning. Much of this research has been guided by Carroll's (1963) model of learning in school. He proposed five sets of variables that can account for variation in achievement. Three of these sets of variables are expressed in terms of time (Carroll, 1989). These are (a) aptitude (defined as the amount of time a student requires to learn a task to mastery), (b) opportunity to learn (e.g., the amount of time available for learning the task), and (c) perseverance (the amount of time a student is willing to spend on learning the task). The remaining two sets of variables in the model are (d) quality of instruction and (e) student ability to understand instruction. Carroll (1989) admitted that in designing his model he was not very specific about the variables that make up these last two sets. Under quality of instruction he would include telling students what they are supposed to learn, providing adequate materials, planning and ordering the steps in learning. Student ability to understand would encompass such variables as language comprehension and ability to figure out what the task is and how to go about learning it (Carroll, 1989). Educators and educational researchers have concentrated on the model's emphasis on time as an important variable in learning, with little attention paid to the possibility that the type of instruction provided may be just as important as the amount of engaged time.

There is a growing consensus among educational researchers that empirical findings based on this type of model have provided mixed benefits for teaching practice. Slavin (1984) argued that the time on task research has proved to be very disappointing. In reviewing studies of the relationship between time and achievement he concluded that the relationship tends to be so small that it often fails to achieve statistical significance, much less substantive importance. (In the studies reviewed by Slavin [1984], time on task accounted at best for 2% of the variance in achievement at posttest, with pretest achievement levels controlled.) Furthermore, the relationship between time and achievement across grade levels seems inconsistent and unstable. In Slavin's view, the failure to find large effects of engaged time on learning is because models linking these variables do not give appropriate consideration to the impact of factors like quality and level of instruction and student motivation. Similarly, Sirotnik (1983) concluded that time on task research may have diverted attention from critical instructional variables concerned with how that time is spent. In his study of more than 1,000 elementary and secondary classrooms Sirotnik (1983) found that in accordance with the research focus on quantity of learning time, the larger part of class time was indeed spent "on task" but the on-task activity consisted mostly of teachers lecturing to the class and students working independently on written assignments. Rarely observed were teaching practices such as discussion, demonstration, and student question generation and decision making. Dole et al. (1991) took a more positive view of this body of research, arguing that it helped researchers distinguish between classroom management (i.e., getting and maintaining students on task) and instruction (helping students develop understanding), paving the way for research on qualitative aspects of instruction.

Limitations of the traditional engaged time models have contributed to the view that a new approach to research on effective instruction is called for. There is consensus that new approaches must be solidly built on contemporary models of learning. Accordingly, the cognitive processes and structures fundamental to the development of expertise, and the instructional procedures that promote them, should be appointed a major role. Some cognitive developmental prescriptions for the content and process of instruction are discussed in the remaining sections of this chapter.

Targeting Cognitive Processes for Instruction

For some years now, researchers in education and cognitive development alike have argued that if students are to develop robust, useful knowledge some instruction should be focused on the cognitive processes underlying learning in the different subject domains (e.g., Brown & Reeve, 1987; Glaser & Takanishi, 1986; Slavin, 1984). Careful analyses of the cognitive processes and knowledge structures involved in the development of reading (Brown, Armbruster, & Baker, 1986; Stanovich, 1986), mathematics (Nesher, 1986; Resnick & Omanson, 1987), and the sciences (Carey, 1986) have been performed. Furthermore, there is impressive evidence from a variety of subject areas that some of these processes can be taught and that students benefit from such instruction (e.g., Cunningham, 1990; Oka & Paris, 1987; Palincsar & Brown, 1984). Although considerable research and model building still remains to be done, sufficient, useful knowledge has been established to warrant some instruction of cognitive processes in schools. What this instruction might include in the areas of reading and memory is described next.

Teaching Reading

The past 20 years have witnessed tremendous advances in reading research and in our understanding of the cognitive processes involved in reading. Currently, we have powerful models of componential reading processes and considerable understanding of skilled reading, reading development, and reading disability (Vellutino, 1991). There is no doubt that some of the knowledge produced by reading researchers has immediate application to the teaching of reading. In classrooms, however, little use of this knowledge is evident. Two examples will be used to illustrate this situation. The first is concerned with phonological processing in early reading development and the second with reading comprehension.

Initial Reading Instruction: Phonological Processing

In an alphabetic orthography like English the letters of the writing system encode the speech segments (phonemes) of the speech system. This is the alphabetic principle. The evidence is clear that to become a fluent reader a child must master this principle by acquiring functional spelling to sound knowledge (for a review see Wagner & Torgesen, 1987). The principle may be induced or acquired through direct instruction, but it must be mastered if the child is to progress successfully in reading (Stanovich, 1986). This is because mastery of the alphabetic principle is essential for independent decoding, which is necessary for practice. Through practice with reading, decoding becomes relatively automatic, freeing up resources for comprehension (Stanovich, 1986).

It is also well established that phonological processing skill—the ability to manipulate and make judgments about sound segments at levels below the word (Stanovich, 1991)—can play a critical role in the child's mastery of the alphabetic principle. Presumably, learning to associate phonemes with graphemes depends on the ability to attend to the phoneme (Perfetti, 1991). Measured levels of phonological processing in preschoolers are better predictors of subsequent reading achievement than IQ (Juel, Griffith, & Gough, 1986; Vellutino & Scanlon, 1987) and deficits in phonological processing skill are implicated in most cases of severe reading difficulty (Bruck & Treiman, 1990). Further, level of phonological processing skill can be reliably assessed before school entry (Blachman, 1989) and training in these skills is associated with significant increases in word recognition and spelling (Bradley & Bryant, 1983; Cunningham, 1990).

There are a number of ways that this knowledge might be applied in education. First, there is converging evidence that a clear principle of early reading instruction (i.e., the first three grades) should be to teach children the system by which letters encode speech segments (Calfee, 1991; Perfetti, 1991). Indeed, programs that include some "code emphasis" (e.g., providing some instruction on word analysis or letter-phoneme synthesis) tend to produce better readers than programs that do not (for a review see Adams, 1990). Despite the evidence, there is a long-standing and continuing controversy in education about including code-oriented instruction in early reading programs (see Carbo, 1988; Chall, 1967, 1989, for examples of the "Great Debate") and currently, there is a strong and increasingly popular movement away from teaching the code (Vellutino, 1991).

A second way to apply knowledge about phonological processing is in the prevention of reading difficulties. Routine assessment of phonological processing skills among preschoolers or Kindergartners, with training provided for children who have difficulty, is indicated. Further, assessment and remediation of these skills among children with severe reading difficulties offers great promise. Unfortunately, prospective teachers are not being taught the critical role that phonological processing plays in early reading development (Liberman, 1988). Consequently, few applications of this knowledge are evident and teachers often seem more influenced by fashionable trends and popular movements in education than by scientific evidence (Vellutino, 1991).

Why is it that findings concerning the role of phonological processing in reading development are not being incorporated more into early reading programs? One reason is that in the arena of educational decision-making, philosophy, values, and scientific evidence all come into play. In the case of early reading programs, the prevailing philosophy holds that reading is fundamentally a matter of comprehension and the code is incidental at best. Consequently, including a code emphasis is considered irrelevant, unnecessary, and maybe even detrimental. Stanovich (1991) argued that when scientific evidence conflicts with the dominant philosophy of the reading establishment, the philosophy almost always reigns supreme. This is because the fundamental assumptions on which the philosophy is based tend to be carved in stone and not easily altered by empirical evidence. Unfortunately, it is this philosophy that is transmitted to prospective teachers in colleges of education and to practicing teachers through professional publications and workshops (Perfetti, 1991). Both practicing and prospective teachers need to be educated about the empirical findings on phonological processing and their implications for initial reading instruction. If this knowledge is not being imparted to teachers then we cannot expect them to incorporate it into their personal theories about reading. Because personal theories guide teaching practices in the classroom (Richardson, 1990), we must find ways to influence those theories so that they come closer to the scientific reality.

Teaching Comprehension

Recent research in reading comprehension emphasizes the role of knowledge that students bring to the task and the strategies they use to build and maintain understanding (e.g., Baker & Brown, 1984; Oka & Paris, 1987; Pressley, Forrest-Pressley, Elliott-Faust, & Miller, 1985). Successful readers seem to have a repertoire of cognitive strategies (e.g., rereading, skimming) that they use to help build an understanding of the text, and metacognitive strategies (e.g., summarization as a process of self-review) that they use to monitor and evaluate their progress (Brown et al., 1986; Pressley et al., 1987). Further, successful readers have detailed metacognitive knowledge about the comprehension process and they use it to guide the deployment of cognitive and metacognitive strategies (Baker & Brown, 1984; Pressley, Forrest-Pressley et al., 1985). Findings from numerous instructional studies indicate that these processes and knowledge can be taught and result in impressive reading comprehension gains for young readers and children with reading difficulties (e.g., Oka & Paris, 1987; Palincsar & Brown, 1984; Paris & Jacobs, 1984). These instructional effects have been demonstrated in both laboratory and classroom settings (Paris & Oka, 1986) with both researchers (Lysynchuk, Pressley, & Vye, 1990) and teachers (Duffy et al., 1987) providing instruction.

A number of innovative training packages have been developed to teach comprehension processes to children. For example, Paris and his colleagues (Paris, Cross, & Lipson, 1984) have developed Informed Strategies for Learning (ISL), a curriculum that is designed to teach the strategies and metacognitive awareness important in skilled reading. The effectiveness of this program has been demonstrated in a number of studies (e.g., Oka & Paris, 1987). Palincsar and Brown (1984) developed reciprocal teaching, a method of instruction designed to teach reading comprehension strategies to children. Reciprocal teaching improves standardized reading comprehension for students in grades 4 through 7, and its effectiveness has been demonstrated when delivered by researchers (Lysynchuk et al., 1990) as well as professional teachers (Palincsar & Brown, 1984).

Although comprehension instruction plays an important role in today's reading curriculum, what students and teachers actually do during instruction often stands in sharp contrast to current knowledge about reading comprehension development (Paris & Oka, 1986). Explicit instruction of comprehension processes rarely occurs in classrooms (Pearson & Dole, 1987). Instead, the typical approach to instruction consists of round robin oral reading, with periodic questions from the teacher about the selections read, and students independently completing workbook exercises that supposedly break down the comprehension process into skill compenents like finding the main idea (Pearson & Dole, 1987). This workbook activity can occupy up to two thirds of reading instruction time in the average elementary classroom (Stevens, Slavin, & Farnish, 1991). The rationale seems to be that through practice students will figure out what these comprehension skills are, how they can apply them, and when and why they should use them. Durkin (1978–1979) pointed out that there is nothing in this approach that can help students learn directly what these skills are. Similarly, Paris and Oka (1986) refer to this process as the "mirage of strategy instruction" because most teachers do not give sufficient guidance or explanation so that students understand what skills they are supposed to apply. When teachers do explain how to execute a particular strategy they usually present it as a rule to be memorized as a procedural algorithm, rather than as a flexible plan for reasoning about how to remove blockages to understanding (Duffy et al., 1987). Indeed, many teachers seem to have difficulty conceptualizing reading as a strategic activity at all and others hesitate to focus on cognitive processes arguing that process cannot be separated from content (Duffy et al., 1987).

The situation surrounding comprehension instruction is not too surprising given that the reading comprehension curriculum in use today is built on the model of reading prevalent in the 1950s (Dole et al., 1991). At that time reading comprehension was considered to be a skill that could be divided into a component set of subskills. Further, it was believed that reading comprehension could be improved by practicing each of the individual subskills until mastery was achieved. While we await changes that will bring curriculum in line with contemporary models of reading comprehension, the work of Duffy, Roehler and their colleagues (e.g., Duffy, Roehler, & Rackliffe, 1986; Duffy, Roehler, Meloth, et al., 1986) stands as a testament to the fact that teachers can be trained to recast traditional comprehension skills as strategies and teach children how, when, where, and why to apply these strategies. Furthermore, teachers can provide this instruction within the context of the regular prescribed reading curriculum using standard basal text materials. For example, Duffy et al. (1987) successfully trained third-grade reading teachers to make decisions about when and how to explain the reasoning associated with using reading strategies. The students of trained teachers were more aware of the strategic nature of reading and demonstrated significantly higher reading achievement than students of untrained teachers. These authors point out that there are tremendous individual differences between teachers in their ability to profit from this training; the most successful teachers were those who tailored their explanations to students' restructured understanding (Duffy et al., 1987).

Teaching Memory

During the last three decades cognitive developmental psychologists have produced a substantial body of research on memory development in school-age populations (for a review see Schneider & Pressley, 1989). In general, current models of memory emphasize the interplay of conceptual knowledge (Bjorklund, 1987), resources (Kee & Davies, 1991), strategies (Pressley & Van Meter, this volume), and metamemory (Pressley, Borkowski, & O'Sullivan, 1985) (for a review of the role of all of these factors see Howe & O'Sullivan, 1990). Important developments occur in all of these areas during the school years, including the acquisition and restructuring of knowledge, the increasingly efficient allocation of resources, the development of more powerful strategies, and the construction of more elaborate metamemory, including metamemory with motivational properties.

The development of strategic memory has received particular attention from researchers. As part of this focus an impressive literature on memory strategy instruction for school-age children has been produced (for a review see Pressley, Borkowski, & O'Sullivan, 1985). The evidence is clear that, given appropriate training, children acquire new memory strategies and are motivated to transfer and use them to improve their memory performance on different tasks. This line of research has led to the development of specific guidelines that can be used to design strategy training routines for the school setting (Levin, 1986; Pressley, Forrest-Pressley et al., 1985; Pressley, Goodchild, Fleet, Zajchowski, & Evans, 1989). The extent to which this knowledge is being applied in schools is addressed next, followed by an overview of a recently developed school-based program for teaching memory processing to elementary schoolers.

Schools place considerable demands on students' memory abilities, especially the ability to recall facts and definitions. For example, in the U.S., teachers typically use textbooks that emphasize specific to-be-remembered content and approximately 90% of questions on tests (both teacher-made and standardized) are concerned with factual information (Bloom, 1984). The message that memorization is important for progress in school is not lost on students. More than two thirds of school children believe that learning in school involves memorization of facts in contrast to developing new ways of thinking (Entwistle, 1988). This emphasis on memorization is present from the early grades, and as children progress through elementary school they are faced with increasing demands on their memory abilities. At the same time, teachers are gradually withdrawing organizational supports from their lesson plans and placing more responsibility for the use of memory strategies on the students (e.g., Brown & Sproson, 1987; Rogoff & Mistry, 1985).

Participation in formal schooling is associated with the development of memory strategies that might not ordinarily occur, or develop as rapidly, in nonschool environments (Morrison, 1987). However, the available evidence suggests that memory developments associated with participation in formal education are induced as a result of the task demands placed on children in school (Folds, Footo, Guttentag, & Ornstein, 1990), because little memory instruction is evident in classrooms (Kurtz, Schneider, Carr, Borkowski, & Rellinger, 1990; Moely et al., 1986; Morrison, 1987). For example, in the Moely et al. (1986) study involving teachers from kindergarten to grade 6, memory strategy instruction was very infrequent, only occurring during 2.28% of 300 observation intervals. Metamemory instruction was even less frequent, with teachers rarely providing a rationale for strategy use or instructing self-monitoring activities. German teachers report more memory instruction than their U.S. counterparts but, like U.S. teachers, they offer instruction in strategies far more frequently than instruction in metamemory (Kurtz et al., 1990). Although rare, teacher-provided memory instruction is associated with early emerging strategy use (Schneider, Borkowski, Kurtz, & Kerwin, 1986), enhanced metamemory knowledge, and increased benefits from strategy training on experimental tasks (Moely et al., 1986). Moely et al. (1986) suggested that the paucity of memory instruction in schools may be simply because teachers know very little about memory at all. This is not surprising given that teacher training programs rarely include courses in cognition or cognitive development and textbooks in educational psychology generally contain limited coverage of memory development, how to facilitate memory processing, or the effects of training on memory behavior and performance (Moely et al., 1986). Many teachers seem to believe that efficient, effective memory processing is innate and unfolds gradually with age (Brown & Sproson, 1987).

A Program of Instruction

During the past 2 years I have been developing a program of memory instruction to be delivered by teachers in the context of a regular or a special education elementary school classroom (O'Sullivan, 1991). Following current models of memory development (Howe & O'Sullivan, 1990), the program is designed to teach strategies and metamemory (including those components of metamemory with motivational properties). These processes were targeted for instruction because, although the knowledge base is important in memory processing (e.g., Pressley et al., 1987), teaching conceptual knowledge for the diversity of school-based memory tasks would likely amount to a massive enrichment campaign (Baker & Brown, 1984). Children in the 6- to 12-year-old age range (with typical or atypical memory development) can be included in the program, provided that they demonstrate the ability to benefit from strategy instruction (determined through memory assessment for children with atypical memory).

The program is a set of instructional methods and activities designed to provide students with the motivation to use memory strategies and the knowledge to direct intelligent strategic processing. Students are taught how to execute a number of memory strategies and are given considerable practice applying those strategies across different tasks and subject areas. Initially, the teacher provides considerable support during practice, prompting, directing, and encouraging strategy application and metamemory acquisition. As student competence increases, teacher support is gradually withdrawn. A major focus is the instruction and induction of metamemory knowledge (O'Sullivan & Pressley, 1984; Pressley, Borkowski, & O'Sullivan, 1984). Teachers provide general guidelines about where, when, and why to use different strategies. However, students are encouraged to elaborate on those guidelines by monitoring and evaluating the cost-benefit ratio of each strategy across different tasks. Through elaborated feedback, the teacher helps students to see relations between their strategic behavior and their memory performance, encouraging the development of attributions reflecting self-control of memory processing. Self-control is also encouraged through group activities, with groups coming together to plan for strategic processing and to pool feedback about ease, effectiveness, and drawbacks of strategies. Throughout the program teachers discuss, explain, and model their own (a) use of memory strategies, (b) updating of their metamemory about the strategies, (c) metacognitive planning, monitoring, and evaluation of their memory behavior and performance, and (d) attributions of their own memory performance to their appropriate or inappropriate strategic efforts. Teachers can vary the strategies they include for instruction in accordance with the needs of the students involved. However, regardless of strategy content, the core instructional focus and procedures remain invariant. Consequently, once teachers have successfully delivered the program they should be able to transfer the instructional methods to teach strategies and metacognition in other domains.

To date, the program has been used with a small sample of children who, following normal development, experience significant and debilitating memory difficulties secondary to cerebral injury (Lawson & Rice, 1989). It was necessary to begin instruction for some of these children at a very basic level; for example, developing their understanding of the concepts of remembering and forgetting. Strategies taught to these children ranged from simple list making (writing a list or, for those children with acquired dyslexia, recording it on audiotape) to elaboration and categorical organization. The children's teachers (both special education and homeroom) and parents were involved in program delivery, prompting application of program content across curriculum areas, in school and at home. Preliminary evidence indicated that although there were considerable individual differences in the extent to which children benefitted from program involvement, all of the children demonstrated some gains in memory functioning. Each child learned to use at least some of the trained strategies appropriately, transferred them to new tasks and across curriculum areas, and demonstrated some significant gains in memory performance. Improvements in the children's general and strategic metamemory, especially the tendency to attribute performance to their strategic efforts, were considerable. Interestingly, parents and teachers reported significant gains in the children's general orientation and responsiveness to instruction and their confidence about their ability to tackle academic tasks.

The participating volunteer teachers required considerable education about memory development, together with encouragement and guidance in explaining and modeling their own memory behavior. It was clear that there were tremendous individual differences between teachers in their ability to carry out the program in its intended form. Considerable research is required to elaborate the influence of a host of teacher, student, and classroom variables on both the delivery and effectiveness of this program. Also, the necessity and sufficiency of the individual program components will have to be determined empirically. However, the demonstrated effectiveness of the program for the small group of brain-injured children included to date is extremely encouraging.

Summary

Cognitive developmental psychologists have produced a large literature on the cognitive processes involved in reading and memory development. Findings from instructional studies demonstrate that many of these processes can be taught by professional teachers in regular classroom settings, resulting in significant performance benefits for children. However, little application of these findings is evident in classrooms. Reasons for this include the fact that instructional practices are often dictated by educational philosophy rather than science, that curriculum is driven by outdated models of learning, and that in teacher-training programs little attention is paid to the development of cognitive processes and how to modify them. The end result is that knowledge about cognitive developmental principles and their educational applications is not reaching prospective and practicing teachers. There is little prospect for widespread change in educational practice unless we can find ways to influence teachers' own thinking about the nature of expertise and how to promote it.

The Process of Instruction

Cognitive developmentalists have not only highlighted those cognitive processes that can be targeted for instruction but have developed procedures for successful training of those processes. Twenty years of instructional research have witnessed considerable changes in both the methods and the effectiveness of strategy training routines. Procedures used to train strategies during the 1970s promoted acquisition and implementation of strategies but rarely produced maintenance over time or generalization across tasks or settings (Pressley, Borkowski, & O'Sullivan, 1985). Implications for instructional practices in the school system were few and far between. Indeed, educators often used the failure to produce transfer in these studies as an argument against trying to teach cognitive strategies at all (Perkins & Salomon, 1990). In the past 10 to 12 years the picture has changed considerably. Researchers are increasingly reporting successful use of instructional methods that enable children to take control of their learning, applying newly acquired strategies in intelligent ways across tasks and settings. At least three common denominators of successful strategy training routines can be identified. These are (a) a dynamic, interactive instructional process, (b) the provision of metacognitive instruction, and (c) incorporating training in the context of authentic cognitive activity. These three factors and their implications for instruction in school settings are discussed next.

Interactive Instructional Processes

The current interest in dynamic learning situations has seen a shift away from traditional experimenter controlled instruction and toward an emphasis on interactive processes (Baker & Brown, 1984). Many of the successful training studies now being reported have been influenced by Vygotsky's notion of guided learning within the student's "zone of proximal development." Vygotsky (1978) emphasized the social nature of learning and argued that much of cognitive development is mediated by masters providing expertise to novices (e.g., parents to children, teachers to students). It is through these interactions with a supportive, knowledgeable adult that children are led to the limits of their own understanding. Initially, the master provides considerable support to the novice and acts as a model, coach, and interrogator, leading children to use more powerful strategies. Observing the master, practicing, and explaining/defending their position to the master helps children internalize those cognitive functions that are within their zone of proximal development. In time, children increase in competence by adopting the activities of the master who, in turn, gradually withdraws support. This process, where provision of expert support gradually diminishes as student competence increases, has been called *scaffolded instruction* by Palincsar and Brown (1984) and has been incorporated into successful reading strategy programs, like Palincsar and Brown's reciprocal teaching and Paris, Cross, and Lipson's (1984) Informed Strategies for Learning, as well as memory strategy programs such as that designed by O'Sullivan (1991).

The role and function of the teacher in this interactive, instructional process is considerably different from the traditional teaching role. In interactive instruction the teacher acts as a partner, sharing responsibility for learning with the student, rather than the traditional manager of time and practice. Interactive instruction calls on teachers to demonstrate and share their expertise with students, instead of simply telling students what to do and leaving them to get on with it. Finally, interactive instruction requires that the teacher engage in continuous assessment of the student, tailoring instruction to the student's emerging understanding. In contrast, the traditional approach consists of administering regularly scheduled tests and corrective feedback (i.e., simply indicating if an answer is correct or incorrect).

To evaluate the validity of such an approach, it would naturally have to be implemented in the classroom. To date, such instruction has typically been restricted to specific programs introduced by researchers at a local level (e.g., a specific school or classroom), rather than more extensive implementation in mainstream education. Widespread adoption of interactive instruction may have to await policy changes at the school board level as well as changes in many teachers' acceptance of, and ability to implement successfully, this type of approach to instruction (Pearson & Dole, 1987).

Metacognitive Instruction

Successful strategy training studies with children invariably include a metacognitive component (for a review, see Pressley, Borkowski, & O'Sullivan, 1985). It is clear from this body of research that successful strategy training involves more than teaching the strategies themselves. Rather, it requires that some knowledge of the strategy beyond the simple mechanics of its execution be imparted to children. For example, knowing the type of task where a particular strategy can be used and understanding its effectiveness relative to other strategic alternatives is necessary. This is because successful maintenance and transfer of strategies relies on children's understanding of how strategies work, and where, when, and why to use them (O'Sullivan & Pressley, 1984; Ringel & Springer, 1980). Children's metacognition about strategies can be instructed or induced in a variety of ways, including feedback about performance (Kennedy & Miller, 1976), providing rules for generalizing trained strategies (O'Sullivan & Pressley, 1984), and training children in monitoring routines that generate metacognitive knowledge (Lodico, Ghatala, Levin, Pressley, & Bell, 1983). However, metacognition must be included in training for effective, generalized strategy use. This principle seems to hold for training memory (Pressley et al., 1987), reading comprehension (Paris & Oka, 1986), and phonological processing (Cunningham, 1990) strategies.

Very little metacognition is imparted to children in classrooms (Kurtz et al., 1990; Moely et al., 1986; Paris & Oka, 1986). Introducing metacognitive instruction offers a number of challenges for the school system. Teachers will need to accept that there are no hard and fast metacognitive rules. Instead children must be encouraged to develop their own personal metacognitive knowledge. Teachers will, in addition, need to become aware of and be able and willing to share their thinking processes publicly. They will have to go beyond simple effort-outcome attributions for students' performance and develop more complex understandings about how cognitive effort can be deployed through strategies to impact on performance. The design and delivery of metacognitive instruction will also have to take account of the motivational systems operating at both the classroom and the individual level. For example, there is little point in educating children about the benefits of strategy use if strategic behavior is inconsistent with an individual child's academic goals or the goals espoused by the teacher. There is some evidence that individual differences in student motivation (Nolen, 1988) and in classroom goal structures (Ames & Ames 1984; Ames & Archer, 1988) are associated with different valuing and use of cognitive strategies.

Training Activities

Modern strategy instruction research is carried out in the context of actual reading and studying with the goal of understanding and remembering (Baker & Brown, 1984; Pressley et al., 1987, 1989). There is little doubt that transfer, especially for the young child, is more likely when training proceeds in the context of authentic activity. It follows that school-based strategy instruction should be incorporated into the curriculum and proceed in the context of authentic reading and remembering activity. Surprisingly, implementing this apparently simple practice may prove to be quite a challenge. This is because in education, the activity and context in which learning takes place are regarded as ancillary to learning, distinct, and even neutral with respect to what is learned Brown, Collins, & Duguid, 1989). Arguing that learning is in fact situated in activity and context Brown et al. (1989) concluded that, contrary to the aims of education, much of school learning is welded to the classroom context and to the type of tasks and procedures used there (e.g., workbook skill exercises that are isolated from authentic reading or studying). Because activity and context have been considered incidental to learning in school, issues relating to the design, selection, and evaluation of learning activities have been relatively neglected in educational research (Brophy & Alleman, 1991). These issues will need to be considered empirically if cognitive processes are to be instructed successfully in schools.

Summary

Successful cognitive instructional studies (a) are built on dynamic systems of tutelage, (b) emphasize metacognition, and (c) incorporate training in the context of authentic reading and remembering activity. Application of these principles in school settings would present a number of challenges for the school system. These include a reappraisal of the role and function of the teacher and a critical examination of the influence of the classroom context on what students learn, including what they learn about learning. If these instructional principles are implemented in schools, then cognitive developmentalists could take advantage of this research opportunity to map the influence of school variables (including teacher, student, and administrative factors) on the effectiveness of cognitive instructional procedures. Equally important, those data should afford critical tests of the more general theories of cognitive development on which these instructional principles are based.

Concluding Comments

It is clear that research in cognitive development has produced the type of knowledge that can be profitably applied in school settings, although little application of this knowledge is currently evident in mainstream education. This situation is changing, however. Educators are acknowledging the limitations of current instructional practices for promoting the type of competence and expertise required in today's society. Increasingly, they are calling for instructional models that are grounded in the science of cognition and cognitive development. We must take advantage of this opportunity to introduce cognitive developmental principles in the school system. This would not only benefit education but would allow cognitive developmentalists to carry out critical tests of the associated underlying theories, contributing substantially to progress in our own field.

Acknowledgments. Preparation of this chapter was supported by Grant No. OGP0046514 from the Natural Sciences and Engineering Research Council of Canada.

References

Adams, M.J. (1990). *Beginning to read: Thinking and learning about print.* Cambridge, MA: MIT Press.

Ames, C., & Ames, R. (1984). Systems of student and teacher motivation: Toward a qualitative definition. *Journal of Educational Psychology, 76,* 535–556.

Ames, C., & Archer, J. (1988). Achievement goals in the classroom: Students' learning strategies and motivation processes. *Journal of Educational Psychology, 80,* 260–267.

Baker, L., & Brown, A.L. (1984). Metacognitive skills of reading. In P.D. Pearson, M. Kamil, R. Barr, & P. Mosenthal (Eds.), *Handbook of reading research* (pp. 353–393). New York: Longman.

Bjorklund, D.F. (1987). How age changes in knowledge base contribute to the development of children's memory: An interpretive review. *Developmental Review, 7,* 93–130.

Blachman, B.A. (1989). Phonological awareness and word recognition: Assessment and intervention. In A.G. Kamhi & H.W. Katts (Eds.), *Reading disabilities* (pp. 133–158). Boston, MA: College-Hill Press.

Bloom, B.S. (1984). The 2 sigma problem: The search for methods of group instruction as effective as one-to-one tutoring. *Educational Researcher, 13,* 4–6.

Bradley, L., & Bryant, P.E. (1983). Categorizing sounds and learning to read—a causal connection. *Nature, 301,* 419–421.

Bransford, J., Sherwood, R., Vye, N., & Rieser, J. (1986). Teaching thinking and problem solving: Research foundations. *American Psychologist, 41,* 1078–1089.

Brophy, J., & Alleman, J. (1991). Activities as instructional tools: A framework for analysis and evaluation. *Educational Researcher*, *20*, 9–23.

Brown, A.L., Armbruster, B.B., & Baker, L. (1986). The role of metacognition in reading and studying. In J. Orasanu (Ed.), *Reading comprehension: From research to practice* (pp. 49–76). Hillsdale, NJ: Erlbaum.

Brown, A.L., & Reeve, R.A. (1987). Bandwidths of competence: The role of supportive contexts in learning and development. In L.S. Liben (Ed.), *Development and learning: Conflict or congruence* (pp. 173–223). Hillsdale, NJ: Erlbaum.

Brown, G., & Sproson, R.N. (1987). The involvement of memory and metamemory in the schoolwork of secondary school pupils. *Educational Studies*, *13*, 213–221.

Brown, J.S., Collins, A., & Duguid, P. (1989). Situated cognition and the culture of learning. *Educational Researcher*, *18*, 32–42.

Bruck, M., & Treiman, R. (1990). Phonological awareness and spelling in normal children and dyslexics: The case of initial consonant clusters. *Journal of Experimental Child Psychology*, *50*, 156–178.

Calfee, R. (1991). Decoding and spelling: What to teach; when to teach it; how to teach it. *Psychological Science*, *2*, 83–85.

Carbo, M. (1988). Debunking the great phonics myth. *Phi Delta Kappan*, *70*, 226–240.

Carey, S. (1986). Cognitive science and science education. *American Psychologist*, *41*, 1123–1130.

Carroll, J.B. (1963). A model of school learning. *Teachers College Record*, *64*, 723–733.

Carroll, J.B. (1989). The Carroll model: A 25 year retrospective and prospective view. *Educational Researcher*, *18*, 26–31.

Chall, J.S. (1967). *Learning to read: The great debate.* New York: McGraw-Hill.

Chall, J.S. (1989). Learning to read: The great debate twenty years later. A response to "Debunking the great phonics myth." *Phi Delta Kappan*, *71*, 521–538.

Cunningham, A.E. (1990). Explicit versus implicit instruction in phonemic awareness. *Journal of Experimental Child Psychology*, *50*, 429–444.

Dole, J.A., Duffy, G.G., Roehler, L.R., & Pearson, P.D. (1991). Moving from the old to the new: Research on reading comprehension instruction. *Review of Educational Research*, *61*, 239–246.

Duffy, G.G., Roehler, L.R., Meloth, M.S., Vavrus, L.G., Book, C., Putnam, J., & Wesselman, R. (1986). The relationship between explicit verbal explanations during reading skill instruction and student awareness and achievement: A study of reading teacher effects. *Reading Research Quarterly*, *21*, 237–250.

Duffy, G.G., Roehler, L.R., & Rackliffe, G. (1986). How teachers' instructional talk influences students' understanding of lesson content. *The Elementary School Journal*, *87*, 3–16.

Duffy, G.G., Roehler, L.R., Sivan, E., Rackliffe, G., Book, C., Meloth, M.S., Vavrus, L.G., Wesselman, R., Putnam, J., & Bassiri, D. (1987). Effects of explaining the reasoning associated with using reading strategies. *Reading Research Quarterly*, *22*, 347–368.

Durkin, D. (1978–1979). What classroom observations reveal about reading comprehension. *Reading Research Quarterly*, *14*, 481–533.

Dweck, C. (1986). Motivational processes affecting learning. *American Psychologist, 41*, 1041–1048.

Entwistle, N. (1988). Motivational factors in students' approaches in learning. In R.R. Schmeck (Ed.) *Learning strategies and learning styles* (pp. 21–51). New York: Plenum.

Folds, T.H., Footo, M.M., Guttentag, R.E., & Ornstein, P.A. (1990). When children mean to remember: Issues of context specificity, strategy effectiveness, and intentionality in the development of memory. In D.F. Bjorklund (Ed.), *Children's strategies: Contemporary views of cognitive development* (pp. 67–91). Hillsdale, NJ: Erlbaum.

Glaser, R. (1982). Instructional psychology: Past, present, and future. *American Psychologist, 37*, 292–305.

Glaser, R., & Takanishi, R. (1986). Introduction: Creating a knowledge base for education: Psychology's contributions and prospects. *American Psychologist, 41*, 1025–1028.

Howe, M.L., & O'Sullivan, J.T. (1990). The development of strategic memory: Coordinating knowledge, metamemory, and resources. In D.F. Bjorklund (Ed.), *Children's strategies: Contemporary views of cognitive development* (pp. 129–155). Hillsdale, NJ: Erlbaum.

Iran-Nejad, I. (1990). Active and dynamic self-regulation of learning processes. *Review of Educational Research, 60*, 573–602.

Juel, C., Griffith, P.L., & Gough, P.B. (1986). Acquisition of literacy: A longitudinal study of children in first and second grade. *Journal of Educational Psychology, 78*, 243–255.

Kee, D., & Davies, L. (1991). Mental effort and elaboration: A developmental analysis of accessibility effects. *Journal of Experimental Child Psychology, 52*, 1–10.

Kennedy, B.A., & Miller, D.J. (1976). Persistent use of verbal rehearsal as a function of information about its value. *Child Development, 47*, 566–569.

Kurtz, B., Schneider, W., Carr, M., Borkowski, J.G., & Rellinger, E. (1990). Strategy instruction and attributional beliefs in West Germany and the United States: Do teachers foster metacognitive development? *Contemporary Educational Psychology, 15*, 268–283.

Lawson, M.J., & Rice, D.N. (1989). Effects of training in the use of executive strategies on a verbal memory problem resulting from closed head injury. *Journal of Clinical and Experimental Neuropsychology, 11*, 842–854.

Levin, J.R. (1986). Four cognitive principles of learning-strategy instruction. *Educational Psychologist, 21*, 3–17.

Liberman, I.Y. (1988). Discussion. In J.F. Kavanagh & T.J. Truss (Eds.), *Learning disabilities: Proceedings of the national conference* (pp. 168–173) Parkston, MD: York Press.

Lodico, M.G., Ghatala, E.S., Levin, J.R., Pressley, M., & Bell, J. (1983). The effects of strategy monitoring on children's selection of effective memory strategies. *Journal of Experimental Child Psychology, 35*, 263–277.

Lysynchuk, L.M., Pressley, M., & Vye, N.J. (1990). Reciprocal teaching improves standardized reading-comprehension performance in poor comprehenders. *The Elementary School Journal, 90*, 469–484.

Moely, B.E., Hart, S.S., Santulli, K., Leal, L., Johnson, T., Rao, N., & Burney, L. (1986). How do teachers teach memory skills? *Educational Psychologist, 21*, 55–71.

Morrison, F.J. (1987, November). *Making the cut: Contrasting developmental and learning influences on cognitive growth.* Paper presented at the annual meeting of the Psychonomic Society, Seattle.

Nesher, P. (1986). Learning mathematics: A cognitive perspective. *American Psychologist, 41*, 1114–1122.

Newell, A., & Simon, H.A. (1972). *Human problem solving.* New York: Prentice-Hall.

Nolen, S.B. (1988). Reasons for studying: Motivational orientations and study strategies. *Cognition and Instruction, 5*, 269–287.

Oka, E.R., & Paris, S.G. (1987). Patterns of motivation and reading skills in underachieving children. In S.J. Ceci (Ed.), *Handbook of cognitive, social, and neuropsychological aspects of learning disabilities* (Vol. 2, pp. 115–146). Hillsdale, NJ: Erlbaum.

O'Sullivan, J.T. (1991). *Remember "M," remember "E" put them together and remember "ME": A program for teaching memory to children.* Unpublished manuscript, Memorial University of Newfoundland.

O'Sullivan, J.T., & Pressley, M. (1984). Completeness of instruction and strategy transfer. *Journal of Experimental Child Psychology, 38*, 275–288.

Palincsar, A.S., & Brown, A.L. (1984). Reciprocal teaching of comprehension-fostering and comprehension-monitoring activities. *Cognition and Instruction, 1*, 117–175.

Paris, S.G., Cross, D.R., & Lipson, M.Y. (1984). Informed strategies for learning: A program to improve children's reading awareness and comprehension. *Journal of Educational Psychology, 76*, 1239–1252.

Paris, S.G., & Jacobs, J.E. (1984). The benefits of informed instruction for children's reading awareness and comprehension skills. *Child Development, 55*, 2083–2093.

Paris, S.G., & Oka, E.R. (1986). Children's reading strategies, metacognition, and motivation. *Developmental Review, 6*, 25–56.

Pearson, P.D., & Dole, J.A. (1987). Explicit comprehension instruction: A review of research and a new conceptualization of instruction. *The Elementary School Journal, 88*, 151–165.

Perfetti, C.A. (1991). The psychology, pedagogy, and politics of reading. *Psychological Science, 2*, 70–76.

Perkins, D.N., & Salomon, G. (1989). Are cognitive skills context bound? *Educational Researcher, 18*, 16–25.

Pressley, M., Borkowski, J.G., & O'Sullivan, J.T. (1984). Memory strategy instruction is made of this: Metamemory and durable strategy use. *Educational Psychologist, 19*, 94–107.

Pressley, M., Borkowski, J.G., & O'Sullivan, J.T. (1985). Children's metamemory and the teaching of memory strategies. In D.L. Forrest-Pressley, G.E. MacKinnon, & T.G. Waller (Eds.), *Metacognition, cognition, and human performance* (pp. 111–153). Orlando, FL: Academic Press.

Pressley, M., Borkowski, J.G., & Schneider, W. (1987). Cognitive strategies: Good strategy users coordinate metacognition and knowledge. In R. Vasta & G. Whitehurst (Eds.), *Annals of Child Development* (Vol. 5, pp. 89–129). New York: JAI Press.

Pressley, M., Forrest-Pressley, D.J., Elliott-Faust, D.J., & Miller, G.E. (1985). Children's use of cognitive strategies, how to teach strategies, and what to do if they can't be taught. In M. Pressley & C.J. Brainerd (Eds.), *Cognitive learning and memory in children* (pp. 1–47). New York: Springer-Verlag.

Pressley, M., Goodchild, F., Fleet, J., Zajchowski, R., & Evans, E.D. (1989). The challenge of classroom strategy instruction. *Elementary School Journal, 89*, 301–342.

Resnick, L.B. (1985). Instructional psychology. In T. Husen & T.N. Postlethwaite (Eds.), *International encyclopedia of education: Research and studies* (pp. 2569–2581). Oxford: Pergamon Press.

Resnick, L.B. (1987). Constructing knowledge in school. In L.S. Liben (Ed.), *Development and learning: Conflict or congruence* (pp. 19–50). Hillsdale, NJ: Erlbaum.

Resnick, L.B., & Omanson, S.F. (1987). Learning to understand arithmetic. In R. Glaser (Ed.), *Advances in instructional psychology* (Vol. 3, pp. 41–95). Hillsdale, NJ: Erlbaum.

Richardson, V. (1990). Significant and worthwhile change in teaching practice. *Educational Researcher, 19*, 10–18.

Ringel, B.A., & Springer, C.J. (1980). On knowing how well one is remembering: The persistence of strategy use during transfer. *Journal of Experimental Child Psychology, 29*, 322–333.

Rogoff, B., & Mistry, J. (1985). Memory development in cultural context. In M. Pressley & C.J. Brainerd (Eds.), *Cognitive learning and memory in children* (pp. 117–142). New York: Springer-Verlag.

Schneider, W., Borkowski, J.G., Kurtz, B.E., & Kerwin, K. (1986). Metamemory and motivation: A comparison of strategy use and performance in German and American children. *Journal of Cross Cultural Psychology, 17*, 315–336.

Schneider, W., & Pressley, M. (1989). *Memory between two and twenty*. New York: Springer-Verlag.

Sirotnik, K.A. (1983). What you see is what you get—consistency, persistency, and mediocrity in classrooms. *Harvard Educational Review, 53*, 16–31.

Slavin, R.E. (1984). Component building: A strategy for research-based instructional improvement. *The Elementary School Journal, 84*, 255–269.

Stanovich, K.E. (1986). Matthew effects in reading: Some consequences of individual differences in the acquisition of literacy. *Reading Research Quarterly, 21*, 360–407.

Stanovich, K.E. (1991). Cognitive science meets beginning reading. *Psychological Science, 2*, 70–81.

Stevens, R.J., Slavin, R.E., & Farnish, A.M. (1991). The effects of cooperative learning and direct instruction in reading comprehension strategies on main idea identification. *Journal of Educational Psychology, 83*, 8–16.

Vellutino, F.R. (1991). Has basic research in reading increased our understanding of developmental reading and how to teach reading? *Psychological Science, 2*, 70–83.

Vellutino, F.R., & Scanlon, D. (1987). Phonological coding, phonological awareness, and reading ability: Evidence from a longitudinal and experimental study. *Merrill-Palmer Quarterly, 33*, 321–363.

Vygotsky, L.S. (1978). *Mind in society*. Cambridge, MA: Harvard University Press.

Wagner, R.K., & Torgesen, J.K. (1987). The nature of phonological processing and its causal role in the acquisition of reading skills. *Psychological Bulletin, 101*, 192–212.

8
Organizing Principles of the High/Scope Curriculum

David P. Weikart and Mary N. Hohmann

The development of a curriculum to assist disadvantaged children and their families relies on more than the transmittal of beliefs and traditions gained from educational training and on more than the accumulation of incremental research knowledge gleaned from academic studies. Curriculum development is a complex undertaking. Curriculum developers must possess these attributes: a commitment to a broad-based philosophy, in-depth knowledge of young children's growth and development, and practical knowledge about children's interests and activities. In addition, curriculum developers must have the ability to consolidate and interpret information gathered over an extended period of time.

The developers of the High/Scope Curriculum possess such a philosophical and intellectual orientation and commitment. This chapter examines the origin of the High/Scope Curriculum, how it has evolved over time, its central principles, and why it works so well for children, families, and society.

History of the High/Scope Curriculum

In 1962, the Perry Preschool Project was initiated by Special Services staff in the Ypsilanti, Michigan, public school system. It was a response to the embarrassing predictability of educational and psychological evaluations of disadvantaged adolescent boys and girls. Referred to psychological services because of their persistent school failure, children from Ypsilanti's poorest districts consistently scored in the lower ranges (upper 70s and low 80s) on various intelligence tests and in the bottom quartile on academic achievement tests. As early as the 1950s, school evaluators, alarmed by these trends, searched for causes and cures. Staff concluded that the children's IQ scores were the result of limited opportunities for adequate school preparation and were not accurate predictors of students' innate ability.

They also realized that the achievement problems of minority students were concealed by the segregated elementary school system prevalent at the time. As in most districts nationwide, the Ypsilanti Public Schools attendance patterns were based on neighborhood boundaries. Only when students from the segregated elementary schools moved into the district's two junior high schools were their problems fully revealed. At this level, what had been an endemic problem became a systemic one.

In 1958, after much consideration, school officials concluded that the system could not alter its basic approach to education, which was successful for the majority of the district's students. Nevertheless, a committee of three elementary principals and the Special Services director informally agreed that something had to be done regardless of the school's official position. This group—Pete Kingston, principal of George Elementary School; John Salcau, principal of Erickson Elementary School; Gean Beatty principal of Perry Elementary School; and David Weikart, director of Special Services—began a series of discussions in 1959. They explored several key issues: teaching methods, test scores, achievement patterns, referrals to outside agencies, and school boundaries. In addition, a second, more informal committee was established within the Special Services Department itself. This committee—John Mader, director of the county's Special Services unit; Norma Radin, school social worker; Byron Aldrich, school psychologist; and David Weikart, director of Special Services—looked for practical programs that might be implemented by the Special Services division.

The committee conceived the concept of *early intervention* for 3- and 4-year-olds to counter what Special Service staff perceived to be the intransigent attitudes of the majority of public school staff (as an assistant high school principal said, "We don't make adjustments for individuals"). Intervention at this level could be operated "outside" normal public school channels, avoiding the controversial issue of districtwide school reform.

The idea was to prepare disadvantaged minority preschool-age children to be as ready for school as other children. The two committees cooperated fully in this plan. The "Principal" Committee found space in a community center for the first year of the project's operation (1962–63) and then arranged for the program to move into Perry Elementary School for its remaining 5 years of operation. The "Special Services" Committee obtained permission from the state to operate the preschool education program (the first in the state-funded system) and hired the teachers and other staff.

Locating qualified teachers was an especially difficult task because there was a severe national teacher shortage at the time. Also, to ensure program effectiveness, the state required those hired to be licensed as elementary school teachers with a preschool endorsement and as special education teachers. Nevertheless, four teachers were found who met the state's requirements, and were also representative of the local community.

Another critical issue the Special Services Committee faced was the selection of a curriculum. The typical play school and cooperative nurseries of the time employed a free-play and theme-based orientation focused on children's social and emotional growth (Sears & Dowley, 1963). The committee believed, however, that, considering the population being served, they needed to focus more attention on academic and intellectual development. The committee's visit to a unique afterschool preschool program in Detroit in the fall of 1961 lent credence to this belief. Children in this innovative program had "play time" with the usual preschool toys and supplies, followed by a juice and cookie snack time. To leave the table after snack, each child had to say "Excuse me" to the remaining children at the table. The teacher stood back from the table, next to the door. The last child sat for a long time at the table, although obviously finished. Finally the teacher asked him if he knew what to do. He said, "Yea." She said, "Well, do it." So the young lad stood and said the required "Excuse me" to the empty table. The Committee decided they did not want this type of "manners and morals" program, but rather a program with a "cognitive" orientation that would support children's intellectual and academic growth. There was not, however, a clear path to follow to attain this goal.

Given the absence of a suitable curriculum, the Special Services Committee invited a small group of university experts to consult on the organization and operation of the proposed preschool program. However, one of these experts advised the group not to proceed with the program because it would probably harm the children! The experts cautioned that 3- and 4-year-olds were not old enough for a "school-based" program because they lacked mental and emotional maturity.

In response to this caution, the committee established the Perry Preschool Project as a true experiment in preschool effectiveness. They randomly assigned children to treatment and control groups to test the project's validity and to answer the question, "Does high quality early education make a difference in the lives of children?" In addition, the committee decided to develop a curriculum that met the goal of "teaching" appropriate content in an informal, nondirective manner—contrary to the prevailing free-play theories of the time.

Staff believed that to be effective the curriculum must meet three basic criteria. First, curriculum theory must provide the vision and the limits to guide the teaching and learning process. The theory must support the group's fundamental belief in the capacity of each child to develop his or her internal talents and abilities through ongoing opportunities for active involvement with people, materials, events, and ideas. Second, to support the active teaching and learning approach, the curriculum must incorporate specific "key" experiences in learning and employ child observation techniques as standard processes in daily program operations. Thus, the teachers must be involved in all aspects of curriculum development as equal partners with researchers and administrators. Third, the curriculum must achieve a balance between theory and practice after careful consideration of the viewpoints of theorists and practitioners. The project director would assume ultimate decision-making authority in this area.

After the first year of operation of the Perry Preschool Project, staff firmly believed a more systematic, coherent approach was needed if they were to achieve their goals. In the spring of 1963 the Special Services Committee discovered the writings of Jean Piaget as summarized in *Intelligence and Experience* by J. McVicker Hunt (1961). Clearly, this theory supported the philosophical orientation of project staff, and they found much in it to guide their thinkng. However, the Special Services Committee, now expanded to include the researchers and teachers in the project, gradually split into a "research" group and a "teacher" group. The researchers wished to maintain strict interpretations of Piaget's theories in classroom settings. The teachers, however, pressed for more informal interpretation tempered by their observations of children, their professional experience, and their desire to maintain traditional "tried-and-true" nursery school practices. Because of this situation, the Special Services Committee decided to translate Piaget's theories into daily operations (Weikart, Rogers, Adcock, & McClelland, 1971; Hohmann, Banet, & Weikart, 1979). Although not entirely pleasing to some theoreticians even today (DeVries & Kohlberg, 1987), this "blended" approach is reasonable to others (Forman & Fosnot, 1982).

The basic form of the High/Scope Curriculum took shape in the spring of 1964 with the "plan-do-review" sequence as a core, and staff made a firm commitment to support children in their construction of knowledge, relationships, and ideas. Staff devised key experiences in learning essential to development. In the early 1970s the key experiences were stated more systematically to provided a framework to help teachers understand more clearly children's development as active learners. Today, the High/Scope Curriculum's active learning approach is based on more than 25 years of classroom implementation and training experience.

The staff's debate about how to interpret Piagetian theory for classroom practice was tempered by an awareness that learning does not occur under carefully controlled conditions. After all, a child does not develop wisdom through discussions with genetic epistemologists trained by Piaget (1952, 1970, 1973), or by treading the "zone of proximal development" under the guidance of Vygotsky (1978). Rather, the child uses complex abilities when engaging in the learning opportunities presented by the real world. Our responsibility as teachers, parents, and administrators is to assess key issues in the realms of theoretical knowledge, experience, culture, and aspirations in order to provide the best possible program for children. This ongoing effort is what produces high quality programs.

Today we know much more about what constitutes high quality early childhood education than we did in 1962. From following the Perry Preschool Project participants into adulthood, we know that their early education experience had significant, positive long-term effects—greatly improving their life chances (Berrueta-Clement, Schweinhart, Barnett, Epstein, & Weikart, 1984). This improvement occurred because the 3- and 4-year-old children where given ample opportunities to construct their own knowledge of the world with the support of well-informed, dedicated staff and involved parents, within a rich, "active learning" environment. Using Piagetian concepts as a base, the staff provided time for the children to plan their play activities, carry them out, and reflect on the actions they had taken. Further, through home visits, staff engaged parents in thinking about the process of schooling. The home visits also encouraged teachers to think about the needs of parents. The teaching staff served as a resource, introducing ideas as needed but not "crowding" children or parents.

Apparently, giving the children control of their environment and their relationships with peers and adults had a significant impact on children's long-term development. The long-term effects of the High/Scope Curriculum indicate that a high quality preschool education program has great value for children and families. Children who participated in the program—in contrast to the children in a nonparticipating control group—experienced increased success in school, increased employment, and reduced social problems such as crime, teen pregnancy, and welfare dependency (Berrueta-Clement et al., 1984).

Although other approaches to early childhood education have been implemented over the last 30 years, few have developed a research base that documents as clearly the success of the program on the lives of the participating children (Roopnarine & Johnson, 1987). The next section presents the design and findings from the study through age 19 years.

The High/Scope Perry Preschool Study

Design

The High/Scope Perry Preschool study identified young children living in poverty, randomly assigned them to preschool and no-preschool groups, operated a high quality child development program for the preschool group at ages 3 and 4 years, and collected data on both groups of children throughout their childhood, adolescence, and in young adulthood—ages 19 and 28.

The longitudinal sample consists of 123 persons who, at least during the 1960s, lived in the attendance area of the Perry Elementary School in Ypsilanti, Michigan. This sample was accumulated over a 4- year period, beginning with 28 4-year-olds and 17 3-year-olds in 1962, followed by 26 3-year-olds in 1963, 27 in 1964, and 25 in 1965. These children were invited to join the study sample because their families lived in poverty, as assessed by parent's years of schooling and employment status, and because the children had low intelligence-test scores at age 3 years (or age 4 years in the 1962 sample). Their mothers had completed a median of 9.7 years of schooling and their fathers, 8.8. In 58% of the families at least one parent was employed—usually in unskilled labor. Half the families received welfare assistance; 47% had no father living with them. All members of the study sample were black, as was virtually everyone living in the attendance area of the Perry Elementary School where every household was surveyed to locate qualified samples. The preschool group had 58 members and the no-preschool group had 65.

The internal validity of the study rests on the accomplishment of random assignment to groups: neither parents nor teachers had a choice about which children attended the preschool program—no parent refused to cooperate at any stage of the selection process.

Sources of data include parent interviews when children were 3 and 15 years of age; annual intelligence and language tests from ages 3 to 10 and at age 14 years; annual achievement tests from ages 7 to 11 and at ages 14 and 19 years; annual teacher ratings from ages 6 to 9 years; participant interviews at ages 15 and 19 and now at age 28 years; school record information collected at ages 11, 15, and 19 years; and police and social services records information collected at age 19 years. Age-28 data are now being collected, therefore information is not yet available. The median percentage of missing cases across all data sources is under 5%, with only four measures exceeding 25%. Only two cases were missing for the crucial age-19 interview.

In this chapter, we report only those findings whose probability of chance occurrence is less than 0.05, based on conservative, nondirectional two-tailed tests of statistical significance. Thus, *all* differences between groups mentioned the following results section are significantly different at this alpha level unless they are specifically said not to be.

Results

The preschool group surpassed the no-preschool group in intellectual performance from ages 4 to 7 years. Probably because of this intellectual boost and the increased language skills, problem solving, and sense of control of self supported by the curriculum, the preschool group achieved significantly greater school success than the no-preschool group—higher school achievement and literacy, better placement in school, stronger commitment to schooling, and more years of school completed. It is also likely that it was because of this greater school success that the preschool group surpassed the no-preschool group in teenage socioeconomic success and social responsibility: higher rates of employment and self-support, a lower welfare rate, fewer acts of serious misconduct, and a lower arrest rate. Analysis of financial costs and benefits revealed that the program provided a substantial return on public investment.

Initial Boost in Intellectual Performance and Motivation

On the average, the preschool group outperformed the no-preschool group on the Stanford-Binet Intelligence Scale from ages 4 to 7 years. The average intelligence test scores of the two groups differed by 12 points at ages 4 and 5, six points at age 6, and five points at age 7 years. The two groups had the same mean intelligence test scores before the preschool program and again at ages 8, 9, 10, and 14 years.

The preschool group also had a significantly higher average—across ages 6 through 9 years—than the no-preschool group on teacher ratings of school motivation (such items as "shows initiative," "alert and interested in schoolwork," and "motivated toward academic performance"). In kindergarten through sixth grade, members of the preschool group averaged 11.9 days absent per school year, whereas, members of the no-preschool group averaged 16.3.

Improved School Success

The average score of the preschool group on the California Achievement Test was slightly but not statistically significantly higher at ages 6 through 10 years, and both statistically significantly and substantially higher at 14 years. At age 19 years, the preschool group outscored the no-preschool group in basic literacy on the Adult Performance Level Survey.

Despite the fact that subjects' intelligence test scores at age 3 years theoretically placed them on the borderline of mental impairment at that time, only 15% of the preschool group and 35% of the no-preschool group were subsequently classified as mentally impaired. Preschool-group members averaged 1.0 school years receiving supplementary compensatory education classes, in addition to regular education classes, as compared to 0.4 school years averaged by members of the no-preschool group. Combining the two types of extra educational services, preschool-group members averaged 3.0 school years in special and compensatory education, whereas no-preschool group members averaged 4.0 school years. These differences would have been even greater if the no-preschool group's high school graduation rate had been as high as the preschool group's.

Sixty-seven percent of the preschool group, but only 49% of the no-preschool group, graduated from high school. The preschool group's graduation rate equaled that of all black 19- and 20-year-olds in the U. S. in 1980, according to U. S. census data. At age 19 years, 38% of the preschool group, but only 21% of the no-preschool group, were receiving postsecondary education, either academic or vocational.

Greater Success as Adolescents in the Community

Half of the preschool group, but only one-third of the no-preschool group, were employed when interviewed at age 19 years. Since leaving school, the preschool group had averaged 4.9 months without work, whereas the no-preschool group averaged 10.3; moreover, the preschool group reported greater job satisfaction than the no-preschool group. In the preschool group 45% compared to only 25% of the no-preschool group said they supported themselves by their own and/or their spouses' earnings.

When interviewed at age 19 years, 18% of the preschool group, but 32% of the no-preschool group, reported they were currently receiving welfare assistance. According to the records of the Michigan Department of Social Services, 19% of the preschool group, as compared to 41% of the no-preschool group, had ever received General Assistance (in poverty, but not qualified for AFDC—Aid to Families with Dependent Children) as an adult or principal grantee, with most of these people receiving Food Stamps as well. Although the forgoing differences were significant, the groups did not differ to a statistically significant extent in their overall use of Food Stamps, AFDC, or Medicaid.

At age 15 years, the preschool group reported significantly fewer acts of misconduct than did the no-preschool group, including fewer acts of serious misconduct—233 compared to 319 acts per 100 people. At age 19 years, although similar differences in self-reported misconduct were not statistically significant, the preschool group reported fewer involvements in serious fights, gang fights, inflictions of injuries needing medical attention, and run-ins with the police than did the no-preschool group (Schweinhart, 1987, p. 141).

Police arrest records confirm this pattern. Only 31% of the preschool group, but 51% of the no-preschool group, where ever arrested as juveniles or as adults. Seven percent of the preschool group, as compared to 17% of the no-preschool group, had been arrested five or more times. The arrest rate of the no-preschool group, 230 arrests per 100 people, was nearly twice that of the preschool group, which was only 126 arrests per 100 people; there were statistically significant group differences in the numbers of both major and minor charges. The rate per 100 people of property and violence charges was 81 for the preschool group, as compared to 117 for the no-preschool group (Schweinhart, 1987, p. 142).

Teen girls in the preschool group reported fewer pregnancies than did teen girls in the no-preschool group (68 compared to 117 pregnancies per 100 girls), but this is a marginal difference statistically.

Substantial Return on Investment

Taxpayers received substantial returns on their investment in the Perry Preschool Program—$3.00 for every dollar invested in the 60-week program at age 3 and 4 years and $5.95 for every dollar invested in the 30-week program at age 4 years. The dollar figures reported in this section are the per-child costs and benefits expressed in 1988 constant dollars discounted at 3% annually. The ledgers of the Ypsilanti Public Schools provided a thorough accounting of program costs for personnel, overhead, supplies, child selection, and building space. Due largely to the high teacher-child ratios, the costs were high, about $6,500 per child-year. Reducing the ratios from 1:6 to 1:10 would have reduced the cost per child-year to $3,900.

The benefits of the program generated $39,278 per child in financial benefits to taxpayers. Taxpayers saved $7,005 per child because of reduced special education costs, $4,252 because of reduced crime costs to victims and the criminal justice system, and $22,490 because of reduced welfare payments. It cost them $964 per child because more of the preschool group than the no-preschool group received postsecondary education, but this higher education attainment meant that the preschool group would have higher lifetime earnings and therefore pay $6,495 in additional lifetime taxes.

Preschool Curriculum Approaches

In 1967, the Special Services Committee launched another research effort, the Curriculum Comparison study, to examine the relative effectiveness of the High/Scope Curriculum against other major alternative curriculum approaches. Figure 8.1 provides an overview of the major emphasis of these early childhood curriculum approaches. (See Weikart, 1972, and Weikart, Epstein, Schweinhart, & Bond, 1978, for an earlier discussion of this study; Kohlberg & Mayer, 1972, for a similar overview; and Johnson, 1987, for a description of curriculum models organized along a continuum.)

In all curriculum approaches, adults and children interact. However, the role the adult plays relative to the child and the role the child assumes as learner vary across curricula depending on the program's theoretical model of learning and social development. Adults employ a wide range of roles in their interactions with children in all curricula approaches, yet

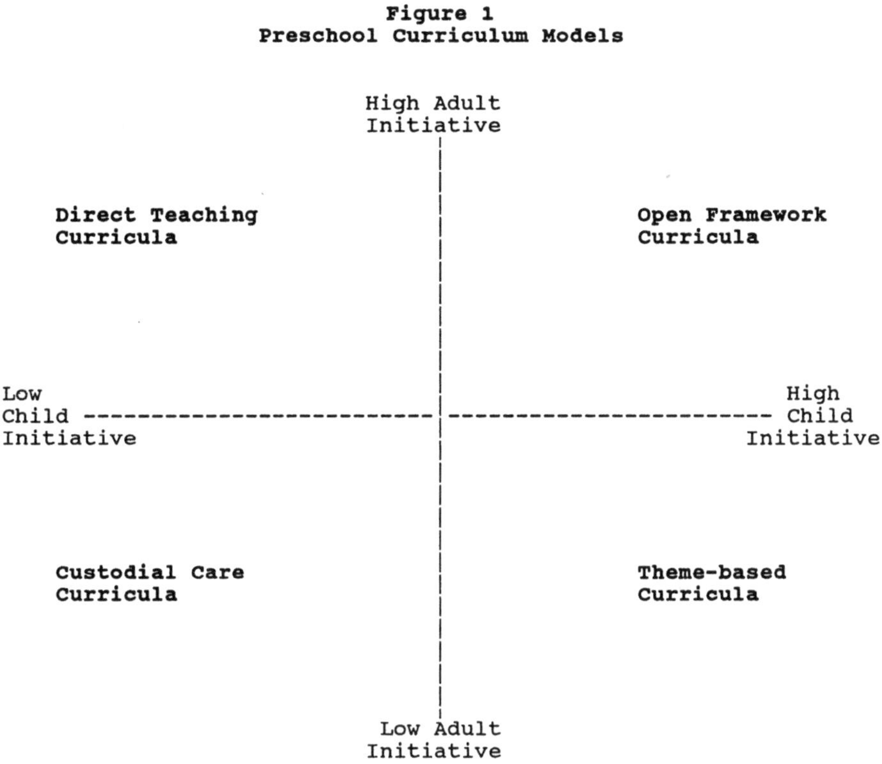

FIGURE 8.1. Preschool curriculum models.

when viewed in terms of curriculum implementation, distinctive belief systems and interaction styles prevail.

First, adults can be "active, high-level" initiators as they approach children and curriculum, or they can be "low-level, less active" initiators. Regardless of their level of initiative, however, effective adults in all curriculum approaches are supportive, observant, and willing to accommodate children's interests and desires within the curriculum framework they employ.

Second, across programs children exhibit a wide range of behaviors, but certain actions characterize each curriculum model. Children can be "active, high-level" initiators responsible for their decisions, or they can be "receptive, low-level" initiators who spend considerable time waiting, listening to adults, and following adult directions. Of course, well-run programs of any type have cooperative, motivated children, although the percentage of such children depends on instructional and management methods.

Direct Teaching Curricula

Depending on the level of initiative in adults and children, different curricula are manifested, as illustrated in Figure 8.1. A Direct Teaching curriculum is characterized by "high-initiative" adults and "low-initiative" children—generally found in traditional classrooms. In such classrooms, an adult is in charge of children, who receive knowledge organized by either the teacher or textbooks. Lawrence Schweinhart, a High/Scope Foundation researcher, refers to these programs as "keyboard" curricula—all the knowledge is stored (in adults, texts, computer programs) and the child's job is to learn to press the right keys to release information about colors, numbers, state capitals, multiplication tables, shapes, and so forth. These "programmed curricula" include many computer-assisted instructional programs and most textbooks. In these methods, adults use a system of rewards and related behavior modification techniques to motivate children and encourage cooperation. (For one of the best examples of this approach, see Bereiter and Engelmann, 1966.).

Custodial Care Curricula

It is interesting to note that custodial care programs are also content-oriented. Rather than providing information on colors and numbers, however, the program focuses on feeding, nap, and toilet schedules, washing and bathing routines, and a limited amount of free play. The adult's role is "low-initiative" in terms of supporting children's active learning and social development, and without adult support children also tend to be "low-level" initiators of active learning experiences and social interactions. We have seen such programs in some family and center-based day care in this country and in nutrition and health programs in other countries (Kagitcibasi, Sunar, & Bekman, 1988).

Theme-Based Curricula

Traditional preschool programs have involved children in Theme-Based curricula (Katz & Chard, 1989). Here, the teacher establishes "themes"—a trip to the dentist or the market, seasons, holidays—around which to focus children's energies and inventive natures. If the children do not focus on the theme, however, adults tend to become more directive. Some theme-based programs tend to resemble direct-teaching programs. On the other hand, others tend to look more like custodial care programs because adults leave children to their own devices rather than interacting with them.

Open Framework Curricula

In an Open Framework curriculum children build or construct their own knowledge through direct participation and involvement with people, materials, events, and ideas. They take control of their own learning opportunities. By constructing knowledge through active engagement, children gain the dispositions that support successful life-long learning. Adults and children share control over the content of learning, but adults support and rely on children's inventive energies to create their own understanding of the world. The High/Scope Curriculum is one example of an Open Framework curriculum (Hohmann et al., 1979).

The High/Scope Preschool Curriculum Study

Design

The preschool curriculum study (Schweinhart, Weikart, & Larner, 1986), operating in the public schools of Ypsilanti, Michigan, served children 3 and 4 years old between 1967 and 1970 who lived in families of low socioeconomic status and who, according to test scores, were at risk of failing in school.

Children were assigned to one of the three curriculum models described above by a random-assignment procedure that was also designed to assure the initial comparability of the groups. The curriculum models were all operated under similar administrative conditions to high standards of quality.

Common Characteristics of the Programs

All three programs in the study were part of the same research project, with the same director (Weikart), funding source, personnel policies, and position in the school system. All three programs in the study had two components—classroom sessions and educational home visits. Classroom sessions lasting $2\frac{1}{2}$ hours were held 5 days a week, Monday through Friday. A teacher visited each mother and child at home in 90-min sessions every 2 weeks, during the part of the day when the class was not meeting. During the home visits, the teacher encouraged the mother to engage her child in learning activities that fit the curriculum approach used in that classroom.

Classes, operating between 1967 and 1970, consisted of either 15 or 16 3- and 4-year-olds. Two teachers were assigned to each classroom group, making the typical ratio of teachers to children about 1 to 8. In addition, each classroom had a teacher assistant who also drove the bus; and, in each classroom, a female high school special education student was employed and received school credit to provide custodial care, particularly on bus rides to and from school and on field trips.

Each of the three teaching teams engaged in daily evaluation and planning sessions, reviewing activities and the progress of individual children, but the teams did not engage in joint planning or meetings. A staff supervisor provided guidance to all three teams and used the daily evaluation and planning sessions to help them maintain curriculum model goals and meet the needs of individual children. Whereas it is possible that the director or supervisor could have exhibited subtle biases for or against a particular curriculum model, elaborate managerial procedures militated against it. Each program was frequently reviewed for faithfulness of curriculum implementation by nonteaching staff and outside consultants, who observed the classroom and met with the teachers and supervisor.

The teaching team implementing the Distar model received training from University of Illinois consultants trained and employed by the Bereiter–Engelmann curriculum development team. The team implementing the High/Scope model engaged in the development of that model and continued to work with High/Scope curriculum consultants on further refinement. The team implementing the nursery school model developed it themselves, drawing on their early childhood education training, experience with children, and teacher intuition, which is highly valued in this approach.

Sample Selection

Sixty-eight children met the study's criteria for inclusion: they were residents of Ypsilanti, Michigan, they became 3 years old between 1967 and 1969 inclusively, they lived in families of low socioeconomic status, and they were at risk of school failure according to test scores.

Participants in the study were selected from among the three age cohorts of Ypsilanti children who became 3 years old between 1967 and 1969. Participants in the study were born between 1964 and 1966, attended the preschool programs at ages 3 and 4 years between 1967 and 1970, and responded to interviews at age 10 years between 1974 and 1976 and again at age 15 years between 1979 and 1981.

Each September from 1967 to 1969, the 3-year-olds in these families took the Stanford-Binet Intelligence Scale (Form L-M; Terman & Merrill, 1970). Children with IQs between 60 and 90, with no evidence of physical disability, became eligible for enrollment in the preschool programs of the study. The mean IQ of the sample at program entry was 78.3. On this basis, before they attended the preschool programs the children in the study could have been temporarily classified as slow learners, at risk of school failure.

Assignment to Curriculum Models

Each year, the children in a new wave were randomly assigned to three groups, with reassignments until the three groups were comparable in race, gender, and mean IQ at program entry. The three groups were then randomly assigned to the three preschool curriculum models. In a departure from random assignment, siblings were assigned to the same curriculum models to prevent confusion of the effects of two curriculum models within families; this procedure affected 9 of the 68 children.

Each school year, the preschool programs brought together two waves of children—one as 4-year-olds and one as 3-year-olds. Because of this feature, two additional waves of children participated in the preschool programs with the study participants—one wave of children before the study sample, one after—but were not part of the study.

Initial Sample and Group Characteristics

Characteristics at program entry of the 68 children in the program sample and their families are as follows: 65% were black; 54% were female; the families lived in poverty, one out of three receiving welfare assistance; in the 75% of families for whom fathers were present, 98% of the fathers were employed in unskilled labor; 38% of the mothers were employed in unskilled labor; fathers averaged 9 years of schooling, mothers 10; the average household had 6.7 persons, or one person per room.

Curriculum groups were similar on the key characteristics of gender, family socioeconomic status, and child IQ at program entry. However, the nursery school group did have some initial advantages over the other groups, particularly the High/Scope group: a higher level of mothers' schooling and fewer single-parent families. Also, fewer blacks and more whites were in the nursery school group.

Preschool Curriculum Effects on Intellectual and Scholastic Performance

The three preschool programs in the High/Scope Preschool Curriculum study were designed with the goal of giving children at risk of school failure the skills they would need to meet the demands of schooling. Evidence from other studies has shown that preschool experience can produce at least a temporary improvement in intellectual and social skills (McKey et al., 1985) that then should help children establish positive patterns of school performance—leading to increased motivation, commitment, and expectations for success on the part of students themselves, parents, and teachers (Schweinhart & Weikart, 1980; Lazar, Darlington, Murray, Royce, & Snipper, 1982).

Preschool Curriculum Effects on Intellectual Performance

When the mean IQs of the three preschool curriculum groups are compared, the differences between them are quite small. During the first year of the preschool program, mean IQs rose between 23 and 29 points, moving the groups of children out of the at-risk category. During the second preschool year, mean IQs of the High/Scope and nursery school groups dropped 9 to 10 points, whereas that of the Distar group dropped only 3 points and thereby achieved the only statistically significant intellectual advantage among groups at any testing. From the end of kindergarten onward, curriculum groups did not differ in mean IQs and stabilized in the range of 90 to 100.

Preschool Curriculum Effects on School Achievement

The achievement scores gathered on all the children were the California Achievement Tests at the end of first through fifth grades. Although each of the groups gained between 50 and 60 points between testings (using the same test form), the groups were not significantly different from one another at any time. This is to be expected, since the early IQ differences that separated the groups diminished by kindergarten and disappeared by the second grade. The modest early advantage that the Distar group had over the other two was not translated into superior achievement in elementary school.

Rounding out our understanding of the achievement abilities of the youths in the study is the Adult Performance Level (APL) Survey (American College Testing Program, 1976), which measures a person's competence in solving real-world problems and coping with the cognitive demands of adult life. The APL total and subscale scores of the three preschool groups show that the Distar group scored the lowest on 9 of the 11 APL scales, to a statistically significant extent for occupational knowledge and approaching a statistically significant extent for writing.

Preschool Curriculum Effects on Social Behavior

Juvenile delinquency and other aspects of social behavior were examined for the Curriculum study sample by self-reports at age 15 years. According to these data, the Distar group engaged in twice as many delinquent acts as did the other two curriculum groups, including five times as many acts of property violence and twice as many acts of drug abuse and such status offenses as running away from home. Other areas of social behavior corroborate this pattern of relatively poor social performance by the Distar group—poor family relations, less participation in sports or school job appointments, lower expectations for educational attainment, and less reaching out to others for help with personal problems. For most of these variables, the sharpest contrast was with the High/Scope group, whose social behavior was relatively positive. The curriculum groups performed similarly to each other in the spheres of employment and money, in measured self-esteem, and in perceived locus of control.

Preschool Curriculum Effects on Juvenile Delinquency

The average member of the Distar group engaged in 13 self-reported delinquent acts, the average nursery school group member engaged in seven, and the average High/Scope group member engaged in five. On all but one item of the 18-item scale, the Distar group reported the highest frequency, or was tied for the highest frequency, of the three groups.

The 18-item delinquency scale is divided into five subscales: personal violence, property violence, stealing, drug abuse, and status offenses. The Distar group engaged in twice as many acts of personal violence as the other two groups, but this difference was not statistically significant because of the large variation among individuals within groups, particularly the Distar group. The Distar group had the highest frequencies of the three groups on each of the five items in that subscale.

The Distar group engaged in five times as many acts of property violence as did the other two groups, reporting 1.7 acts per person as compared to only 0.3 acts per person in the other two groups. The Distar group had the highest frequencies of the three groups on each of the three items in that subscale; the difference in the arson category approached statistical significance. Groups did not differ significantly in frequencies reported for the stealing subscale.

The Distar group reported that they engaged in twice as many acts of drug abuse as did the other two groups, in use of both marijuana and other illegal drugs. The Distar group reported that they engaged in twice as many activities that we have labeled "status offenses," exceeding the other two groups in fights with parents, trespassing, and, to a statistically significant extent, running away from home.

Curriculum groups at age 15 years did not yet manifest statistically significant differences in the official consequences of juvenile delinquency. Gold (1970) reported similar findings, that group differences in self-reported delinquency did not yet show up in arrest rate differences for 15-year-olds. Regardless of curriculum group, half the members of the sample reported having been picked up or arrested by police by age 15 years; the average sample member reported contact with the police 0.5 times.

Preschool Curriculum Effects on Other Social Variables

The one statistically significant group difference in the family domain was that one out of three members of the Distar group said their families felt they were doing poorly, a response made by only 1 out of 36 members of the other two curriculum groups combined. Similarly, although not to a statistically significant extent, one out of five members of the Distar group reported getting along poorly with their families, whereas no one in the High/Scope group made this response. Finally, one out of three members of the High/Scope group reported contributing to household expenses, whereas fewer than one out of six members of the Distar group did so. Given the substantially higher rates of delinquent behavior reported by the Distar group, their greater frequency of poor family relations should come as no surprise.

In the activities domain, the biggest group difference was in sports participation: nearly all of the High/Scope group participated in sports, whereas fewer than half of the Distar group did so. Compared to members of the Distar group, twice as many members of the High/Scope group had recently read a book.

No one in the Distar group had ever been appointed to an office or special job at school. The strongest contrast here was with the nursery school group, which reported one out of three members with some school appointment. Only half of the Distar group expected to pursue postsecondary education, whereas two thirds of the nursery school group and three quarters of the High/Scope group expected to do so.

The general picture of group differences that emerges at age 15 years is that, when compared to the other two groups, more of the Distar group members reported that they were not socially well adjusted.

Summary

The High/Scope Curriculum accepted the challenge of becoming an Open Framework program and balancing adult responsibilities with child-initiated learning. The validity of this decision has been strengthened by the findings from the High/Scope Curriculum Comparison study, established by High/Scope to test the efficacy of the Open Framework, Theme-Based, and Direct Teaching approaches. Children who participated in a Direct Teaching approach (Bereiter & Engelmann, 1966) performed the same on tests and academic measures as children in the Theme-Based and Open Framework programs during their early school years. As adolescents, however, those youth from the Direct Teaching preschool program reported more delinquency and alienation from family and school than the children who had participated in the other preschool approaches. This particular study suggests that curricula that permit children to initiate their own learning are more effective in helping them become socially responsible adults. (See Karnes, Schwedel, & Williams, 1983, and Miller & Bizzell, 1983, for cautions about the effectiveness of direct teaching with preoperational children.)

How is an Open Framework curriculum organized so that children can move naturally through the stages of development; can deal with direct information as needed (children do not need to invent social conventions

TABLE 8.1 High/Scope curriculum organization: birth through adolescence.

	Sensorimotor years	Preoperational years	Concrete operational years	Formal operational years
Age	$0-2\frac{1}{2}$ years	$2\frac{1}{2}-6$ years	7–10 years	11 years and up
How children learn	Direct experience, active learning Interaction with adult caregivers	Verbal intentions Direct experience, active learning Verbal reflection	Verbal intentions Direct experience, active learning Verbal reflection Generative use of direct information	Verbal intentions Direct experience, active learning Verbal reflection Generative use of direct information Group work Engagement with the hypothetical
Key program elements	Interactive play based on child's interests	Plan-to-review Represent: tell, draw, invented writing	Plan-do-review Represent: tell, draw, build, write	Plan-do-review Represent: tell, draw, build, write, verify, and present
What children learn	Explore physical reality Develop trust, autonomy, initiative, and empathy	Language Explore classification, seriation, number, space, time, movement Develop curiosity, initiative, interests, and friendships	Reading, math, science writing, music, movement, art, and drama Develop social network	History, literature, philosophy, science, dance, languages, art, religion, math, music, civics Develop peer, social, activity groups
Adult role	*Observant teaching* Provide materials, opportunities Support active learning	*Supportive teaching* Provide materials and opportunities Support active learning Provide information as needed Encourage reflection	*Emergent teaching* Provide materials and opportunities Support active, learning Provide information as needed Encourage reflection Encourage production	*Dialogue teaching* Provide materials and opportunities Support active learning Provide information as needed Encourage reflection Encourage production Support hypothetical thinking

although they have to construct their own understanding of them); and can maintain a high level of initiative and active involvement in their own learning and social development? Table 8.1 provides a means of organizing this rather complex process.

High/Scope Curriculum Framework

The High/Scope Curriculum is organized around the developmental stages defined by Piaget: sensorimotor (infancy–$2\frac{1}{2}$ years); preoperational ($2\frac{1}{2}$–6 years); concrete operational (7–10 years); and formal operational (11 years–adult). High/Scope's curriculum implementation efforts have also been shaped over time by broad interpretations of the implications that children's development at each stage have for teaching and learning. Neo-Piagetians, like Donaldson (1978), believe that Piaget's age ranges are useful guides for children's development, but must be viewed with great flexibility. Children develop and mature at different rates, depending on their inborn natures and the range of opportunities provided in their specific environments. Some 3-year-olds, for example, may still exhibit characteristics of the sensorimotor stage of development. Other children may think and express themselves in "preoperational" terms, and others may actually teach themselves to read. High/Scope views children's ages as general rather than strict guidelines.

Looking at how children learn, key program elements, what children learn, and the role adults play in the process are effective ways to examine the central issues of learning from birth onward.

The Role of Language and Direct Experience in Early Learning

From birth, the direct experience of language profoundly impacts children's learning and social development. Sensorimotor and preoperational children develop language through a complex process that is both genetic and environmental. Basically, very young children acquire words to match their growing experience and knowledge of their particular world. They build their understanding and use of language through their trial-and-error experiences with people and materials. For example, a child learns what "hot" means through direct, tactile experiences with heated liquids, stoves, lighted candles, and so forth. "Twist the block; then it will fit in the hole," makes sense only when the child has matched the block and the hole many times through practice. Children learn the meaning of words through their own experiences and use words to convey and reflect this understanding.

Direct experience of the physical world is also essential to children's growth and development. Young children learn best from direct physical experience with people, materials, events, and ideas. Whereas older children can wrestle with concepts, theories, and hypotheses, such abstractions are not sufficient in themselves to promote and strengthen young children's learning.

How Children Learn

Indeed, the High/Scope Curriculum assumes that direct experience and active learning are absolutely essential to all children at all stages of development. This commitment is in contrast to the tendency in schools and society at large to substitute passive language and visual learning experiences gradually for active engagement and to encourage indirect rather than direct experiences. To explain this position, let us consider the effectiveness of a movie-viewing experience as a learning activity. The movie "Lawrence of Arabia," for example, creates a vivid image of the Sinai Desert and the privations people undergo as they cross it. Simply watching Lawrence and his men suffer from lack of water and searing heat, however, does not evoke equivalent understanding in a viewer sitting in an air-conditioned theater sipping an iced soft drink. Unless one has experienced desert thirst, one cannot truly understand the actual suffering of those who have. Although this is an extreme example, it does highlight the importance of direct experience in education. Children do not really understand what sand is until they have had experiences playing with it.

For sensorimotor children, an essential aspect of direct experience and active learning is their ongoing interaction with positive, supportive adults. Infants and toddlers need to make eye contact with their caregivers. Infants need touching and close body contact with adults who rock them, pat their backs to a steady beat, bath, feed, care for, and play with them. These types of interactions with attentive adults are critical to infants' learning and social development.

Rapid verbal development characterizes the preoperational child. In addition to direct experience and active learning, adult support for children's verbal intentions and reflection becomes increasingly important. Whereas children communicate and follow their interests from birth onward, indicating their intentions, making their own decisions, and describing their experiences in their own words emerge as distinctive patterns during the preoperational stage of growth and development. For example, when a child engages in a conversation about a topic of personal interest and an adult listens attentively, makes comments, and asks specific questions, the child has the opportunity to think out loud, decide on the direction and content of the conversation, and experience adult respect and partnership.

At the concrete operational level children are developing language skills to the point where they can use written words as tools for learning.

It is important at this point, however, that adults do not substitute reading and writing for experience-based learning. In learning to read and write, children need to continue to construct their own understanding of words and make decisions about how to use what they know and understand. Although adults can and must provide information to children, at the same time they must turn that information over to children to use for themselves. For example, an adult might suggest, "Tap your shoulders and then your knees," to introduce the concept of steady beat, which children might never discover or invent on their own. "What other parts of your body can you tap?" turns control over to the children who then generate their own creative solutions. Or an adult might introduce a science concept: "Seeds grow and create new plants. What conditions make seeds sprout and grow? Let's find out." If the children are ready for science problems, then they are ready to generate their own solutions.

Providing information to concrete operational children is easy. The challenge lies in creating a supportive active learning environment where they can use information to generate their own solutions. Otherwise, schooling breaks down. Adults, textbooks, and tests take control over learning, and students become bored. On the other hand, when students put new information to use, they actively engage in making decisions and constructing knowledge. In this context, test scores, although useful for some accounting or screening needs, are virtually irrelevant indicators of children's success. Rather, it is children's capacity to plan, try out their ideas, think about them, and express their findings that builds success and competence.

By the time formal operations emerge, children have developed great capacity to think and work "like an adult." Although children of all ages work in groups, the formal operational student, in particular, needs to discuss ideas and experiences and focus on group work processes. The success of the new industrial models in providing quality control and self-governing work teams and employee initiatives to improve productivity point to the importance of fostering group work skills. The shift to this intense type of verbal exchange is possible because by this time students are able to engage in hypothetical reasoning. Although a teenager's "What ifs" can drive parents and teachers to distraction, such thinking characterizes their developing ability to construct and integrate new ideas and viewpoints into their daily lives. Supported by their ongoing active learning experiences and opportunities for decision-making, teenagers are motivated to wrestle with hypothetical ideas.

Plan-Do-Review: A Key Program Element

During the sensorimotor period infants and toddlers need to play to develop a sense of independence and to explore things that attract their attention. Yet simply providing a rich environment with ample opportunities to explore is not sufficient for promoting development at this stage. Infants and toddlers also need to interact in two-way communication with positive, supportive adults. By taking turns with children, observing and following children's interests and initiatives, and allowing them to control the pace of events, adults support and respond appropriately to children's needs. Children, in turn, develop a sense of trust and efficacy.

During the preoperational period, the plan-do-review cycle supports child-initiated action. Adults encourage children to express their intentions by asking, for example, "What would you like to do?" "How do you plan to make it?" Children then carry out their plans, which may last a few minutes or for an hour or more. Dramatic play involving several children, cooking enterprises to "feed" playmates, block structures, and drawings are common activities during this "Do" stage. After each play period, adults encourage children to review their experiences. The children may talk about what they did or express themselves in drawings and "writings." Representing their work in these ways, children begin to retain knowledge and develop insights about their experiences.

The plan-do-review cycle continues to be important for concrete operational and formal operational children by ensuring that direct experience and active learning are not neglected. At these more mature levels, children are increasingly able to write about their plans and evaluations. At the formal operational level, students are able to verify their findings, use the scientific method to construct knowledge, and represent ideas and experiences through speeches, dramatic presentations, summary charts, and written documents.

What Children Learn

As sensorimotor infants and toddlers explore their worlds, they are learning about physical reality. Since everything they encounter is brand new to them, they have to "discover" things for themselves by tasting, chewing, smelling, pushing, pulling, banging, throwing, holding, hearing, and seeing. When they explore the physical world with the full support of caregivers who play with and care for them as partners, infants and toddlers also begin to relate to people in a way that allows them to form a positive, hopeful view of themselves and trustful relationships with others.

The preoperational child is involved in matching language to actions and finding out about the physical world from a more logical perspective, with a focus on the relationships of classification, seriation, number, space, and time. The child can use materials, toys and tools, work next to and in partnership with others, and relish the joy of trying things out and making them work through practice. Out of these active experiences come the disposition to be curious, initiate relationships with others, and enjoy exploring and learning. Strangely, it is not only the actual knowledge of logical relationships gained during this period but also the manner in which children interact with people, materials, events, and ideas to gain this knowledge that is critical to preoperational learning and its lifelong consequences.

At the concrete operational and formal operational levels, children are still grounded in experience and physical reality. The content of their knowledge, however, shifts increasingly toward the abstract as they wrestle with the collective wisdom of various disciplines recorded through the ages and interpreted by different cultures. As adults present this more formal content, the tendency is to lecture to students when, in fact, these older children still need to wrestle with new information through planning, direct experience, active learning, verbal reflection, generating alternatives, working in groups, and exploring hypothetical situations. Again, it is the meshing of appropriate content with the experience of active learning that leads to thinking and unleashes the innate energy and drive within each individual.

The Adult Role

The term *observant teaching* captures key aspects of the adult's role with infants and toddlers. By observing children's actions and interactions, parents and caregivers can interact and communicate as partners with infants and toddlers, allowing children to set the tone, pace, and focus of the play or "conversation." To give children the control and attention they need, caregivers in this role serve a small number of infants at a time and adjust their schedules to children's needs.

Supportive teaching begins to define the adult role with preoperational children. As children become increasingly verbal, thoughtful, and physically able, adults continue to support children's initiatives and interact as partners in children's play by listening, imitating, offering related comments, and asking questions. Whereas adults cannot tell a child, for example, that beans and peas are seeds and that 10 beans and 2 peas means that there are more seeds than beans, they can provide materials and experiences that encourage children to think about number and amount and construct the best understanding possible based on both appearances and an emerging logic.

Emergent teaching links the role of adults with concrete operational children. These children are "emergent" thinkers—bursting with ideas, energy, and the will to push ahead with projects in their own way. They create their own stories, for example, and depend on adults to understand their meaning and intent despite unconventional spellings and unusual logic. The role of the teacher at this time is to recognize skills emerging and support wholeheartedly the diverse ways children pursue their interests while overlooking children's "mistakes" in logic and presentation.

Dialogue teaching describes an important aspect of the educative relationship between adults and formal operational youngsters. By dialogue, we intend to conjure up the image of Socrates' lengthy discourse with his students. Like Socrates, the role of the adult with teenage students is to converse with them in a way that reflects authoritative knowledge but not the control and dominance of authoritarian logic. In addition to dialogue, adults encourage and support direct experience and students' efforts toward working to a high standard of accuracy, performing on time, cooperating with peers in long-term projects, and persevering through the arduous construction of knowledge that characterizes the work of poets, scientists, and anyone pursuing a serious interest. Although teaching this level is challenging and complex, it is also rewarding, engaging, and exciting.

Why the High/Scope Curriculum Works

What makes an early education experience at 3 to 5 years of age so powerful that it changes children's lives and experiences as they reach young adulthood? Why do early childhood experiences last a lifetime? In the early 1960s the theory was that early intervention through education would improve children's intelligence. Yet most studies have failed to provide evidence that such experiences raise children's IQ significantly for any length of time. Even the Perry Preschool study findings report similar IQ levels for both control-group and experimental-group participants a decade after intervention. The data from the Consortium of Longitudinal Studies (1983) and Head Start (Cicerelli 1969; McKey et al., 1985) all report the same outcome. A few studies such as the High/Scope Curriculum Comparison study (Schweinhart et al., 1986) do report long-term IQ gains, but such findings are atypical.

Since IQ does not seem to be responsible for the long-term changes in children's lives, what is? Perhaps it is the academic content that early education provides. Most adults agree that children need to learn certain skills early on to be successful in later schooling. Yet the High/Scope Curriculum Comparison study, among others, found that children who participated in the Direct-Teaching curriculum with its structured approach to teaching reading, math, and language did not do any better academically in a decade of follow-up than children who participated in child-initiated learning programs. In fact, the young adults who as children had participated in the direct-teaching model demonstrated serious social alienation from school, family, and society. Clearly, academic content, at least as a structured objective, is not the link between the experiences of early childhood and successful adult performance.

The best estimate of what permits a high quality early childhood experience to influence later adult performance significantly seems to be

TABLE 8.2 High/Scope curriculum processes and outcomes.

Processes	Outcomes
Children express intentions	Initiative
	Responsibility
Children generate experiences	Curiosity
	Independence
Children reflect on experiences	Divergent thinking
	Trust
	Confidence

the development of specific personal traits. Erik Erikson (1950) pointed out that the natural psychological thrust of 3- to 5-year-olds is toward developing a sense of initiative, responsibility, and independence. Katz (1985) discusses the importance of dispositions such as curiosity, friendliness, and cooperation that young children develop at this age range, and how effective preschool programs support the development of such traits. However, these personal traits and dispositions are elusive. They cannot be "taught" or inserted as a "theme" into a program of instruction. They can only develop under appropriate circumstances. So, what specific circumstances and program strategies support the development of such traits?

Attempts to answer this question are important undertakings for early childhood policy and training organizations. The National Association for the Education of Young Children (Bredekamp, 1987) has outlined a set of standards for developmentally appropriate education that form a basis for educational quality. The High/Scope Curriculum Comparison study helped validate developmentally appropriate curricula that provide ample opportunity for child-initiated learning processes that result in positive, life-long outcomes.

The processes described in Table 8.2 are the key events in child-initiated, adult-supported events that High/Scope's curriculum planners believe lead to the outcomes listed—positive habits, traits, and dispositions.

High/Scope's high quality early childhood curriculum relies heavily on active learning and child-initiated experiences during which children express their intentions, plan and carry out their play experiences, and reflect on their accomplishments.

Children Express Their Intentions

High quality programs provide numerous, ongoing opportunities for children to express their own intentions. Initially, children express their intentions through both gestures and actions. For example, an infant picks one toy rather than another, or a preschooler points to a toy or takes the adult's hand and walks to the material she or he wants to play with. As children mature, they can inform others of their intentions: "I want the wagon" or "I'm gonna play with the blocks." As they become writers and readers, children begin to express their intentions in more detail, through written plans, models, blueprints, and detailed discussions with peers and adults. The High/Scope Curriculum calls children's expression of intent *planning*; children not only plan during the designated "planning time" but also throughout the day.

Children Generate Experiences

As well as encouraging children to express their intentions, a high quality program must offer opportunities for the children to act on them. Effective action comes about when a child makes choices; is actively involved with people, materials, events, and ideas; and has enough time for trial and error, generating new ideas, practicing, and succeeding. Personal independence is the key to active learning by self-motivated children. In the High/Scope Curriculum children act on their intentions during "work time." Throughout other parts of the day children's choices are somewhat limited by specific materials or decisions made by others, but they are still free to use materials and respond to situations in ways that makes sense to them.

Children Reflect on Their Experiences

Along with providing opportunities for children to express their intentions and generate their own experiences, a high quality curriculum must provide opportunities for children to reflect on their activities and accomplishments. Children reflect on their experiences with increasing verbal ability and logic as they mature. Through this process, they begin to match words to their actions and construct memories and insights they can modify as their understanding increases. In the High/Scope Curriculum the time set aside for this process is called *recalling* or *review*.

These three essential aspects of high quality curriculum—children's expression of intent, their independently generated experiences, and their reflections—are central to our definition of child-initiated learning. Their outcomes, important to life-long learning, include the development of important traits, such as initiative, curiosity, trust, confidence, independence, responsibility, and divergent thinking. These are traits valued by society.

Children Gain Control

When children experience the High/Scope program they develop control and self-discipline. This control is real power, not over people or things, but over oneself. Understanding what is happening in our environment, realizing that those around us are genuinely interested in what we say and do, and knowing that our work and effort will often lead to success is the type of control that promotes personal satisfaction and motivates us to be productive. Although no single factor assures success in life, the sense of personal control is certainly a major factor. And high quality early childhood programs can support and strengthen this feeling.

Summary

Since 1962 the High/Scope Curriculum and its related research has explored the issues that lead to high quality educational programs for all children. The High/Scope Curriculum builds on the experience of staff working with children both in the United States and overseas and applies a consistent theoretical framework that has been validated by longitudinal research. The essential ingredients of high quality educational programs are known. The challenge is to apply these principles in programs throughout the country to improve the lives of children and families.

References

American College Testing Program. (1976). *User's guide: Adult APL Survey.* Iowa City, IA: Author.

Bereiter, C., & Engelmann, S. (1966). *Teaching disadvantaged children in preschool.* Engelwood Cliffs, NJ: Prentice-Hall.

Berrueta-Clement, J.R., Schweinhart, L.J., Barnett, W.S., Epstein, A.S., & Weikart, D.P. (1984). Changed lives: The effects of the Perry Preschool Program on youths through age 19. *Monographs of the High/Scope Educational Research Foundation, 8* (pp. 94–104). Ypsilanti, MI: High Scope Press.

Bredekamp, S. (Ed.) (1987). *Developmentally appropriate practice in early childhood programs serving children from birth through age 8.* Washington, DC: National Association for the Education of Young Children.

Cicerelli, (1969). *The impact of Head Start: An evaluation of the effects of Head Start experiences on children's cognitive and affective development.* Athens, OH: Westinghouse Learning Conjunctive and Ohio University.

Consortium of Longitudinal Studies. (1983). *As the twig is bent . . . lasting effects of preschool programs.* Hillsdale, NJ: Erlbaum.

DeVries, R., & Kohlberg, L. (1987). *Programs of early education.* New York: Longman.

Donaldson, M. (1978). *Children's minds.* London: Cromm Helm.

Erikson, E.H. (1950). *Childhood and society.* New York: Norton.

Forman, G.E., & Fosnot, C.T. (1982). The use of Piaget's constructivism in early childhood education programs. In B. Spodek, (Ed.), *Handbook of research in early childhood education* (pp. 185–214). New York: Macmillan.

Gold, M. (1970). Delinquent behavior in an American city. Belmont, CA: Brooks/Cole.

Hohmann, M., Banet, B., & Weikart, D.P. (1979). *Young children in action: A manual for preschool educators*. Ypsilanti, MI: High/Scope Press.
Hunt, J.McV. (1961). *Intelligence and experience*. New York: Ronald Press.
Johnson, J.E. (1987). Evaluation in early childhood education. In J.L. Roopnarine & J.E. Johnson (Eds.). *Approaches to early childhood education* (p. 21). Columbus: Merrill.
Kagitcibasi, C., Sunar, D., & Bekman, S. (1988). *Comprehensive preschool education project: Final report* (Report for International Development Research Centre, Ottawa, Canada). Istanbul, Turkey: Bogazici University.
Karnes M.B., Schwedel, A.M., & Williams, M.B. (1983). A comparison of five approaches for educating young children from low-income homes. In Consortium for Longitudinal Studies, *As the twig is bent... lasting effects of preschool programs* (pp. 133–170). Hillsdale, NJ: Erlbaum.
Katz, L. (1985). Dispositions in early childhood education. *EAC/EECE Bulletin*. *18*(2), 1, 3.
Katz, L.G., & Chard, S.C. (1989). *Engaging children's minds: The project approach*. Norwood, NJ: Ablex.
Kohlberg, L., & Mayer, R. (1972). Development as the aim of education, *Harvard Education Review*, *42*(4), 449–496.
Lazar, I., Darlington, R., Murray, H., Royce, J., & Snipper, A. (1982). Lasting effects of early education. *Monographs of the Society for Research in Child Development*, *47*(1–2, Serial No. 194).
McKey, R.H., Condelli, L., Ganson, H., Barrett, B., McConkey, C., & Plantz, M. (1985). *The impact of Head Start on children, families and communities* (Final report of the Head Start Evaluation, Synthesis and Utilization Project). Washington, DC: CSR.
Miller, L.B., & Bizzell, R.P. (1983). The Louisville experiment: A comparison of four programs. In Consortium for Longitudinal Studies, *As the twig is bent... lasting effects of preschool programs*. Hillsdale, NJ: Erlbaum.
Piaget, J. (1952). *The origins of intelligence in children*. New York: International Universities Press.
Piaget, Jean. (1970). The stages of intellectual development in the child. In J. Conger, P. Mussen, & J. Kagen (Eds.), *Readings in child development and personality* (2nd ed.). New York: Harper and Row.
Piaget, J. (1973). *To understand is to invent*. New York: Grossman.
Roopnarine, J.L., & Johnson, J.E. (Eds.). (1987). *Approaches to early childhood education*. Columbus: Merrill.
Schweinhart, L.J. (1987). Can preschool programs help prevent delinquency? In J.Q. Wilson & G.C. Loury (Eds.), *From Children to citizens: Vol. 3, Families, schools and delinquency prevention*. New York: Springer-Verlag.
Schweinhart, L.J., & Weikart, D.P. (1980). Young children grow up: The effects of the Perry Preschool program on youths through age 15. *Monographs of the High/Scope Educational Research Foundation*, *7*. Ypsilanti, MI: High/Scope Press.
Schweinhart, L.J., Weikart, D.P., & Larner, M.B. (1986). Consequences of three preschool curriculum models through age 15. *Early Childhood Research Quarterly*, *1*, 15–45.
Sears, P.S., & Dowley, E.M. (1963). Research on teaching in the nursery school.

In N.L. Gage (Ed.). *Handbook of research on teaching* (pp. 811–864). Chicago: Rand McNally.

Terman, L.M., & Merrill, M.A. (1970). *Stanford-Binet Intelligence Scale, Form L-M: Manual for the third revision*. Boston: Houghton Mifflin.

Vygotsky, L. (1978). *Mind in society*. Cambridge, MA: Harvard University Press.

Weikart, D.P. (1972). Relationship of curriculum, teaching, and learning in preschool education. In J.C. Stanley (Ed.), *Preschool programs for the disadvantaged* (pp. 22–66). Baltimore, MD: Johns Hopkins University Press.

Weikart, D.P., Epstein, A.S., Schweinhart, L.J., & Bond, J. (1978). The Ypsilanti preschool curriculum demonstration project: Preschool years and longitudinal results. *Monographs of the High/Scope Educational Research Foundation, 4* (p. 40). Ypsilanti, MI: High/Scope Press.

Weikart, D.P., Rogers, L., Adcock, C., & McClelland, D. (1971). *The Cognitively Oriented Curriculum: A framework for teachers*. Urbana, IL: NAEYC.

Part III
Afterword

9
New Approaches to the Development of Cognitive Competence

ROBERT PASNAK AND MARK L. HOWE

The first volume in this set was concerned primarily with some fundamentals of cognitive development; that is, capacities, processes, and abilities that constitute part of the foundation for further development. This volume has been concerned with cognitive competence. By competence we mean the higher level abilities that a child erects on the basis of, or in addition to, more fundamental abilities such as those described in Volume I. For example, a child who remembers verbatim information and gist, and who has a suitable knowledge base, must still acquire mnemonic strategies (Pressley & Van Meter, this volume). The acquisition of strategies and metacognitive assessment of their use is a step in the direction of competence, and in some sense may be considered to be an effective superstructure built on the foundation acquired earlier. Similarly, competence in reading results from the interaction of several underlying processes and working memory. Weakness in this foundation causes inordinate delays in the development of reading competence, as Siegel (this volume) pointed out. In perhaps its grandest sense, competence can be equated with intelligence, which involves not just simple abilities, but their combination and elaboration into increasingly effective problem-solving mechanisms and expertise employable in a plethora of arenas. Volume II has been concerned with some definitions and modes of acquisition of such competencies, ranging from the very simple to the very complex.

There is, of course, no hard and fast demarcation of where foundation ends and superstructure begins. Competence is above all relative. The initial steps taken by a young child in categorizing things by causal inferences rather than perceptual similarity represent an increase in competence, but the competence is not as great as that which the child will possess at a later age. Still, whether competence is as simple as primitive categorization or as complex and comprehensive as that measured by Spectrum, it is a unifying characteristic of the chapters in this volume. All refer to the relative ability of children to interpret their environment successfully, and to how they may improve their abilities to do so.

In fact, one of the hallmarks of the study of cognitive development as it enters the last decade of the 20th century is the recent emergence of more definitive, detailed, and specific definitions of different types of competence. Sometimes these advances are on a narrow but important front, as when the basis of a learning disability is defined (Siegel, this volume) or when the principles by which children form categories are elucidated (Gelman & Kalish, this volume). At other times, they have been on the broadest of fronts. The view that intelligence, the *sine qua non* of cognitive competence, develops as a relatively stable combination of general ability and specific abilities has been altered by new theorists. Now the identification of many distinct intelligences (Feldman, 1980; Gardner, 1983) and the nonuniversal development or arrest of competence at different stages within those domains has captured the attention of psychologists. New measurement techniques must be devised to measure cognitive development in terms of these new definitions (Adams & Feldman, this volume). The guidance that these improved descriptions of cognitive development can offer to psychologists who wish to help children reach their full potential may be as important as the theory building that is facilitated.

The second hallmark of cognitive developmental psychology at this time is increasing knowledge on a broad variety of fronts of the behaviors, processes, and methodologies by which children's cognitive competence advances or can be advanced. The belief that the discipline is by now sufficiently mature to offer effective guidance to parents, teachers, or professionals working with children is voiced by many authors in this volume. New ways in which the behavior of children and parents facilitates cognitive development have been discovered (Bjorklund, Gaultney, & Green, this volume; Rosengren, Behrend, & Perlmutter, this volume), and effective ways in which instruction and curricula can benefit the child have likewise been identified (O'Sullivan, this volume; Pressley & Van Meter this volume; Weikart & Hohmann, this volume). Such efforts, innovative and building on the successes and failures of past decades, appear to form a major theme of cognitive developmental psychology in the years ahead.

Definitions of Cognitive Competence

The Nature of Categorization

The accuracy with which children respond to similarities and differences and the facility with which they express them verbally are key components of cognitive competence. Tasks assessing such capabilities play an important role in the major tests traditionally used to assess children's intelligence (Terman & Merrill, 1973; Thorndike, Hagan, & Sattler, 1986; Wechsler, 1974) and sorting and classification skills are taught in most curricula. Yet, the basis by which children naturally form categories and organize their environment in the ordinary course of development has scarcely been investigated.

Gelman and Kalish (this volume) captured the importance of this issue with the statement that "without the capacity to organize experience into categories, we would have extremely limited abilities to extend knowledge to new examples, and so to learn from experience." The potential importance of knowing the principles by which children categorize is very great for assessing competence (Adams & Feldman, this volume) and efforts to increase competence (O'Sullivan, this volume; Weikart & Hohmann, this volume).

Gelman and Kalish pointed out that similarity of features would not be a sufficient basis for children's categorizations, as there are an infinite number of possible features, of potentially different weights, that may be unknowable. Instead of developing a feature differentiation approach, as was attempted by developmental psychologists studying form perception (Gibson & Gibson, 1955; Gibson, Gibson, Pick, & Osser, 1962), they presented a constructive synthesis of Piaget's early work on causality (Piaget, 1930; Piaget & Inhelder, 1951/1975) and recent discoveries of the role naive theories play in children's understanding and knowledge (Carey, 1985; Wellman, 1990).

The gist of their synthesis is that children's categorizations are based on naive theories about causal relations between features. These theories constrain the features used to form categories (Kalish & Gelman, 1990), because the causal linkages theorized determine which features are primary for category members, and which are only secondary. The categories are organized around the features that are thought to generate or cause other features (Gelman & Kalish, this volume).

The emergence of this and similar fine grain understandings of why children's ideas develop as they do is potentially of great importance to psychologists working to improve cognitive function. Weikart and his collaborators had to devise the "key experiences" for their Piagetian-based curriculum to promote the cognitive growth and learning of preschoolers before important parts of Piaget's writings were translated, and before the role of naive theories in organizing preschoolers knowledge was imagined (Weikart & Hohmann, this volume). Consider the advantage that psychologists developing the new wave of preschool programs will have.

The Nature of Dyslexia

Siegel undertook no less ambitious a definition of cognitive competence when she undertook to define dyslexia (Siegel, this volume). Dyslexia is significant because it is a disorder in which some normal cognitive competencies are weak or lacking; identification of these competencies is an essential first step in understanding and, in the future, devising remediation strategies for this developmental disability. Heretofore, the definition was made by exclusion, at a relatively coarse level. Difficulty in reading, absent emotional, neurological, or instructional problems, or deficiencies in general cognitive competency (usually expressed as IQ) constituted dyslexia. Such a definition is of limited utility, because the reason for the difficulty in reading is not specified. By a careful consideration of recent research (much of it her own) on the nature of reading comprehension, phonological processing, syntactic awareness, working memory, semantics, and orthographics, Siegel was able to demonstrate that deficiencies in phonological processing, syntactic awareness, and working memory are the major components of dyslexia. It is just this sort of knowledge, in this and other domains, that makes possible the advances in instruction by application of cognitive developmental psychology that O'Sullivan (this volume) advocates.

Stanovich's (1988a, 1988b) model of phonological processing as an independent cognitive process is important in this context. This independence of competence in one domain from general cognitive competence (intelligence, in this case) is a recurring theme in models of cognitive competence that are emerging at this time. The domain of phonological processing is a small, if critical, one. The existence of such a module of cognitive functioning, relatively independent of central processing, is quite compatible with the model of nonuniversal intelligence described by Adams and Feldman (this volume). Excellence or deficits in the limited domain of phonological processing could, and perhaps should, be orthogonal to excellence or deficits in other cognitive functioning. A further investigation of the nature of syntactic awareness (a sensitivity to grammar that facilitates prediction of what word comes next) may lead to similar hypotheses—or to quite different ones.

The Nature of Intelligence

Competence in one or another aspect of cognition is one thing; a broadly based competence in many aspects of cognition is another. It is just this far-ranging competence in cognitive pursuits that many scientists have tried to capture in definitions of intelligence.

The nature of intelligence has intrigued many of the best minds in psychology and other disciplines. Galton's (1869) research on cognitive excellence, although primitive by today's standards, led to the postulation of the general, or "g," factor, that is still supposed by many to underlie much intelligent behavior. As developed by Spearman (1904, 1927) this concept of general cognitive excellence (or mediocrity) was intrinsic to the early psychometric approach to definition and measurement of cognitive competence throughout the life span. Yet, discrepancies between cognitive competence of one sort and that of another sort demand explanation, and successive views have emerged. Thurstone (1938) proposed that seven specific factors combined to define intelligence, and advanced psychometric evidence to substantiate this definition. A flurry of research and debate followed. The obvious issues—whether cognitive competence should be properly viewed as a general characteristic, as a combination of several specific kinds of abilities, or as a combination of general and specific abilities, and how many of the latter should be encompassed in a valid definition—commanded much attention and effort. Eventually, the stage theory of Piaget, derived via an entirely nonpsychometric approach, captured the attention of researchers in cognitive development. The novel demonstrations of cognitive competence and cognitive errors developed by Piaget and his collaborators fueled much of the research into cognitive competence on both sides of the Atlantic.

Piaget's conceptions of cognitive development continue to have an important influence, manifested in part by neo-Piagetian formulations of cognitive competence in certain domains (e.g., Case & Sowder, 1990). Yet much excitement has been generated by newer models of intelligence. One of the most important is Sternberg's (1977, 1984, 1985) information theory approach, which features the role of metacognition. Metacognition was defined by Flavell (1977), a Piagetian, as the observation and regulation of one's own cognitive processes. Sternberg refers to metacognition as the child or adult's ability to selectively apply, monitor, and evaluate lower order components of cognition. The lower order components are those that govern some aspect of acquisition, retention, transfer, or performance. One difficulty with this formulation is whether it sufficiently specifies both the domains of competence needed for competent behavior and their developmental aspects. Increasingly, researchers are identifying new aspects of metacognition that may be relatively independent and age specific, a tendency evident in this volume.

A second important new development is Gardner's (1983) definition of at least seven different intelligences—logical, mathematical, linguistic, spatial, musical, interpersonal, intrapersonal, and bodily-kinesthetic. By according each of these full status as a separate kind of intelligence, Gardner has attempted to say that they are more than specific abilities that contribute to overall intelligence. It appears, however, that the interest generated by his approach lies in part in the unusual nature of the last three kinds of intelligence he has posited. The first two, although not identical with specific factors identified by earlier researchers, are not qualitatively different, and the question of whether they merit full status as "intelligences" is not likely to interest more than a limited cadre of researchers. The last three, however, show clearly the breadth of the domains in which one must have some level of cognitive competence and specify some domains in which its development may be traced. The ultimate importance of Gardner's theory may lie in the stimulus it provides for the next generation of researchers in cognitive development.

The theory delineated by Adams and Feldman (this volume) is in many respects a culmination of Gardner's approach and the emerging view that cognitive competence can be domain-specific (Fischer, 1980; Case, 1985; Keil, 1986; Horowitz, 1987). The theory is a stage theory; within any domain of competence, ability develops through a sequence of qualitatively different stages. Its most distinguishing aspect, however, is its emphasis on nonuniversal development, as opposed to general ability. This emphasis is that competence in one domain is relatively independent of competence in another, and develops only with specific input that is determined by culture, environment, and individual choice. The developmental assessment of competence or intelligence described by these researchers fully deserves its label "Spectrum," as the range of abilities measured reflects the diversity of "intelligences" suggested by Gardner, including but not limited to social analytic, bodily-kinesthetic, and musical ability.

This emphasis on the multifaceted nature of cognitive competence is one of the more striking trends of recent theory. Perhaps even more important is the specific emphasis on the temporal and sequential development of one cognitive competence or another. The Spectrum approach described by Adams and Feldman is designed to assess just where a child is at a given point in time in each of many aspects of cognitive development. It is also designed to do so in a way that will permit mentors, whether psychologists, instructors, or parents, to help a child progress to higher levels of mastery within a chosen domain of competence. Such movement with the aid of a mentor from a current stage of development to a higher stage is a specification of movement across a zone of proximal development (Vygotsky, 1962, 1978) in the context of the 1990s. In this respect, Spectrum (and its potential successors) provides the type of assessment needed for parents and mentors to function most effectively (Rosengren, Perlmutter, & Behrend, this volume). It also provides the kind of assessment most necessary for O'Sullivan's recommendations to be put in place, and one that would show more fully the impact of effects to raise cognitive competence in a broad sense. The coordination of efforts such as those, in the context of applied research like that described by Weikart and Hohmann, will be key themes of research in the next two decades.

Advances in Cognitive Competence

Imitation and Meta-Imitation

Children's observations of others are the source of many of their own cognitive advances. Bjorklund, Gaultney, and Green (this volume) made the point that during free play a preschooler may imitate other children every 4 or 5 minutes (Abramovitch & Grusec, 1978). Hence, their interest in imitation as a source of learning and acquisition of competence is well taken. Although the role of imitation in the acquisition of new understandings and behaviors has been studied for decades, Bjorklund, Gaultney and Green have introduced the construct of meta-imitation—children's understanding of their own imitative abilities. This kind of enterprise—the identification and examination of a heretofore unexamined type of metacognition—is characteristic of research in cognitive development at this time, and meta-imitation seems to obey some of the same parameters as other metacognitions. That is, Bjorklund, Gaultney, and Green found that children's estimates of the imitative abilities are usually overoptimistic, just as are their estimates of their own mnemonic abilities (see the early reviews by Cavanaugh & Perlmutter, 1982, or Flavell & Wellman, 1977), and that accuracy increases with age (Schneider & Pressley, 1989). Bjorklund, Gaultney, and Green's suggestion that the overestimation associated with meta-imitation may be productive fits well with the role assigned to self-esteem and self-concept in cognitive development by other authors in this volume (e.g., consider the recommendations of Adams and Feldman, O'Sullivan, and Weikart and Hohmann). Greater metacognitive accuracy could reduce the child's motivation to imitate, if motivation were based in any part on comparisons of real achievements to internal standards for achievement, as Bandura suggested (Bandura, 1981, 1986, 1989). (Note Bjorklund, Gaultney, and Green's suggestion that such comparisons may be domain-specific—a recurring theme in the 1990s.) To the extent that imitations are poor, these metacognitive assessments need to be inaccurate and positively biased to maintain a positive perception of self-efficacy. It is this perceived self-efficacy that in large part determines the time and effort spent on task (Bandura, 1981, 1986, 1989). The effect may be to produce a positive feedback circle, as trying hard (time and effort) is often perceived by preschoolers to be as essential as doing well in their judgments of a "success." As Bjorklund, Gaultney, and Green pointed out, preschools tend to reinforce this sort of evaluation (O'Sullivan, this volume, and Pressley and Van Meter, this volume, made the same point about elementary schools), and Stipek (1984) urged that preschoolers' environments be designed to maintain such positively biased metacognitions. Bjorklund, Gaultney, and Green's observation that, for young children, such overly positive meta-imitation may be associated with greater cognitive competence reinforces this point. The implication is that preschool curricula that emphasize self-directed learning (i.e., Weikart & Hohmann, this volume) rather than direct reinforcement of accurate decisions may have an unforeseen advantage. At early ages, the lack of emphasis on accuracy and on metacognitive accuracy can produce increased effort, self-esteem, and learning. This is an advantage that psychologists who emphasize metacognition in the development of intelligence (Sternberg, 1985) or in curricula and instruction (O'Sullivan, this volume; Pressley & Van Meter, this volume) can profitably explore.

Parent-Assisted Learning

Children certainly are the source of much of their own cognitive development, through self-engendered interactions with their environment, observation, and responsiveness to many opportunities for learning. Imitation of others is only one of the tools that they use for this purpose. Yet, interaction with others, especially in the broad sense, certainly has a crucial role in cognitive development. Psychologists' views of what that role is has been changing, and may have to change more as the place and interactive role of social intelligence in cognitive development become better understood. As Rosengren, Behrend, and Perlmutter (this volume) indicated, Piaget's formulation has been dominant until recently. That theory is, in essence, that social interaction could not be the origin or cause of new cognitive structures. Rather, its role is to refine those already in place. Piaget (1962, 1968) felt that social interaction became more important as children passed through the late preoperational period to concrete operations. Interactions with peers were held to be more important aids to cognitive development than those with adults, because the equality (symmetry) of peer interactions allowed children to see how their views differed from those of peers. Children were likely to be more passive with an adult, and so change their thinking less (Piaget, 1932, 1968).

This view was, as Rosengren, Behrend, and Perlmutter pointed out, quite different from that of Vygotsky (1962, 1978). One of Vygotsky's main assumptions was that cognition originates in social interaction, which is important from birth onward. The development of social cognition is a key developmental process. Others (parents at the early ages) regulate children's behavior, gradually transferring skills and information so that the children can self-regulate. Language soon plays an important role in this, as the parents talk their children through problem-solving processes and the children later talk themselves through similar processes. This instruction works well, according to Vygotsky, within the zone of proximal development. A key is that the parent must modify the level of regulation and instruction as a function of the child's ability or success.

Several factors led in the late 1980s to the recognition that parental instruction of children does in fact plays a key role in cognitive development (Rosengren, Behrend, & Perlmutter, this volume). Ellis and Rogoff (1986) found that even though children were more active in problem solving with a peer, they learned more from adults. Adults tend to query a child rather than waiting to be queried; the children appear passive, as Piaget observed, but the learning experience is effective. Azmitia and Perlmutter (1989) advanced several cogent arguments to the effect that close relations (parents) should be unusually effective in instructive interactions, and several more were advanced in the chapter by Rosengren, Behrend, and Perlmutter.

The question for the 1990s must be in part what parent and child characteristics govern the success of parent–child instruction in the cognitive arena. Rosengren, Behrend, and Perlmutter presented empirical research on the effects of the social emotional support, structuring, and control the parents offer; in general the first two characteristics were most important. The research represents a fair beginning, but much more remains to be done. There are many other contexts in which these three parental characteristics, and other parental characteristics, should be studied. Characteristics of the child, including but not limited to age, gender, personality variables, relative cognitive competence, and experience with the adult await investigation.

It is noteworthy that the High/Scope preschool curriculum set up in the early 1970s anticipates philosophically many of the points made in a research context by Rosengren, Behrend, and Perlmutter. Weikart and Hohmann (this volume) attribute the long range success of this curriculum, which is mainly in the social sphere after initial gains in overall IQ, to the manner in which adults and children interact. The role of the adult as a partner in the construction of knowledge, rather than as a direct imparter of knowledge, is the essence of the key Plan-Do-Review program element. This is scaffolding expressed in different words, and the emphasis on responsiveness and support for children's initiatives is very strong (with more control needed when the children are infants, as Rosengren, Behrend, and Perlmutter suggest). It would be of great interest to have Adams and Feldman's measures of social intelligence applied here, and also to have them for children who have long experience with particular parental styles.

Instruction of Children in Cognitive Strategies

As children age, two phenomena change that have important impacts on their cognitive development. One is that group instruction from adults other than their parents occupies a major portion of their day, and that much of this instruction makes demands on one or another form of cognitive competence. Another is that as their cognitive development continues, they become more amenable to instruction in cognitive strategies.

Of all cognitive strategies, memory strategies are certainly among those most particularly demanded by formal schooling. Pressley and Van Meter (this volume) elucidated the history of three waves research on the development and employment of such strategies.

They identified the first wave, in the 1960s, as research into variation in the use of strategies, thought to be the source of many differences in memory development. This was followed in the 1970s by investigations of metamemory and its effects on the employment of strategies (Pressley, Borkowski, & O'Sullivan, 1984, 1985). Now, in Pressley and Van Meter's assessment, the focus is on the interaction of these two aspects of cognitive development with basic processes, motivation, and the knowledge base, whose rules were emphasized in the 1980s. Thus, a fourth wave of research may be emerging, one that features integration of phenomena previously elucidated.

Pressley and Van Meter made the point that new methodologies have arisen because research has moved from the laboratory to the classroom, and that this will be a continuing trend. The issue now to be resolved is what type of instruction will be most effective. The two premier possibilities are improving the knowledge base or improving metacognition about strategies while offering instruction in strategies. Pressley and Van Meter suggest that the answer depends in part on what is being learned. If the information to be acquired is strongly related to the knowledge base, strategy instruction might be unnecessary. But a child may sometimes need a mnemonic strategy to use fully the knowledge base, and such strategies are likely to be useful when the information is not related to the knowledge base.

O'Sullivan (this volume) traced the history of strategy instruction. In the 1970s, strategy instruction was not focused sufficiently on children's continued use of the strategies they were taught or on transfer to situations significantly different from those in which the strategies had been learned. The lack of transfer that resulted left unrequited instructional psychologists' need for a prescriptive theory of instruction, and is part of the reason that little instruction on memory is incorporated in classroom instruction today. The resolution to this problem may be at hand. The mid-1980s review by Pressley, Borkowski, and O'Sullivan (1984) indicated that memory instruction produced its most durable results when instruction on memory strategies was combined with the teaching of metacognition about the value of the strategy. O'Sullivan and Pressley (1984) also showed that instruction on how strategies work, and on when, where, and why to use them was helpful. It appears that cognitive developmental psychology is poised, with its increased emphasis on the value of metacognition, to have an increased impact on children's instruction. There is no reason to suppose that this impact will be narrowly focused on only a few aspects of cognition. As O'Sullivan pointed out, the 1980s saw careful analyses of the cognitive processes and knowledge structures involved in reading, mathematics, and other domains. There are currently models especially in reading, of componential processes, skills and their development, and disability (Vellutino, 1991; Siegel, this volume), and significant progress has been made in mathematics (cf. Case 1985; Case & Sowder, 1990).

O'Sullivan made a strong case that successful readers use cognitive and metacognitive comprehension strategies, and have sufficient knowledge of the comprehension process to deploy these strategies effectively. An impressive crescendo of research in the mid-1980s showed that children could be taught such strategies and metacognitive processes, that impressive gains in comprehension resulted, and that classroom teachers could carry out the instruction. O'Sullivan described similar efforts in mnemonic instruction, and presents a program to teach strategies and metamemory, based on current models of memory development (Howe & O'Sullivan, 1990). It is important to note that to be successful, long-term instruction that is an integral part of the curriculum is probably necessary (Pressley & Van Meter, this volume).

The emergence of such programs is coupled with the emergence of a new understanding of the importance of the role of children's initiatives and independence in constructing knowledge. Influenced by Vygotsky (1962, 1978), researchers are emphasizing the importance of children's role in their own cognitive development, with support and effective scaffolding from instructors (O'Sullivan, this volume; Pressley & Van Meter, this volume; Rosengren, Behrend, & Perlmutter, this volume; Weikart & Hohmann, this volume). This is a movement away from the model of the teacher as controlling learning and imparting knowledge to the child, a model that has been in vogue since the 1960s. The older model reflects in part the Skinnerian approach, with its emphasis on direct instruction, reinforcement of constructive behavior, and controlled acquisition of knowledge, an approach that may be the main influence of psychology on educational practice today (Dweck, 1986; O'Sullivan, this volume). Educational researchers continue to emphasize those factors most directly under the control of teachers, with little emphasis on the student's knowledge base or cognitive processing, and less on social interaction during learning. Carroll's (1963) model, which gives no scope to such factors, still guides much educational research, and reflects little of what is known about cognitive development today (O'Sullivan, this volume).

The new wave of psychological research in cognitive development features student–teacher interaction, not teacher control (O'Sullivan, this volume). The focus is on the highly social, interactive nature of effective strategy instruction, with emphasis on teaching students how, when, and why strategies work (O'Sullivan & Pressley, 1984). When authentic metacognitive activity is generated, children are guided away from the view that success is a function of effort—a view that, as Rosengren, Behrend, and Perlmutter point out, is taught even in preschool and is a lynch pin of education today (Carroll, 1963; Weikart, 1979). Instead, elementary school children can be helped to view success as a function of cognitive and metacognitive strategies matched to task requirements (Pressley & Van Meter, this volume). In essence, children can be guided to the discovery of ways to work smarter, not harder—the essence of intelligent behavior.

Instruction of Children in Preschools

There have always been hopes that the development of general cognitive competence could be accelerated even if it were through sharpening the mind by training in mathematics or Latin or some other disciplines. Inherent in such claims is the belief that relative cognitive competence, or intelligence, could be increased if only we could teach young minds how to think at more advanced levels for their age.

Interestingly, the emergence of psychometric techniques for measuring cognitive development objectively and quantitatively put a damper on efforts to increase it. The prediction of success in academics through measurement of IQ gave rise to a common understanding that intelligence does not change much, and subsequently to the belief that it could not be changed much. This was hardly the position of Binet, the inventor of the first great psychometric instrument for measuring cognitive competence. He also invented a program designed to raise IQ (Blagg, 1991). But the relative stability of IQ scores from preadolescence onward and the knowledge that biological inheritance made an important contribution led to the idea that intelligence was fixed within a narrow range.

Piaget's assertion that physiological maturation of the brain and nervous system was a necessary condition for advances in levels of thinking reinforced this notion. And Piaget's further observation was that children did not profit much from lessons that should have promoted higher levels of thought, and instead continued to employ their existing, more primitive cognitive processes. This "assimilation" of discordant information also applied to lessons offered by the environment. Younger children ordinarily make little of opportunities for increasing their cognitive competence, whereas at an older age they will profit greatly from the same lessons. This resistance to learning to function at a higher level of cognitive competence, as distinguished from other types of learning, was observed by both researchers and educators (Flavell, 1963) with sufficient regularity that "readiness" for learning cognitive skills became a watchword. The convergence of these observations, Piaget's theoretical position, and the psychometrically based notion of a stable IQ combined to slow efforts to create broadly based increases in cognitive competence.

One group of psychologists who were never deterred were those well versed in operant learning procedures, and they have persistently tried to teach more intelligent behavior to children who were not making normal progress. These efforts, sparked by the early analyses of Bijou (1963, 1966), have led to the currently commercialized Distar approach and seem to have an independent zeitgeist of their own. They do not borrow much from cognitive developmental psychology, and depend to a great extent on sophistication in eliminating unsuccessful behavior while promoting acquisition of more competent behaviors.

Of course, even without special interventions cognitive competence increases in an absolute sense as one progresses through childhood and adolescence. But relative competence also changes, a phenomenon that has slowly begun to make itself known. Longitudinal studies, especially that of McCall, Appelbaum, and Hogarty, (1973) have shown that general competence as measured by psychometric IQ tests changes importantly for a majority of children, and that often these changes occur at the stage changes posited by Piaget. (Sonntag, Baker, and Nelson [1958] earlier made similar but more limited observations that were essentially ignored; they came too soon.) These findings that IQ is mutable even in the absence of special interventions can be expected to have an increasing influence on specialists in cognitive development as they become better known. Second, Vygotsky's (1962, 1978) discussions of zones of proximal development, translated at about the same time as the longitudinal research on IQ, has given hope to those who wish to accelerate cognitive development. The zone of proximal development—the difference between what a child can do independently and what the same child can do when guided by adults or more able children—is in one sense the difference between the child's usual cognitive competence and the current ceiling for that competence. Thus, the observation that a child's functioning can be lifted to a higher level by relatively brief episodes of guidance and support suggests that more extensive, long-term, and ingenious guidance might move the child across such zones in many types of cognitive endeavors. Given sufficient investment of instructional resources and careful selection of key cognitive competencies, speeded progress toward greater cognitive prowess is foreseeable.

In fact, numerous studies have shown that IQ changes as a result of instructon, at least when the instruction is offered to disadvantaged children in preschools (Bronfenbrunner, 1974). At the present time, for such children the issue is really whether programs designed by cognitive developmental psychologists to increase cognitive competence would do that better than the more up to date of the educational programs in which such children are ordinarily enrolled.

On the other hand, numerous intervention programs have been invented and put into practice that produced little empirical evidence that they accomplish what was intended. In many cases, this is because the developers of these programs have not carried out appropriate research studies, preferring instead to operate on the basis of consensus and testimonial, so important in educational settings. This enduring tendency of educators to respond to fashionable trends and philosophy, rather than empirical evidence (Stanovich, 1991; O'Sullivan, this volume), has been, as O'Sullivan so eloquently argues, a major stumbling block. In other cases, validation studies have been conducted, often at great effort and expense, but have produced ambiguous or negative evidence (cf. Blagg, 1991; Spitz, 1986).

Conceptual and Methodological Problems

There are special problems for researchers in this field. One is that it is difficult to constitute a control group, particularly one to which children are randomly assigned. A control group is traditionally one that receives a zero or very low value of the independent variable. Educators have legitimate objections to assigning a substantial number of children to receive no special assistance while others receive a great deal of it, and of course parents and preschool administrators do also, so zero value control groups are not easy to obtain.

Good control does not really mean a traditional control group, in any case. Whereas in almost any type of sociobiological research it is a standard procedure to evaluate the effect of an independent variable by contrasting scores made under a high or representative value of that variable with those made under a low or zero value of that variable, that procedure is inadequate in educational settings. It is commonly conceived that the control group would be short changed if it did not receive as much special attention, and equivalent investment of instructional resources, so as to engender equal expectations of success; absent these and related equalizations, the experiment would be confounded. The advantage of the experimental group might arise not from the nature of the instruction it received, but from the advantages of attention, expectation, etc. The ordinary answer would be placebo control, but there is seldom the equivalent of a sugar pill in instruction. Instructing children in such a way that they will not benefit is not usually acceptable, and not likely to match the experimental instruction adequately if it were attempted. Thus, the real criterion for testing an innovation is to contrast it with an equally intense application of another method that is known to work well—an "active" control group. The task, for a cognitive developmental psychologist who wishes to influence instruction, is not to show that an innovation is effective. It is to show that it is more effective than equal investment in tried and true methods that also assist cognitive development! The null hypothesis is that both procedures accelerate cognitive competence equally.

Another problem, peculiar to cognitive developmental psychology rather than research in educational settings (or almost any other setting), is the expectation that effects of any effort expended to help children be permanent. Particularly if the effort is to increase cognitive competence, efforts are often considered unsuccessful if their results do not endure for many years, perhaps even until adulthood (Spitz, 1986; Weikart & Hohmann, this volume).

This is a conceptual problem. Most applied researchers are not interested in temporary increases in competence, although these maybe of some theoretical importance. (Consider Rosengren, Behrend, and Perlmutter's discussion in this volume of short-term effects of parenting styles.) A temporary increase would be the acquisition of some advanced cognitive strategies, metacognition, or other cognitive abilities that were quickly forgotten or not employed or unemployable for some reason so that the improvement was quickly lost, and of little practical importance. A permanent increase in competence would be gains in such competencies that were not lost, and continued to be employed whenever appropriate. The nature of cognitive development, however, is that such a permanent increase in competence would not lead to a permanent increase in relative competence. As Adams and Feldman (this volume) demonstrate with the Spectrum profile, cognitive development reflects competencies at a point in time.

This is one of the major points of the Spectrum assessment. Relative competencies are those that exist in various domains at a given time, not fixed abilities. Movement from one stage to another in some domain is so dependent on support and individual choice that continued movement at the same rate in that domain is in no sense guaranteed, whether the movement was accelerated by intervention, or proceeded from natural causes. As time passes, competencies that were relatively advanced for a child's age may be relatively inappropriate for a child's new age, unless the competencies change apace. What is necessary for interventions to have life-long effects is for the intervention to create self-propagating changes. That is, if instruction in memory strategies at age 6 years, for example, were to produce a permanent grasp and use of those strategies, and their mastery led at a later age still more advanced strategies, and those to still more at later ages, the change would be self-propagating. This is a tall order, and certainly need not be accomplished for a child to achieve benefits from instruction on memory strategies (Pressley, Borkowski, O'Sullivan, 1984, 1985; Pressley & Van Meter, this volume), componential reading processes (O'Sullivan, this volume), or phonological processing skills (O'Sullivan, this volume; Siegel, this volume), which are not of the temporary sort. Yet, especially when gains in competence are broad, even broad enough to show up in traditional psychometric measures of intelligence, the expectation is often advanced that they should convey a relative advantage from preschool even into adulthood (e.g., Spitz, 1986), rather than an advantage limited to the ages for which the competencies are useful. Researchers in cognitive development must contend with this expectation in one way or another if their research involves assisting children's cognitive development.

A Zero Value Control Group Study

These issues are pertinent for the last chapter of this volume, in which Weikart and Hohmann presented two classic studies of preschool intervention programs, classic because of the rigorous experimental designs and because of the unique follow-up of the children into the late teens. The first of these, the Perry Preschool Project, involved random assignment of 3- and 4-year-olds to a special preschool curriculum or to a zero value control group, and began in 1962, a time when preschools conventionally offered free play and focused on social and emotional growth. Weikart and Hohmann's description of the process by which a curriculum emphasizing specific opportunities for active involvement in learning based on a blend of Piagetian theory and teacher wisdom and experience was devised, conveys a sense of dé jà vu; that was the cutting edge at that time. The faithfulness of this synthesis to Piaget's theory eventually received mixed reviews, as they acknowledge; perhaps just some useful ideas were borrowed. The curriculum featured ample opportunity for children to construct their own knowledge with the well informed support of adults in a rich environment—a prescription that anticipated recommendations emerging on a broad front today (O'Sullivan, this volume; Pressley & Van Meter, this volume; Rosengren, Behrend, & Perlmutter, this volume). Time was earmarked for the children to plan, carry out, and reflect on numerous key experiences, and home visits engaged parents in this agenda, albeit in the absence of recent research on parent–child interactions (Rosengren, Behrend, & Perlmutter, this volume).

Weikart and Hohmann summarized the major results of this study in their chapter. These included early increases in general cognitive competence, as measured by the Stanford-Binet, and motivation for schooling that endured for several years. There was a long-term impact on school success and on socioeconomic success during the middle and late teenage years. Weikart and Hohmann suggested that the better language skills, problem-solving capabilities, and sense of self the experimental group derived from the preschool program led to the greater long-term school success, and that the school success led to the greater socioeconomic success. This suggestion seems plausible, even if domain and specific cognitive competencies taught in preschool at ages 3 and 4 years became irrelevant after several years. It is also possible, of course, that gains were made in social intelligence that were self-propagating; either explanation or a combination of the two could account for the results observed. The potential application of a Spectrum-type assessments in intervention studies during the ensuing decade is obvious.

An Active Control Group Study

Besides summarizing the results of the previously published Perry Preschool Project, Weikart and Hohmann previewed new longitudinal findings from the High/Scope Preschool Curriculum Study. This study involved random assignment of disadvantaged preschoolers to active control groups. One of the "control" groups employed the Distar curriculum, which is probably the best of the behavioral programs rooted in Skinnerian psychology; the other featured theme-based teacher input, which is highly regarded in many educational circles. The "experimental" group experienced the High/Scope curriculum, which is an advanced form of that used in the Perry Preschool project. The rigor of this design is remarkable for the time at which the research was initiated and now we have a 19-year follow-up; developmental psychologists are unlikely to have the luxury of examining any similar study soon.

It was predictable (Brofenbrunner, 1974) that psychometric IQ scores stabilized at near normal levels regardless of the type of intervention, a probability that was not so clear at the time the study was initiated. At the present time it seems likely that this will usually be the most favorable outcome of preschool intervention studies as far as IQ measures are concerned. It is more interesting that the Distar program (Direct Instruction System in Arithmetic and Reading) did not lead to greater school achievement than the other programs. The emphasis of Distar on academics should have produced an academic head start, which was never manifested. The essence of Distar is that intelligent behavior is operant behavior, operant behavior is learned, cognitive processes are operant behaviors that can be taught through their observable manifestations, and the teacher can control the environment and its reinforcement contingencies to make such learning occur. This Skinnerian approach to intervention in cognitive development has probably reached its peak, and seems likely to be superseded by the social-interactive approaches that are expounded so consistently in this volume.

Weikart and Hohmann suggested that since the Distar curriculum produced inferior long-term socioeconomic results and (ultimately) lower expectations of education achievement, models of direct instruction should be avoided. Instead, by emphasizing the child's control, the opportunity for keeping instruction within the zone of proximal development for each child can be maximized, and the opportunity for self-instruction through observational learning and imitation increased. This emphasis on child control is made by Rosengren, Behrend, and Perlmutter, (this volume), by Pressley and Van Meter (this volume), and by O'Sullivan (this volume). Furthermore, the regular child observations—"observant teaching"—Weikart and Hohmann recommend lend themselves to effective scaffolding, and the active involvement of pre-operational children in learning in an instructive physical environment is likely to promote cognitive progress.

Emerging Trends

Weikart and Hohmann's chapter presented two main findings. One was that three different preschool interventions produced substantial broadly based cognitive advances reflected in IQ changes that lasted at least 2 years. For Weikart and Hohmann, this was the lesser point. Their focus was on long-range social, educational, and economic advantages that were especially likely following the early spur to cognitive development offered by the High/Scope curriculum. This could well be seen as an emerging trend in cognitive development. If such development proceeds well in early life, with the right kind of assistance from experts in cognitive development, then longer term benefits in personal and social domains may result. This finding was recently echoed, on a much smaller scale, by Dudek, Thomas, and Strobel's (1987) finding of intermediate-range personal and social concomitants of early standing on Piagetian measures of cognitive development. It has already been effectively argued that cognitive competence has important personal and social domains (Adams & Feldman, this volume; Feldman, 1980; Gardner, 1983). The benefits may be greater or longer term when the cognitive competence is developed in these domains or comes at an important time, as on first contact with the peer and adult demands for performance in early educational settings. As we become more aware of the multifaceted nature of cognitive competence, and more accurate in our knowledge of what competence is at certain times, the interaction of components of cognitive and socioemotional development may become an important part of many research programs.

In contradistinction to Weikart and Hohmann, a different theme is emerging from this and related research. That is, children so advantaged would enjoy a relative superiority to their unassisted cohort, but this advantage would not last forever, even though the newly won cognitive advances did. This is because, as Adams and Feldman point out, cognitive development is nonuniversal and domain-specific. Relative superiority at one point in time in some domains, gained because the child has been helped to enter some stages that would otherwise not have been entered, does not mean that a child will forever enter still more stages sooner than a child who was not assisted. Only self-propagating increases in cognitive functioning would accomplish that. Although it is certainly plausible that some gains in cognitive competence could be self-propagating, others would only be permanent, and still others just temporary.

The report for Distar and High/Scope by Weikart and Hohmann indicates that we can say confidently that the advances that can currently be accomplished in the traditional cognitive arena as measured by IQ are permanent, but probably not self-propagating. The results for the best of other interventions are similar (Brofenbrenner, 1974) for IQ; the picture has not changed for decades. This leads then to an increasing challenge for researchers in cognitive development.

Since the current state of the discipline has not produced self-propagating changes in broadly based measures of cognitive competence, an alternative approach is likely to emerge. Instead of one-time interventions, comprehensive series of interventions, appropriate to the increasing ages and profiles of abilities of the children, are likely to be attempted. The extent to which the interventions are appropriate and fruitful will depend only in part on the delivery methods devised by educators and applied psychologists. Foremost, they will depend on the accuracy with which cognitive developmental psychologists have identified key ways of learning, understanding, and remembering at each age, and on the breadth with which they have approached the continuum of competence from the simplest memory functions to social cognition. In the next decades, cognitive competence is likely to be much more completely defined, much more so than the pioneers have accomplished. Likewise, the broadly based assessment of development at each point in time pioneered by Spectrum may represent only a necessary beginning. Increasingly sophisticated investigation of what competencies are, the levels through which they progress, and the nature of instruction that facilitates such progress are key themes of research at this end of the century.

References

Abramovitch, R., & Grusec, J. (1978). Peer imitation in a natural setting. *Child Development, 49*, 60–65.

Azimita, M., & Perlmutter, M. (1989). Social influences on children's cognition: State of the art and future directions. In H.W. Reese (Ed.), *Advances in Child Development and Behavior* (Vol. 22, pp. 89–144). New York: Academic Press.

Bandura, A. (1981). Self-referent thought: A developmental analysis of self-efficacy. In J.H. Flavell & L. Ross (Eds.), *Social cognitive development: Frontiers and possible futures*. Cambridge, England: Cambridge University Press.

Bandura, A. (1986). *Social foundations of thought and action*. Englewood Cliffs, NJ: Prentice-Hall.

Bandura, A. (1989). Regulation of cognitive processes through perceived self-efficacy. *Developmental Psychology, 25*, 729–735.

Bijou, S.W. (1963). Theory and research in mental (developmental) retardation. *Psychological Record*, 13, 95–110.

Bijou, S.W. (1966). A functional analysis of retarded development. In N.R. Ellis (Ed.), *International review of research in mental retardation* (Vol. 1). New York: Academic Press.

Blagg, N. (1991). *Can we teach intelligence*? Hillsdale, NJ: Erlbaum.
Brofenbrenner, U. (1976). Is early intervention effective? Facts and principles of early intervention: A summary. In A.M. Clarke & A.D.B. Clarke (Eds.), *Early experience: Myth and evidence*. New York: The Free Press.
Carey, S. (1985). *Conceptual change in childhood*. Cambridge: Cambridge University Press.
Carroll, J.B. (1963). A model of school learning. *Teachers College Record*, *64*, 723–733.
Case, R. (1985). *Intellectual development: Birth to adulthood*. New York: Academic Press.
Case, R., & Sowder, J.T. (1990). The development of computational estimation: A neo-Piagetian analysis. *Cognition and Instruction*, *1*, 70–104.
Cavanaugh, J.C., & Perlmutter, M. (1982). Metamemory: A critical examination. *Child Development*, *53*, 11–28.
Dudek, S.Z., Strobel, J., & Thomas, A. (1987). Chronic learning problems and maturation. *Perceptual and Motor Skills*, *64*, 407–429.
Dweck, C. (1986). Motivational processes affecting learning. *American Psychologist*, *41*, 1041–1048.
Ellis, S., & Rogoff, B. (1986). Problem solving in children's management of instruction. In E.C. Mueller & C.R. Cooper (Eds.), *Process and outcome in peer relationships* (pp. 301–325). Orlando, FL: Academic Press.
Feldman, D.H. (1980). *Beyond universals in cognitive development*. Norwood, NJ: Ablex.
Fischer, K.W. (1980). A theory of cognitive development: The control and construction of hierarchies of skills. *Psychological Review*, *87*, 477–531.
Flavell, J.H. (1963). *The developmental psychology of Piaget*. New York: Van Nostrand.
Flavell, J.H. (1977). *Cognitive development*. Englewood Cliffs, NJ: Prentice-Hall.
Flavell, J., & Wellman, H. (1977). Metamemory. In R.V. Kail, Jr. & J.W. Hagen (Eds.), *Perspectives on the development of memory and cognition*. Hillsdale, NJ: Erlbaum.
Galton, F. (1869). *Hereditary genius: An enquiry into its laws and consequences*. (Reprinted 1907, New York: Dutton.)
Gardner, H. (1983). *Frames of mind: The theory of multiple intelligences*. New York: Basic Books.
Gibson, E.J., Gibson, J.J., Pick, A.D., & Osser, H. (1962). A developmental study of the discrimination of letter-like forms. *Journal of Comparative and Physiological Psychology*, *55*, 897–906.
Gibson, J.J., & Gibson, E.J. (1955). Perceptual learning: Differentiation or enrichment? *Psychological Review*, *62*, 32–41.
Horowitz, F.D. (1987). *Exploring developmental theories: Toward a structural/behavioral model of development*. Hillsdale, NJ: Erlbaum.
Howe, M.L., & O'Sullivan, J.T. (1990). The development of strategic memory: Coordinating knowledge, metamemory, and resources. In D.F. Bjorklund (Ed.), *Children's strategies: Contemporary views of cognitive development* (pp. 129–155). Hillsdale, NJ: Erlbaum.
Kalish, C.W., & Gelman, S.A. *Preschooler's sensitivity to differences in category implications*. Paper presented at the meeting of the Jean Piaget Society, Philadelphia, PA.

Keil, F.C. (1986). On the structure-dependent nature of stages in cognitive development. In I. Levin (Ed.), *Stage and structure: Reopening the debate.* Norwood, NJ: Ablex.

McCall, R., Applebaum, M., & Hogarty, P. (1973). Developmental changes in mental performance. *Monographs of the Society for Research in Child Development*, *38*(3, Serial No. 150).

O'Sullivan, J.T., & Pressley, M. (1984). Completeness of instruction and strategy transfer. *Journal of Experimental Child Psychology*, *38*, 275–288.

Piaget, J. (1930). *The child's conception of physical causality*. London: Kegan Paul.

Piaget, J. (1932). *The moral judgment of the child.* Glencoe, IL: Free Press.

Piaget, J. (1963). *Play, dreams, and imitation in childhood.* New York: Norton.

Piaget, J. (1968). *Six psychological studies*. New York: Vintage Press.

Piaget, J., & Inhelder, B. (1951/1975). *The origin of the idea of chance in children* (L. Leake, Jr., P. Burrell, & H. Fishbein, Trans.). New York: Norton. (Original work published 1951.)

Pressley, M., Borkowski, J.G., & O'Sullivan, J.T. (1984). Memory strategy instruction is made of this: Metamemory and durable strategy use. *Educational Psychology*, *19*, 94–107.

Pressley, M., Borkowski, J.G., & O'Sullivan, J.T. (1985). Children's metamemory and the teaching of memory strategies. In D.L. Forrest-Pressley, G.E. MacKinnon, & T.G. Waller (Eds.), *Metacognition, cognition, and human performance* (pp. 111–153). Orlando, FL: Academic Press.

Schneider, W., & Pressley, M. (1989). *Memory development between 2 and 20.* New York: Springer-Verlag.

Silliphant, V. (1983). Kindergarten reasoning and achievement in grades K-3. *Psychology in the schools*, *20*, 289–294.

Sonntag, L.W., Baker, C.T., & Nelson, V.L. (1958). Mental growth and personality development: A longitudinal study. *Monographs of the Society for Research in Child Development*, *23*(2, Serial No. 68).

Spearman, C. (1904). General intelligence objectively determined and measured. *American Journal of Psychology*, *15*, 201–203.

Spearman, C. (1927). *Abilities of man*. New York: MacMillan.

Spitz, H.H. (1986). *The raising of intelligence*. Hillsdale, NJ: Erlbaum.

Stanovich, K.E. (1988a). Explaining the differences between the dyslexic and garden variety poor reader: The phonological-core variance-difference model. *Journal of Learning Disabilities*, *21*, 590–604, 612.

Stanovich, K.E. (1988b). The right and wrong places to look for the cognitive locus of reading disability. *Annals of Dyslexia*, *38*, 154–177.

Stanovich, K.E. (1991). Cognitive science meets beginning reading. *Psychological Science*, *2*, 70–81.

Sternberg, R.J. (1977). *Intelligence information processing, and analogical reasoning: The componential analysis of human abilities*. Hillsdale, NJ: Erlbaum.

Sternberg, R.J. (1984). Toward a triarchic theory of human intelligence. *The Behavioral and Brain Sciences*, *7*, 269–315.

Sternberg, R.J. (1985). Approaches to intelligence. In S.F. Chipman, J.W. Segal, & R. Glaser (Eds.), *Thinking and learning skills: Research and open questions* (Vol. 2). Hillsdale, NJ: Erlbaum.

Stipek, D. (1984). Young children's performance expectations: Logical analysis or wishful thinking? In J.G. Nicholls (Ed.), *Advances in motivation and achievement: Vol. 3, The development of achievement motivation*. Greenwich, CT: JAI Press.

Terman, L.M., & Merrill, M.A. (1973). *Stanford-Binet* Intelligence Scale: Manual for the third *revision*, form L-M. Boston: Houghton-Mifflin.

Thorndike, R.L., Hagan, E.P., & Sattler, J.M. (1986). *Stanford-Binet Intelligence Scale* (4th Ed.). Chicago: Riverside Publishing Company.

Thurstone, L.L. (1938). *Primary mental abilities*. Chicago: University of Chicago Press.

Vellutino, F.R. (1991). Has basic research in reading increased our understanding of developmental reading and how to teach reading? *Psychological Science*, *2*, 70–83.

Vygotsky, L.S. (1962). *Thought and language*. (E. Hartmann & F. Vakar Eds. & Trans.). Cambridge, MA: MIT Press.

Vygotsky, L.S. (1978). *Mind in society*. Cambridge, MA: Harvard University Press.

Wechsler, D. (1974). *Manual for the Wechsler intelligence scale for children—revised*. New York: The Psychological Corporation.

Wellman, H.M. (1990). *The child's theory of mind*. Cambridge, MA: MIT Press.

Author Index

Note. Italicized entries refer to reference list citations.

Subject Index